THE CAPE TOWN CONVENTION

A Documentary History

This book is the first detailed and comprehensive analysis of the history of the Cape Town Convention and its protocols. It critically engages with the challenges faced by the developers of this treaty, analyses thousands of pages of archived materials and derives important lessons for the development of transnational commercial law globally.

The book is an invaluable addition to the existing literature on the Cape Town Convention. It also informs the debate about harmonisation of secured transactions regimes generally, and as such will be of interest to academics, legal practitioners and the judiciary involved in secured transactions law around the world. Practising lawyers will better understand the rationale behind the key provisions of the Cape Town Convention, while the treaty-making lessons will assist governmental officials, representatives of international organisations and legal advisers engaged in harmonisation of commercial law.

The text covers all four protocols to the Cape Town Convention, including the MAC Protocol adopted on 22 November 2019 in Pretoria.

Hart Studies in Commercial and Financial Law: Volume 5

Hart Studies in Commercial and Financial Law
Series Editor: John Linarelli

This series offers a venue for publishing works on commercial law as well as on the regulation of banking and finance and the law on insolvency and bankruptcy. It publishes works on the law on secured credit, the regulatory and transactional aspects of banking and finance, the transactional and regulatory institutions for financial markets, legal and policy aspects associated with access to commercial and consumer credit, new generation subjects having to do with the institutional architecture associated with innovation and the digital economy including works on blockchain technology, work on the relationship of law to economic growth, the harmonisation or unification of commercial law, transnational commercial law, and the global financial order. The series promotes interdisciplinary work. It publishes research on the law using the methods of empirical legal studies, behavioural economics, political economy, normative welfare economics, law and society inquiry, socio-legal studies, political theory, and historical methods. Its coverage includes international and comparative investigations of areas of law within its remit.

Volume 1: The Financialisation of the Citizen: Social and Financial Inclusion through European Private Law
Guido Comparato

Volume 2: MiFID II and Private Law: Enforcing EU Conduct of Business Rules
Federico Della Negra

Volume 3: Reforming Corporate Retail Investor Protection: Regulating to Avert Mis-Selling
Diane Bugeja

Volume 4: The Future of Commercial Law: Ways Forward for Change and Reform
Edited by Orkun Akseli and John Linarelli

Volume 5: The Cape Town Convention: A Documentary History
Anton N Didenko

The Cape Town Convention

A Documentary History

Anton N Didenko

•HART•

OXFORD • LONDON • NEW YORK • NEW DELHI • SYDNEY

HART PUBLISHING

Bloomsbury Publishing Plc

Kemp House, Chawley Park, Cumnor Hill, Oxford, OX2 9PH, UK

1385 Broadway, New York, NY 10018, USA

29 Earlsfort Terrace, Dublin 2, Ireland

HART PUBLISHING, the Hart/Stag logo, BLOOMSBURY and the Diana logo are trademarks of Bloomsbury Publishing Plc

First published in Great Britain 2021

A catalogue record for this book is available from the British Library.

Library of Congress Cataloging-in-Publication data

Names: Didenko, Anton N, 1985- author.

Title: The Cape Town convention : a documentary history / Anton N Didenko.

Description: Oxford, UK ; New York, NY : Hart Publishing, an imprint of Bloomsbury Publishing, 2021. | Series: Hart studies in commercial and financial law ; volume 5 | Based on author's thesis (doctoral – University of Oxford, 2017) issued under title: Challenges to effective treaty-making in contemporary transnational commercial law. | Includes bibliographical references and index.

Identifiers: LCCN 2021000186 (print) | LCCN 2021000187 (ebook) | ISBN 9781509939770 (hardback) | ISBN 9781509947232 (paperback) | ISBN 9781509939794 (pdf) | ISBN 9781509939787 (Epub)

Subjects: LCSH: Convention on International Interests in Mobile Equipment (2001 November 16) | Export sales contracts. | Security (Law) | Machinery industry—Law and legislation. | Transportation equipment industry—Law and legislation.

Classification: LCC K1028.32001 .D53 2021 (print) | LCC K1028.32001 (ebook) | DDC 343.08/78—dc23

LC record available at https://lccn.loc.gov/2021000186

LC ebook record available at https://lccn.loc.gov/2021000187

ISBN: HB: 978-1-50993-977-0
ePDF: 978-1-50993-979-4
ePub: 978-1-50993-978-7

Typeset by Compuscript Ltd, Shannon

To find out more about our authors and books visit www.hartpublishing.co.uk. Here you will find extracts, author information, details of forthcoming events and the option to sign up for our newsletters.

PREFACE

The Cape Town Convention: A Documentary History

In the area of international harmonisation of commercial law, no other instrument has gone as far, and achieved as much, as the 2001 Convention on International Interests in Mobile Equipment ('Cape Town Convention' or 'CTC'), which has been hailed by some commentators as 'the most successful international secured transactions instrument ever implemented' (Mooney, 2014). This book is the first detailed and comprehensive account of the history of the CTC and its protocols. It critically engages with the challenges faced by the developers of this treaty, analyses thousands of pages of archived materials and derives important lessons for the development of transnational commercial law globally.

The book is an invaluable addition to the existing literature on the Cape Town Convention. It informs the debate about harmonisation of secured transactions regimes generally, and as such will be of interest to academics, legal practitioners and the judiciary involved in secured transactions law around the world. Practising lawyers will better understand the rationale behind the key provisions of the Cape Town Convention, while the treaty-making lessons will assist governmental officials, representatives of international organisations and legal advisors engaged in the harmonisation of commercial law.

The text focuses on the development of the Convention itself and its Aircraft Protocol (as the only protocol in force at the time of writing), however all the other protocols and their history are frequently referred to for comparison or to illustrate specific challenges - including the MAC Protocol adopted on 22 November 2019 in Pretoria.

ACKNOWLEDGEMENTS

This book is based on my DPhil thesis which I defended at the University of Oxford in 2017.

During my years in Oxford I had the rare privilege of being supervised by Sir Roy Goode and Professor Louise Gullifer, whose incredible support inspired me, a practising lawyer at the start of this journey, to pursue an academic career.

I wish to thank Professor Horst Eidenmüller, Professor Thomas Krebs, Professor Anna Veneziano and Professor Stefan Vogenauer for their invaluable critique and inspiring suggestions. My sincere thanks go to Martin Stanford and Professor Jeffrey Wool for their insights into the workings of the various meetings and sessions preceding the adoption of the Cape Town Convention.

I would like to thank the Cape Town Convention Academic Project for the generous scholarship and ongoing financial assistance that made this research possible. I am grateful to all the staff at the Oxford University Faculty of Law and Harris Manchester College for their support throughout the years.

I am indebted to the UNIDROIT Secretariat for the kind permission to study the documents stored in its archives and for helping me locate some of the unpublished records, and for inviting me to attend various working group meetings. I want to thank in particular William Brydie-Watson, Bettina Maxion, Carla Milani and Laura Tikanvaara.

I am grateful to the anonymous reviewers and the Hart Publishing's team, in particular Roberta Bassi, Andrew Devine, Rosemarie Mearns, Emma Platt and Linda Staniford, who made this book a reality.

I owe a debt of gratitude to Professor Ross Buckley, whose support allowed me to finish this book in Sydney, at the University of New South Wales.

My concluding words of gratitude are for the people who are closest: my wife Anastasia and my parents, Liubov and Nikolai. Thank you for helping me when it mattered most and for your endless love, patience and understanding.

CONTENTS

LIST OF ABBREVIATIONS

APG	Aircraft Protocol Group
ASU	Sector Understanding on Export Credits for Civil Aircraft
AWG	Aviation Working Group
CEAL	Center for Economic Analysis of Law
CISG	1980 United Nations Convention on Contracts for the International Sale of Goods
CMI	International Maritime Committee
CTC	2001 Convention on International Interests in Mobile Equipment
CTCAP	Cape Town Convention Academic Project
EBRD	European Bank for Reconstruction and Development
EMEA	Europe, the Middle East and Africa
ESOA	EMEA Satellite Operators Association
EU	European Union
EUROCONTROL	European Organisation for the Safety of Air Navigation
GBP	United Kingdom Pound Sterling
HS	Harmonized Commodity Description and Coding System
IATA	International Air Transport Association
ICMA	International Capital Market Association
ICSID	International Centre for Settlement of Investment Disputes
IMO	International Maritime Organization
INSEAD	European Institute of Business Administration

ISDA	International Swaps and Derivatives Association
ITU	International Telecommunication Union
LBMA	London Bullion Market Association
LIBOR	London Interbank Offered Rate
OECD	Organisation for Economic Co-Operation and Development
OTIF	Intergovernmental Organisation for International Carriage by Rail
PECL	Principles of European Contract Law
REWG	Restricted Exploratory Working Group
SRC	Steering and Revisions Committee
UCC	Uniform Commercial Code
UN	United Nations
UNCITRAL	United Nations Commission on International Trade Law
UNCTAD	United Nations Conference on Trade and Development
UNIDROIT	International Institute for the Unification of Private Law
UPICC	UNIDROIT Principles of International Commercial Contracts
USD	United States Dollar
WCO	World Customs Organization

TABLE OF REPORTS AND WORKING PAPERS

TABLE OF CONVENTIONS AND MODEL LAWS

Instruments Referred to Throughout the Text

Other Instruments

1

Introduction

Treaties have always stood out amidst the many sources of transnational commercial law thanks to their ability to create a degree of uniformity which is beyond the reach of any other instrument. In areas where flexibility is undesirable for the prospects of unification, international conventions remain the instrument of choice. Multilateral treaties – the most ambitious form of unification – can establish a harmonised legal regime on a regional, or, in rare cases, even on a global scale. However, the underlying challenges (such as a substantial commitment of time and resources, opportunity costs, problematic international enforcement, or political sensitivities) frequently outweigh any projected benefits, making successful commercial law conventions a rare breed that deserves attention.

In the area of commercial law, no other treaty has gone as far and achieved as much as the 2001 Convention on International Interests in Mobile Equipment[1] (the 'Cape Town Convention', or 'Convention', or 'CTC').[2]

1.1. Cape Town Convention: A Long Journey Home

In a rather symbolic turn of events, in 2019 the Cape Town Convention 'returned' home to South Africa – the country where it was born back in 2001 – to witness the birth of its fourth protocol. Each of the two South African diplomatic conferences – 18 years apart – was a turning point in the history of the CTC. The first (in Cape Town) gave the Convention its final form and the first protocol (as well as its unofficial name). The second (in Pretoria) finally extended the scope of the treaty beyond the 18-year-old Cape Town design. Indeed, the first three protocols (covering aircraft, railway and space objects) can be called 'implementing protocols', as they were designed to *implement* the blueprints already 'pre-programmed' in Article 2(3) of the CTC. The Pretoria protocol had a different role: it was meant to overcome the gravitational pull of the early design choices and – for the first

[1] Convention on International Interests in Mobile Equipment (adopted 16 November 2001, entered into force 1 March 2006) 2307 UNTS 285.

[2] This book covers the entire history of the Cape Town Convention, from the early drafts, to the newest protocols. Therefore, for simplicity, references to the Convention itself (or any of its protocols) are also used in a historical context to denote the (then) current draft of the relevant instrument.

time – to *expand* the Convention to cover *new types* of assets (mining, agricultural and construction equipment), making it the first 'expansion protocol' to the CTC – a treaty hailed as 'the most successful international secured transactions instrument ever implemented'[3] and as 'one of the most ambitious international commercial law instruments ever to have been fashioned in the field of private transactional law'.[4] What makes the Convention so special?

The high ambition of the CTC stems from its Preamble, which reflects the desire of contracting states to facilitate asset-based financing and leasing transactions by establishing clear rules to govern them. To achieve this, the Convention creates a comprehensive international legal regime protecting secured creditors, conditional sellers and lessors in certain categories of high-value mobile equipment.[5] This new regime is based on unique CTC mechanics: the treaty provides for the creation of an entirely new type of proprietary interest (labelled 'international interest'), the existence and effects of which do not rely on the existence and validity of its counterparts arising through the application of national laws. This *sui generis* concept of international interest is unique and has no equal in the history of international lawmaking.

Notably, the Convention's scope is not limited to the creation of a new type of proprietary interest: the latter is immediately integrated into a comprehensive international system of priorities that supersedes existing domestic regimes. This system of priorities is triggered by the registration of the international interest in a dedicated central international registry, which is another unique feature of the CTC.[6] This gives international interests surprising reach: once registered, they rank ahead of their national law counterparts, even if the latter are not registrable in the international registry (with limited exceptions).

To ensure that the interests of financiers are adequately protected regardless of any differences between domestic legal regimes, the Convention establishes dedicated rules on remedies exercisable upon default of the debtor, providing the creditors with peace of mind and lowering the cost of credit for their clients. In addition, the CTC contains a variety of provisions (eg articles on assignment of associated rights, or subordination of international interests) enhancing legal

[3] Charles W. Mooney, 'Cape Town Convention's Improbable-but-Possible Progeny Part One: An International Secured Transactions Registry of General Application, The Essay' (2014) 55 *Va J Int'l L* 163, 166.

[4] See Roy Goode, *Convention on International Interests in Mobile Equipment and Protocol thereto on Matters Specific to Aircraft Equipment: Official Commentary* (4th edn, International Institute for the Unification of Private Law (UNIDROIT) 2019) 1.

[5] In doing so, the Convention goes further than was initially envisaged by its authors: as discussed further, the CTC was at first conceived as an instrument that would provide greater legal certainty to holders of security and certain quasi-security interests (eg sellers under title retention agreements) in mobile assets in situations when these assets cross national borders.

[6] The international registry for aircraft equipment has had enormous success among private actors: it has recorded over 1 million registrations and produced over 1.2 million search results. See Rob Cowan, 'Comparison of the Aircraft and MAC International Registries' (2018) 7 *Cape Town Convention Journal* 21, 22.

certainty, but at the same time providing sufficient flexibility for asset finance providers in dealing with their counterparties.

Currently the Cape Town Convention covers four types of mobile equipment: aircraft objects (airframes, aircraft engines and helicopters), railway rolling stock, space assets and – since November 2019 – also mining, agricultural and construction equipment. Such broad coverage is achieved by using asset-specific protocols, which reflect the different physical characteristics of these asset types and varying financing techniques applied within the relevant industries (the 'Aircraft Protocol',[7] the 'Rail Protocol',[8] the 'Space Protocol'[9] and the 'MAC Protocol'[10]). The combination of a baseline convention and asset-specific protocols creates a two-level 'umbrella' structure, which not only preserves continuity of the 'core' provisions of the CTC, but also adds flexibility and potential for future expansion. It also provides states with the freedom to apply the CTC only to some, but not all, types of mobile equipment covered by the Convention.

At the time of writing, the Convention and the Aircraft Protocol have been ratified by 82 and 79 contracting states, respectively.[11] This makes the CTC the second most ratified substantive (as opposed to conflict of laws) commercial law treaty in the world. It is second only to the 1980 CISG,[12] which currently has 94 states parties. The success of the CTC within the aviation industry, however, has not translated to the other protocols, neither of which has gained the minimum number of ratifications required for entry into force.

1.2. In Search of Underlying Objectives and Challenges

Almost twenty years have passed since the adoption of the CTC, but many difficult questions remain unanswered. If the Convention is so innovative and successful,

[7] Protocol to the Convention on International Interests in Mobile Equipment on Matters Specific to Aircraft Equipment (adopted 16 November 2001, entered into force 1 March 2006) 2367 UNTS 517.

[8] Luxembourg Protocol to the Convention on International Interests in Mobile Equipment on Matters Specific to Railway Rolling Stock (adopted 23 February 2007).

[9] Protocol to the Convention on International Interests in Mobile Equipment on Matters Specific to Space Assets (adopted 9 March 2012).

[10] Protocol to the Convention on International Interests in Mobile Equipment on Matters Specific to Mining, Agricultural and Construction Equipment (adopted 22 November 2019).

[11] The EU has acceded to both instruments separately from its Member States under Article 48 of the CTC and Article XXVII of the Aircraft Protocol as a Regional Economic Integration Organisation. These articles were introduced at a late stage following a request by the EU, in order to address matters on which it had exclusive competence (such as jurisdiction and the recognition and enforcement of judgments in civil and commercial matters, insolvency proceedings and law applicable to contractual obligations). Later, in 2014, the Rail Protocol was similarly approved by the EU in accordance with its Article XXII.

[12] United Nations Convention on Contracts for the International Sale of Goods (adopted 11 April 1980, entered into force 1 January 1988) 1489 UNTS 3.

then why does it only operate within a single (aviation) industry? If the benefits of the Convention for financiers of mobile equipment are clear, then why is there no shipping protocol? Has the Convention achieved its objects and purposes if its implementation has been drastically different across the industries? These questions highlight a bigger issue: what is the appropriate test to measure the success of a commercial convention in general, and the CTC in particular?

Different criteria can be used to assess whether a particular commercial treaty has been successful, both quantitative and qualitative: the number of ratifications,[13] popularity among end users, the economic benefit generated by the treaty, or even the degree of incorporation of a convention's concepts into other instruments. Assessment of these factors hinges on empirical ex-post analysis of treaty implementation on different levels. However, the usefulness of such analysis is likely to be limited without detailed knowledge of the Convention's history, in particular its underlying *objectives* and *challenges*.

Treaty *objectives* are often reflected in the preamble or otherwise expressed in the text of the treaty itself, but analysis of the final text of a convention is, in this context, of limited usefulness. On the one hand, the relevant provisions are usually drafted last and tend to be used for technical (eg gap-filling) purposes. On the other hand, they generally reflect the status quo that emerged at the *end* of all the relevant negotiations, without capturing the changes introduced at various stages of development, as well as different agendas pursued by the relevant stakeholders. This means that, in order to identify the underlying goals and objectives, one should look beyond any labels and compromise solutions adopted at the end of the development process.

Only a comprehensive analysis of the history of development of a convention can identify its *actual* underlying objectives and challenges associated with its development, track their evolution and eventually assess whether these have been properly addressed by the treaty in question. Indeed, an analysis of implementation patterns or economic benefits alone would be inconclusive. On the one hand, an instrument which does not produce a satisfactory solution to its underlying problems might still be commonly used by the private parties, especially in a situation when there is no working alternative.[14] On the other hand, a treaty proposing an appropriate and rational solution may be disregarded by the industry for reasons which have little to do with the quality of such solution.[15]

[13] The history of transnational commercial law treaty-making suggests that this approach alone is not a reliable measure of success of a treaty: the CISG, with almost 100 contracting states, is so commonly excluded from application by parties to a contract that this phenomenon has become the subject of significant academic interest; see Lisa Spagnolo, *CISG Exclusion and Legal Efficiency* (Kluwer Law International 2014).

[14] See, eg, the International Convention for the Unification of Certain Rules Relating to Maritime Liens and Mortgages (adopted 10 April 1926, entered into force 2 June 1931) LNTS No 2765 (the '1926 Brussels Convention').

[15] See section 3.4 and the corresponding discussion relating to the opposition from the shipping circles to the idea of extending the scope of the CTC to ships.

1.3. Scope of this Book

This book is the first academic study of the documentary history of the Cape Town Convention and its protocols. It provides an in-depth analysis of the history of development of the Convention, from the early discussions in 1988 (and the historical context prior to that period) until the adoption of the CTC in 2001. It also addresses the recurring issues that re-emerged in different forms after adoption (such as the problem of identifying mobile equipment, which remained one of the key difficulties in the development of the MAC Protocol in 2019).

This book should prove useful in the interpretation of the CTC,[16] as well as in practical application of the Convention (particularly in legal proceedings concerning complex or contradictory provisions of the treaty) – since it explains in detail both *how* the key concepts of the treaty developed over time and *why* they took their present form. It may also assist in preparation of new protocols to the Convention, as well as new annotations to the masterly Official Commentaries of Sir Roy Goode. Furthermore, as the research tackles the views of various actors in the treaty-making process, it will be useful for government officials and representatives of international organisations. I hope that, on the whole, this research will help to promote the overall attractiveness and effectiveness of treaty-making as an instrument of harmonising commercial law.

The scope of this book has two main limitations. First, it focuses on the development of the CTC, rather than its subsequent implementation – hence there is no analysis of challenges arising after adoption of the Convention and its protocols, such as seeking ratifications, post-adoption domestication of the treaty and its transposition into national legal systems. Second, the analysis of various challenges is limited to those matters which generated the most difficulties during the development of the CTC and focuses primarily on the defining features of the Convention listed in section 1.1 above. Although most discussions relate to the development of the Convention and the Aircraft Protocol (as the only protocol currently in force), the other protocols and their history are frequently referred to for comparison or to illustrate specific challenges.

1.4. Structure of this Book

Each chapter of the book focuses on a specific challenge in the development of the Cape Town Convention, identifies the corresponding solutions adopted by the drafters, analyses the alternative approaches considered during the preparatory

[16] According to Article 32 of the 1969 Vienna Convention on the Law of Treaties the preparatory work of the treaty and the circumstances of its conclusion constitute 'supplementary means of interpretation' of a treaty. See Vienna Convention on the Law of Treaties (adopted 23 May 1969, entered into force 27 January 1980) 1155 UNTS 331.

stage and explains the reasons behind the particular choices made by the developers of the CTC to critically assess the adopted solutions.

The rest of this book is arranged into chapters as follows.

Chapter two addresses the principal substantive challenges that affected the development of the fundamental concepts shaping the CTC, such as the notion of 'international interest' and the test of 'internationality'.

Chapter three analyses the problem of selecting asset types covered by the Convention.

Chapters four focuses on the establishment of the structure of the CTC.

Chapters five and six examine the main challenges in crafting the key provisions determining the application of the Convention *inter partes* and as against third parties, respectively.

Chapter seven addresses the impact of both the commercial factors and state sensitivities on the development of the CTC.

Chapter eight tackles various process-management challenges relevant to the Convention.

Chapter nine lists the conclusions and formulates the key lessons for commercial law treaty making that follow from the history of the CTC.

For the reader's convenience, section 1.5 of this chapter provides a general overview of the key stages of development of the Cape Town Convention, while Appendix I contains a graphical representation of some of the key milestones of the treaty-making process associated with the Cape Town Convention.

In the interests of brevity and clarity, the text of all chapters includes short-form references to the various reports and working papers. For this reason, Appendix II contains a table of concordance between the full and short forms of such references.

1.5. History of the Cape Town Convention: The Key Stages

The Convention and its protocols were developed by the International Institute for the Unification of Private Law – UNIDROIT (in collaboration with various stakeholders, including the respective industry groups and international organisations) in a multi-stage process. The CTC and the Aircraft Protocol were the first instruments to complete all of the relevant stages as follows.

The first – and longest – stage (1988–98) involved the discussion of the main concepts and ideas in dedicated working groups, culminating in the development of the draft Convention and Aircraft Protocol.[17]

[17] The functions of the various working groups are examined in section 8.2.

During the second stage (1999–2000) the draft instruments were scrutinised by governmental representatives at committees of governmental experts.[18]

Finally, the revised drafts were finalised and adopted during the Cape Town Diplomatic Conference in 2001.

The Rail, Space and MAC Protocols were adopted during the dedicated diplomatic conferences held in Luxembourg (2007), Berlin (2012), and Pretoria (2019) respectively.

[18] All mentions of the 'governmental expert stage' should be read as references to this second step, as applicable to the Convention or the relevant protocol, depending on the context.

2

Defining the Scope of the Convention

2.1. Overview

This chapter goes all the way back to the 'roots' of the Cape Town Convention. In section 2.2, it examines in detail the historical background of the CTC and the main problems the Convention was intended to solve. Sections 2.3 and 2.4 focus on the history of development of two core concepts that ultimately determined the scope of the CTC: 'international interest' and 'internationality'. The chapter tracks the development of each concept from the early days of the CTC and argues that the 'international interest' has its roots in the gradual evolution of the idea of recognition of domestic security interests, and explains that despite the eventual elimination of the principle of 'internationality' from the text of the CTC, its echo has nonetheless remained an important part of the Cape Town Convention due to the state sensitivities that became apparent during the final stages of development of the treaty.

2.2. Identifying the Problem

Two key problems prompted UNIDROIT to initiate the development of a convention on international aspects of security interests in mobile equipment: (i) inappropriateness of the *lex situs* rule in the context of regulating security interests in assets frequently moved between states, and (ii) widely differing approaches to the regulation of security interests (in the broad sense) under national laws. This section 2.2 focuses on these issues to reveal the legal complexities underlying the Cape Town Convention.

2.2.1. Origins of the Convention: The Lex Situs Conundrum

The UNIDROIT's activity concerning the development of a convention in the area of international regulation of security interests in mobile equipment was set in motion by the proposal of the Canadian Government (the 'Canadian Proposal')[1]

[1] The text of the proposal was prepared by Ronald Cuming and was kindly provided to the author by the UNIDROIT Secretariat.

considered during the 67th session of the UNIDROIT Governing Council in June 1988,[2] which was based on three key considerations. First, existing international conventions showed that security interests (or real rights generally) could, in principle, be subject to international regulation in the form of a treaty. Indeed, at the time Article 7 of UNIDROIT's newly adopted Financial Leasing Convention provided for limited recognition of the lessor's real rights in bankruptcy as well as against creditors,[3] while Article I(1)(d) of the 1948 Geneva Convention provided for recognition of certain 'mortgages, hypotheques and similar rights in aircraft'.[4] Second, an attempt to create a broad international agreement regulating security interests *generally* appeared 'entirely unrealistic' in the light of UNCITRAL's recent initiative to harmonise the laws on security interests,[5] which had failed due to its overly ambitious nature: it was seen as an attempt to create a model law for most aspects of both international and domestic security interests. Third, existing research suggested that both the role, and demand for, security interests in international trade were likely to increase in the future.[6] Given the above factors, the paper of the Canadian Government concluded with a proposal for a feasibility study for a project 'directed toward the preparation of a convention on certain international aspects of security interests in mobile equipment'.[7]

Unfortunately, the past examples cited in the Canadian Proposal offered little guidance as to how far the unification could proceed regarding the coverage of substantive rules: the Financial Leasing Convention was still too young to be called a success (the UNIDROIT Governing Council was considering the proposal of the Canadian Government less than a month after the adoption of that treaty), and the 1948 Geneva Convention was, in essence, a conflict of laws instrument, with few substantive rules. Hence, the UNIDROIT Governing Council took a cautious approach and initiated a feasibility study to identify the international elements involved in various types of secured transactions used to finance mobile equipment, assess the corresponding problems, the likelihood of addressing such problems in an international convention and measure the potential support for such convention.[8]

The feasibility study (the 'Study') was prepared by Ronald Cuming (this time acting at the request of UNIDROIT). It highlighted a rather bleak status quo, at

[2] Unidroit, *Governing Council C.D. 67 – Doc. 18 (1988)* 52–53.

[3] Article 7 of the UNIDROIT Convention on International Financial Leasing (adopted 28 May 1988, entered into force 1 May 1995) 2321 UNTS 195 (the 'Financial Leasing Convention').

[4] Article I(1)(d) of the Convention on the International Recognition of Rights in Aircraft (adopted 19 June 1948, entered into force 17 September 1953) 310 UNTS 151 (the '1948 Geneva Convention').

[5] UNCITRAL's project examining the feasibility of developing model rules for security interests in movables (the 'UNCITRAL Project') was carried out between 1968 and 1980. It should be noted that subsequently UNCITRAL did not abandon attempts to prepare such model rules: its efforts culminated in the adoption of the 2016 UNCITRAL Model Law on Secured Transactions.

[6] United Nations, *Report of the Secretary-General: Study on Security Interests (A/CN.9/131) (1978)* 213.

[7] See n 1.

[8] Unidroit, *Governing Council C.D. 67 – Doc. 18 (1988)* 57.

the time: (i) the level of international regulation in the sphere of security interests in movable property was minimal; (ii) national laws regulating security interests in movable property were complex and diverse; (iii) past attempts to harmonise this area of law by way of creation of a model law had failed; and (iv) further harmonisation in the area was possible only in specific areas of commercial activity, provided that they would benefit from such harmonisation.[9] Cuming stressed that, while development of a generic international security interest in movables generally would have been *logical*, this approach was likely to fail: 'necessity and pragmatism and not logic must be the driving forces in the further development of this area of the law'.[10]

Harmonisation of *substantive* rules governing security interests was not seen as a practicable solution from the start: the prospects of 'overcoming national parochialism' in this area of the law seemed highly unlikely.[11] The best step in the circumstances seemed to be in the direction of harmonising *conflict of laws* provisions of national legal systems, to promote uniformity: 'If the conflict of laws rules are substantially similar, there is no need to have substantive international law to secure uniformity of approach'.[12] Cuming stressed, however, that 'uniformity' should not be seen as the *only* objective of unification: 'Uniformly *inappropriate* conflict of laws rules are of no assistance to those whose economic interests depend upon commercially reasonable and fair treatment under the laws of nations in which those interests are being asserted'.[13] In other words, conflict of laws rules not only need to be harmonised: they must contain a solution which is satisfactory for the particular legal relationship.

In his study Cuming examined the connecting factor applied in the majority of European jurisdictions to *in rem* rights, *lex situs* (ie the law of the country in which the asset is located), and found it inadequate in a situation when an asset subject to a security interest created in State A was moved to State B.

First, in this scenario the apparent simplicity of *lex situs* would disappear, as the same connecting factor would point to an entirely different, and often unpredictable, jurisdiction. Apparently, the degree of unpredictability would increase for assets frequently moving from country to country.

Second, the *lex situs* approach would inevitably lead to the 'transposition' problem: whenever the movable asset subject to a security interest created in one country is moved to another state, one needs to compare the status of the foreign security interest with the various security interests allowed under the new *situs* to find the most similar equivalent, either to establish its priority position, or to identify an appropriate remedy in situations when the law of the new *situs* does not provide for a corresponding remedy.[14] This would have a detrimental effect on

[9] Unidroit, *Study LXXII – Doc. 1 (1989)* 2.
[10] ibid 3.
[11] ibid 5.
[12] ibid 6.
[13] ibid (emphasis added).
[14] ibid 8.

predictability: the secured party could end up having less control over collateral moved to another country, compared to the laws of the state in which the security interest was initially created.

Third, a highly problematic area for *lex situs* would relate to mandatory registration and public notice requirements applicable to domestic security interests: if the latter must be registered to ensure efficacy or priority, then foreign security interests are likely to be subject to the same requirements (the contrary would imply that the interests of foreign secured creditors are placed higher than those of their domestic counterparts).[15] While multiple solutions to the problem were identified, all of them required specific substantive law provisions regulating the applicability of domestic public notice requirements to foreign security interests.

According to Cuming, the disruptive effects of *lex situs*[16] could be minimised if a more appropriate choice of law rule was elected to govern the security interests in mobile assets. At the time, examples of displacement of *lex situs* existed both in international instruments and domestic laws of some states. The prevailing connecting factor in the United States and Canada, as well as under the 1965 Convention on the Registration of Inland Navigation Vessels[17] (the '1965 Geneva Convention') was *lex debitoris* (ie the law of the country in which the debtor is located or has its place of business), whereas the relevant international aviation[18] and maritime[19] conventions favoured *lex registri* (ie the law of the country of the relevant register in which the asset is registered).

Both *lex debitoris* and *lex registri* were not without their own flaws, either. Essentially, each of them required the state in which the mobile asset was located to relinquish the application of its own laws with respect to security interests created over such asset in favour of the law of the location of the debtor or the law of the country where the asset was registered.[20] In addition, certain financiers would lack the sophistication to check the laws and records of countries other than the *situs*, whereas the creation and maintenance of an international registry

[15] ibid 9.

[16] During the review of Cuming's report by the UNIDROIT Governing Council in 1989 Roy Goode noted another inadequacy of the *lex situs* rule in situations where the debtor creates security not over a single object, but over the totality of its assets: in this situation the creditor would most likely search the registry at the debtor's location, rather than attempt to physically locate all the relevant assets and then identify the law applicable to *in rem* rights (See Unidroit, *Governing Council C.D. 68 – Doc. 26 (1989)* 33).

[17] Convention on the Registration of Inland Navigation Vessels (adopted 25 January 1965, entered into force 24 June 1982) 1281 UNTS 111. Although the convention formally applies the *lex registri* connecting factor (Article 10 of Protocol No 1), a vessel can only be registered in one state and only provided that this state is (i) the territory from which the operation of the vessel is habitually directed; (ii) the country of nationality or habitual residence of the owner of the vessel; or (iii) the territory on which the owner of the vessel has its registered office or the principal place of business management (Article 3(1)). Effectively this results in the application of the *lex debitoris* connecting factor.

[18] See Articles I(1) and II(2) of the 1948 Geneva Convention.

[19] See Article 1 of the 1926 Brussels Convention. See also Article 1 of the International Convention for the Unification of Certain Rules Relating to Maritime Liens and Mortgages (adopted 27 May 1967) (the '1967 Brussels Convention').

[20] Unidroit, *Study LXXII – Doc. 1 (1989)* 27.

for the purposes of providing public notice of security interests seemed entirely unrealistic at the time.[21]

2.2.2. Seeking Solutions to the Lex Situs Problem

i. Recognition as a Necessary Element of Conflict of Laws Unification

Despite the added legal certainty offered by *lex debitoris* and *lex registri*, it was immediately clear that a simple harmonisation of connecting factors across multiple jurisdictions would not be enough. In addition, Cuming argued, it would be essential to ensure the continued validity of security interests through recognition, regardless of the type of connecting factor used.[22] Indeed, the need for a system of recognition inevitably arises whenever it is physically possible that the same connecting factor (even if uniformly adopted by all states) leads to the application of the law of more than one jurisdiction. Even if *lex debitoris* or *lex registri* is universally applied, courts may still have a dilemma as to which system of law to choose: the law to which the relevant connecting factor points at the time of proceedings (State A), or the law to which the same connecting factor pointed at some earlier time (State B) since the location of the debtor has changed or the asset was reregistered in another registry. Application of the connecting factor by reference to the position existing at the time of proceedings (State A) is inadequate in the sense that it does not provide a necessary degree of predictability (it disregards the fact that the security interest could have been created when the debtor was located, or the asset was registered, in an entirely different state). The need to preserve commercial certainty[23] firmly points towards the application of the laws of State B, supplemented by a rule on recognition of the validity of security interests created under those laws. Depending on the selected conflict of laws provision, this would involve recognition of security interests in cases of: (i) change of the asset's location; (ii) change of debtor's location; or (iii) change of the relevant register.

To ascertain the function of recognition as part of unification of conflict of laws provisions, consider the following example.

Example 1

A financier having its place of business in State X is planning to grant a loan to a borrower whose place of business is in State Y. The loan is to be secured by mortgage over an asset which regularly moves between States X, Y and Z.

[21] ibid.

[22] ibid 28.

[23] The importance of commercial certainty is the subject of detailed analysis in section 7.2.1.

Prior to unification of conflict of laws rules, all *in rem* rights in mobile assets under the laws of State X are regulated by *lex debitoris*, whereas under the laws of States Y and Z *lex situs* applies to *in rem* rights.[24] As a result, the laws of State X mandate the application of the laws of State Y to the security interest regardless of the location of the asset, whereas the conflict of laws rules of States Y and Z require the application of the relevant substantive rules of States X, Y or Z, respectively (with a potential for applying the laws of any other state where the asset may end up).

Following unification of connecting factors States X, Y and Z all apply the same connecting factor to security interests in mobile equipment, *lex debitoris*. The use of the new connecting factor alone results in greatly increased predictability, as the now-harmonised conflict of laws provisions of all states lead to the application of the substantive security laws of the same country (State Y), which is unlikely (although not impossible) to change. From the investor's perspective, compliance with the requirements of substantive law rules of States X or Z yields no added benefit: as long as the security agreement follows the rules of State Y, it will be valid and enforceable in all states (potentially subject to public policy rules of the forum and other factors limiting availability of certain remedies not known to the laws of the forum, but these additional concerns are irrelevant for the purposes of this example).

In this scenario, in addition to the above unification, in order to address the rare situations when the debtor changes its place of business, contracting states additionally agree to recognise the security interests which were validly created in accordance with the connecting factor applicable at the time of their creation, even if at the time of the court proceedings brought by the financier the debtor is located in a different state. However, even without such recognition, the position of the creditor would not be materially prejudiced, since the change of debtor's location is more difficult and potentially time-consuming (compared to the movement of the relevant asset), easier to track and less likely to occur in the first place.

The obvious downside of this scenario lies in practicability: States Y and Z would be required to relinquish the right to apply their own substantive laws to security interests over objects located within their territory and are thus likely to resist unification in the first place.[25] Another problem arises from the need to apply foreign rules, including the rules on remedies, which may not be known to the domestic legal systems of states in which enforcement of security is sought (potentially with the politically unwelcome result of allowing foreign secured creditors greater protection compared to what is permitted domestically).

[24] For the purposes of this example, it is assumed that no *renvoi* applies in any of the cases.

[25] Although in this particular factual scenario State Y may find attractive the extension of the application of its own laws (due to the fact that the debtor appears to be located in State Y, which is completely incidental), in many other situations this will not be the case.

ii. Recognition as an Alternative to Full Conflict of Laws Unification

Even though the unification of conflict of laws rules applicable to security interests in mobile equipment, coupled with a system of recognition mentioned in the previous paragraphs was certainly less ambitious than harmonisation of substantive rules, Cuming's proposal did not contemplate any major revision of conflict of laws rules adopted by states. Instead, the study suggested an even more limited solution: a system of recognition of security interests validly created under the domestic laws of other countries. This solution did not entail any mandatory unification of connecting factors, except for one important scenario: since the ultimate objective was to ensure the recognition of validly created national security interests, it was necessary to provide for a uniform solution to the problem of identification of rules governing the *validity* of such security interests.[26] The solution, according to Cuming, would lie in the abolition of the *lex situs* rule in favour of *lex debitoris*.[27]

Example 2

To identify the different role of recognition envisaged in Cuming's proposal consider the following example.

The starting position is the same as in Example 1 prior to unification, however in this scenario there is no subsequent unification of conflict of laws rules of States X, Y and Z: they continue to apply *lex debitoris* and *lex situs* respectively. In contrast to Example 1, the legal harmonisation here is limited to a single rule on recognition, whereby security interests validly created under *lex debitoris* are to be recognised and enforced by all participating states.

For obvious reasons, this approach is much less intrusive from the perspective of States Y and Z: if there is no security interest validly created under the laws of State Y (or, similarly, if such security interest exists, but is not asserted by the creditor), States Y and Z do not have to relinquish the authority to apply their own substantive rules to the security interest when an asset subject to such security interest ends up in their territory. In this scenario, recognition is not merely an accompanying element of conflict of laws unification aiming to enhance legal certainty (which was the case in Example 1): it is rather an end in itself, as states are free to keep their conflict of laws rules, which are only qualified by the obligation to ensure recognition.

From the financier's perspective, however, this 'light-touch' unification provides a level of certainty which is substantially similar to that of Example 1 (assuming that the problem of foreign remedies unknown to the enforcing court's

[26] In the absence of such uniform connecting factor courts tasked with recognising foreign security interests would have absolutely no indication as to which system of law to analyse for compliance with and would have to search all jurisdictions for signs of compliance with their respective criteria or arbitrarily select such system of law.

[27] See Appendix A in Unidroit, *Study LXXII – Doc. 1 (1989)* iii.

legal system may apply equally in either scenario): to ensure validity of the security interest in other countries, it is sufficient to comply with the laws of State Y. Thus, predictability is achievable through much less interference with the domestic legal system and is less likely to attract opposition from States Y and Z.

A possible alternative to the above concept of recognition could be the creation of a separate *sui generis* international interest governed by the new convention, but the prospects of this approach were not considered at the early stage of the project: in Cuming's own words, the objective of the future convention 'would *not* be to create a supra-national security interest'.[28]

2.2.3. A Functional Approach to Security Interests?

According to Cuming's research, an international regime of recognition of foreign security interests would not be workable without a functional approach (ie a regime whereby the rules governing proprietary interests in mobile assets apply to transactions involving the use of such assets to secure payment or performance of an obligation regardless of the form such transactions may take):[29] 'an undertaking to recognize all foreign generic security interests in mobile equipment would appear to be a sine qua non of a new international structure designed to accommodate modern mobile equipment financing'.[30]

This approach implied that in addition to transactions commonly categorised as creating security interests, such as contractual mortgages and charges, the broad concept of 'security interest' would cover both title reservation agreements and leases having the function of security,[31] which, as shown below, would run contrary to the laws of many jurisdictions.

The proposal to establish an international functional approach to security interests in mobile equipment was first put to the test in the questionnaire prepared by the UNIDROIT Secretariat, together with Ronald Cuming, in 1990 (the 'Questionnaire')[32] to rectify the principal deficiency of Cuming's report, namely the lack of substantial empirical analysis.[33] The document did not merely attempt to assess the commercial need for harmonisation in the area of security interests in mobile equipment: it tested the preliminary legal conclusions made in Cuming's Study.[34]

[28] ibid (emphasis added).

[29] This approach was at the time reflected in Article 9 of the US Uniform Commercial Code and certain Canadian Personal Property Security Acts.

[30] Unidroit, *Study LXXII – Doc. 1 (1989)* 28.

[31] ibid.

[32] Unidroit, *Study LXXII – Doc. 2 (1989).*

[33] Cuming's original assumptions had been tested only by way of inviting comments from a small group of experts.

[34] The Questionnaire was distributed between February and July 1990 in all UNIDROIT member states, as well as in Brazil, Iceland and New Zealand and among a number of international organisations.

Despite the initial assumption that the new convention would not create any kind of supra-national security interest,[35] the Questionnaire nevertheless offered two alternative proposals by which the harmonisation could be achieved: (i) development of an 'entirely new type of secured financing device for use where financing involves collateral in the form of equipment of a kind generally moved from one State to another', or (ii) 'recognition of a generic concept of security interest that encompasses all financing devices used in States … whether or not those devices are conceptualised as such under the laws of the State in which they are used'. The vast majority of respondents (44) supported the latter option, while only 14 sought an entirely different financing vehicle.[36]

2.2.4. Transactions Falling within the Ambit of the New Convention

Preference towards the use of functional approach to identify the categories of transactions covered by the new convention was subsequently affirmed by the UNIDROIT Restricted Exploratory Working Group (REWG) in 1992:

> 'Security interest' should be defined in functional terms, thus avoiding the problems created by differences in the concept of security interest and should encompass, for example, reservation of title under sale agreements as well as security by way of mortgage or charge.[37]

Only consensual non-possessory security interests (ie those in which the debtor is left in physical possession of the asset)[38] were to be covered by the new convention.[39] A similar approach was developed during the first session of the UNIDROIT Study Group for the Preparation of Uniform Rules on Certain International Aspects of Security Interests in Mobile Equipment (the 'Study Group') in 1993: this time, in addition to title reservation agreements, the Study Group for the first time considered the feasibility of covering finance leases, but eventually decided to postpone the decision on that matter.[40]

Subsequent discussions and commentaries received by the Study Group revealed multiple conceptual differences between various legal traditions,[41] particularly with respect to the different treatment of title reservation and leasing agreements by the systems of civil law, which distinguished the right of ownership from security interests as 'fundamentally opposed' categories.[42] In response to

[35] See Appendix A in Unidroit, *Study LXXII – Doc. 1 (1989)* iii.
[36] Unidroit, *Study LXXII – Doc. 3 (1991)* 9–10.
[37] Unidroit, *Study LXXII – Doc. 5 (1992)* 4.
[38] For reasons of exclusion of possessory interests see Unidroit, *Study LXXII – Doc. 11 (1994)* 8.
[39] Unidroit, *Study LXXII – Doc. 5 (1992)* 4.
[40] Unidroit, *Study LXXII – Doc. 7 (1993)* 5.
[41] See, eg, Unidroit, *Study LXXII – Doc. 8 (1993)* 31; Unidroit, *Study LXXII – Doc. 11 (1994)* 7; Unidroit, *Security Interests Study Group Sub-committee 1st Session Misc. 2 (1994)* 3.
[42] Unidroit, *Study LXXII – Doc. 6 Add. 3 (1993)* 1.

these concerns, the Sub-Committee for the Preparation of a First Draft established by the Study Group (the 'First Draft Subcommittee') introduced two substantive changes into the project. First, it was decided that the new convention should be expressed as establishing uniform rules for 'interests' (as opposed to 'security interests'). Second, the subcommittee adopted for the first time the technique that would later persist throughout the whole process of development of the Cape Town Convention: formal separation of interests arising under security agreements from interests created by virtue of a title retention agreement. As a result, all the 'interests' were divided into two distinct categories: security interests *stricto sensu*, on the one hand, and interests arising from retention of title and leasing agreements, on the other.[43] Drawing a distinction between the latter two categories in the text of the new convention was considered unnecessary, as long as they were subject to the same rules.[44] This change marked the formal departure from the concept of a *single* security interest defined 'by looking at the intention and economic effect of the transaction rather than at its particular legal form'[45] and was subsequently reflected in the first set of draft articles of the future Convention.

The first set of draft articles prepared in 1994 differentiated between two types of agreements: a 'security agreement' and a 'title reservation agreement'.[46] The former was defined as 'an agreement which secures performance of an existing or future money obligation owed by one person … to another'.[47] The latter covered both leases and title reservation agreements and was defined as 'an agreement by which mobile equipment is supplied on lease (with or without an option to the lessee to buy the equipment) or is agreed to be sold on terms that ownership does not pass from the seller to the buyer until payment of the sums specified by the agreement'.[48] The combined effect of both definitions was to accommodate the needs of both legal traditions: although the 'security agreement' was still defined in functional terms by reference to its economic purpose,[49] jurisdictions which respected the distinct nature of title retention and lease agreements could continue to do so.

Without challenging the need to differentiate between security interests *stricto sensu* and title reservations (in the broad sense, as defined by the Study Group in 1994),[50] the AWG[51] in 1995 proposed a more technical approach, whereby the two groups were separated on the grounds of allocation of title to the relevant asset. Under this concept, a 'security interest' would be defined as 'a writing containing

[43] Unidroit, *Study LXXII – Doc. 12 (1994)* 5.
[44] ibid.
[45] Unidroit, *Study LXXII – Doc. 7 (1993)* 4.
[46] Unidroit, *Study LXXII – Doc. 13 (1994).*
[47] Article 1(2)(d) in ibid.
[48] Article 1(2)(e) in ibid.
[49] cf Uniform Commercial Code Article 1-201(37); Personal Property Security Act, Revised Statutes of Saskatchewan, 1978.
[50] Unidroit, *Study LXXII – Doc. 12 (1994)* 5.
[51] Aviation working group, a newly formed association of major aircraft financing market participants, represented by Airbus Industrie and The Boeing Company.

obligations … the non-performance of which entitles the interest holder to seize specifically identified assets title to which resides, or will reside, *with the interest holder's contract counterparty* in such writing'. In contrast, a 'title reservation' would mean 'a writing containing obligations … the non-performance of which entitles the interest holder to seize specifically identified assets title to which resides, or will reside, *with such interest holder*'.[52] This new approach captured the common characteristics of title reservation and leasing agreements at a fundamental level: in both types of transactions the ownership vests in the creditor, rather than the debtor. In other words, this solution reached the same objectives as the separation envisaged in the first set of draft articles[53] but abandoned differentiation based on specific transaction mechanics. Despite its conceptual soundness, the proposal of the AWG was never reflected in any of the drafts of the Convention, partly because of the later decision to separate leasing transactions as a separate category not falling under the heading of 'title reservation agreements'.[54]

One problem with the differentiation proposed in the first set of draft articles,[55] which successfully transferred to the second revision of the same in 1995,[56] lay in the fact that it treated in the same manner interests 'arising under' both security agreements and title reservation agreements. Conceptually this is only partly accurate: the only interest a title reservation agreement can possibly create is that of the debtor, since the creditor already holds title to the asset and does not require additional authority over it to be created in its favour.[57] That is not to say, however, that the 'interest' of seller or lessor, which in effect is the right of ownership, cannot be displaced by a security interest: such technique was used in the 1993 EBRD Model Law on Secured Transactions, which in Article 9.1 created a mechanism whereby an unpaid vendor, by operation of law, loses the title to the object of sale (which title is transferred to the purchaser) and instead simultaneously obtains a charge over the same object.[58] This issue was subsequently acknowledged by the First Draft Subcommittee[59] and addressed in the next revision of the first set of draft articles of the future Convention, in which the interest of the seller in a title reservation agreement was expressed as being 'retained' by the seller (Article 1(2)(b)).[60]

In addition, the same set of draft articles abolished the previous practice of treating title reservation and leasing agreements under a single heading, recognising the special characteristics of leasing transactions, which are discussed in the next section.

[52] Unidroit, *Study LXXII – Doc. 16 (1995)* 12 (emphasis added).

[53] Unidroit, *Study LXXII – Doc. 12 (1994)* 5.

[54] The special concerns of the leasing industry which resulted in the formal separation of leases are discussed in section 2.2.4.i below.

[55] Article 1(2)(b) in Unidroit, *Study LXXII – Doc. 13 (1994)*.

[56] Unidroit, *Study LXXII – Doc. 18 (1995)* 6.

[57] Unidroit, *Study LXXII – Doc. 19 (1995)*; Unidroit, *Study LXXII – Doc. 19 Add. (1995)* 3.

[58] See Article 9.1 of the 1993 EBRD Model Law on Secured Transactions.

[59] Unidroit, *Study LXXII – Doc. 21 (1995)* 7.

[60] Unidroit, *Study LXXII – Doc. 22 (1996)* 1.

i. *Leasing Agreements*

In his Study, Cuming, who advocated the functional approach to the definition of security interests, envisaged that the future convention would cover two types of leases: (i) hire-purchase contracts under which the seller leases equipment to a buyer who intends to purchase it, and (ii) leases which under the applicable law are characterised as security agreements.[61] A functional approach would effectively cover leases having the effect of creating security over the leased object and exclude 'true leases' (ie leases which do not serve such function). Difficulties associated with this concept surfaced very quickly.

a. The Distinct Nature of Lessors' Rights

Members of the leasing industry demonstrated their firm opposition to assimilation of leases to security transactions from the early stages of development of the Convention, on the basis that the lessor's ownership right should not be confused with a 'security interest'.[62] In the light of these concerns the UNIDROIT Study Group, which in its first session approved the functional approach as applied to the concept of security interests, decided to defer the consideration of finance leases specifically (leases without the function of creating security were not expected to be covered by the future convention in the first place).[63]

The initial step in the formal separation of leases was taken by the First Draft Subcommittee, which replaced the reference to 'security interests' with a more neutral one, covering 'interests' generally and decided to address both title retention agreements and leasing agreements as a separate (but single) category.[64] Concerned with the opposition emanating from the leasing industry, the subcommittee did not follow the recommendation of Jan-Hendrik Roever[65] to implement, *mutatis mutandis*, an approach similar to that used in Article 9.1 of the 1993 EBRD Model Law on Secured Transactions.[66]

In the next two drafts leasing agreements appeared under the heading of 'title reservation agreements', together with title retention agreements *stricto sensu*.[67]

b. The Special Case of 'True Leases'

The decision to merge both leases and sales with reservation of title into a single category was problematic because, unlike title retention sales, which primarily[68]

[61] See Appendix A in Unidroit, *Study LXXII – Doc. 1 (1989)* ii.

[62] See comments of the French Finance Houses Association in Unidroit, *Study LXXII – Doc. 6 (1993)* 4; see also comments of the European Federation of Equipment Leasing Company Associations in Unidroit, *Study LXXII – Doc. 6 Add. 3 (1993)* 1.

[63] Unidroit, *Study LXXII – Doc. 7 (1993)* 5.

[64] Unidroit, *Study LXXII – Doc. 12 (1994)* 5.

[65] Unidroit, *Study LXXII – Doc. 11 (1994)* 11.

[66] See n 58.

[67] See Unidroit, *Study LXXII – Doc. 13 (1994)* and Unidroit, *Study LXXII – Doc. 18 (1995)*.

[68] An exception would be a contract whereby the transfer of title to the purchaser is subject to an event other than payment.

serve the function of creating security, leases are less homogeneous in this sense and may as well be concluded solely for the purposes of renting the relevant equipment. The inclusion of all types of leases within the scope of the new convention would therefore mean extending its reach to matters which may have nothing to do with security in the first place. This issue could remain a simple policy matter, but the accumulated practical experience dictated otherwise. Differentiation between the two types of leases had proven so difficult that in 1992 Cuming questioned the usefulness of separation of leases based on their purpose: 'experience in North America indicates the futility of attempting to distinguish between "true leases" and "security leases" without clear statutory guidance'.[69]

Four different solutions to the problem emerged in the early stages of development of the Convention. The first was inspired by the recent experience of the EBRD, which had completely excluded leases from the scope of its 1993 Model Law on Secured Transactions in view of the perceived impossibility of drawing a convincing distinction between various leases.[70] The second was formulated by Thomas Whalen, who, essentially for the same reasons, suggested that all leases should be covered by the future convention.[71]

The third and fourth solutions were proposed by Cuming himself. In his view, this problem, which had resulted in 'a great deal of litigation and considerable confusion', was not a good reason to exclude from the scope of the future convention a whole range of leases that were de facto financing transactions. Such exclusion would inevitably result in an uneven application of the treaty in different legal systems: the North American jurisdictions would characterise certain leases as functionally security agreements falling under the convention, whereas courts adopting a more formalistic approach would not look beyond the form of the transaction.[72] Two solutions were envisaged by Cuming. The first would be to make it clear in the text of the convention that the functional concept of 'security interest' was intended to cover finance leases. The second would be to provide in the convention a set of specific tests to determine the categories of leases regulated by the new instrument.[73] Both options were problematic, however: the former did not address the problem of uncertainty, which had plagued the North American jurisdictions, whereas the latter would inevitably result in some transactions that have the function of creating security being left out. As a result, Cuming suggested an alternative definition of 'security lease', which essentially characterised as a security instrument any leasing transaction which: (i) included the lessee's obligation to purchase the leased asset or an obligation to renew the agreement for a term amounting to all or substantially all of the remaining economic life of the equipment; (ii) automatically transferred the title over the leased asset to the lessee after

[69] Unidroit, *Study LXXII – Doc. 4 (1992)* 5.
[70] Unidroit, *Study LXXII – Doc. 11 (1994)* 9.
[71] Unidroit, *Study LXXII – Doc. 10 (1994)* 10.
[72] Unidroit, *Study LXXII – Doc. 8 (1993)* 11.
[73] ibid.

the payment of all, or a specified number of, periodic payments; (iii) effectively gave the lessee a right of possession over the leased asset for all or substantially all of the remaining economic life of the equipment; (iv) gave the lessee the right to purchase the leased asset at a price that was substantially below the market value of the equipment at the date such right was exercised; or (v) permitted the lessee to renew possession of the leased asset at a price that was substantially below the market rental cost of the equipment at the date such right was exercised.[74]

The First Draft Subcommittee did not establish a firm position, but provisionally considered two criteria that could be used to limit the types of leasing agreements covered by the future convention: (i) an option to purchase the leased asset, and (ii) a term of the lease exceeding three years.[75] Nonetheless, the lack of an agreed position on the matter gave the Drafting Group[76] a certain degree of freedom; as a result, neither of the above two requirements were reflected in the following two drafts: the minimum duration was omitted, while the leasing agreements, as defined, included even transactions without an option to purchase the leased asset.[77] Effectively, these drafts covered all types of leasing arrangements.

Opinions relating to the possibility of excluding certain types of leases expressed by various commentators and international organisations in the run-up to the third session of the First Draft Subcommittee were noticeably divided. One group called for the exclusion of 'true leases': on the one hand, the latter were seen as creating conceptual difficulties in jurisdictions that did not recognise the security function of leasing transactions,[78] on the other hand, it was feared that the requirement of registration, if adopted in the future convention as a requirement of validity and/or priority of lessor's interest in bankruptcy, would be excessive when applied to true leases (particularly to those of short-term duration).[79] The other group expressed a general preference towards the inclusion of all leases, mainly for the purposes of increased legal certainty: even in those legal systems which recognised 'security leases' the problems of characterisation eventually increased financing costs.[80] In addition, from the perspective of aviation industry transactions, the requirement of registration, even as applied to short-term leases, would not be seen as a major hurdle, given the relatively high costs of aircraft equipment. In contrast, even if a special exception for short-term leases were introduced, this would, as a minimum, provide a disincentive to enter into short-term leases, not to mention the dual system of rules regulating long-term and short-term leases resulting from such decision.[81]

[74] ibid 12–13.

[75] Unidroit, *Study LXXII – Doc. 12 (1994)* 5.

[76] In this book, mentions of the 'Drafting Group' should be read as references to the specific drafting group operating at the time in question prior to the governmental expert stage – see section 8.2.2.

[77] Unidroit, *Study LXXII – Doc. 13 (1994)*; Unidroit, *Study LXXII – Doc. 18 (1995)*.

[78] Unidroit, *Study LXXII – Doc. 14 Add 2 (1994)* 1; Unidroit, *Study LXXII – Doc. 14 Add 4 (1994)*.

[79] Unidroit, *Study LXXII – Doc. 19 Add. (1995)* 4.

[80] Unidroit, *Study LXXII – Doc. 16 (1995)* 13; Unidroit, *Study LXXII – Doc. 17 (1995)* 5; Unidroit, *International Interests Study-Group Sub-committee 3rd Session Misc. 1 (1995)* 1.

[81] Unidroit, *Study LXXII – Doc. 16 (1995)* 13.

The feasibility of limiting the types of leasing agreements covered by the future convention was next revisited during the third session of the First Draft Subcommittee, which not only reopened the discussion on this matter, but finally separated leasing transactions from title retention agreements.[82] The decision to consider the idea of excluding from the scope of the Convention short-term leases (provisionally identified as those not exceeding three years) was reflected in the next draft, in which a 'leasing agreement' was defined as 'agreement by which one person … leases an object (with or without an option to purchase) to another person … for a period of not less than [three] years'.[83]

The second session of the UNIDROIT Study Group held in 1996 essentially confirmed the same position. Leasing agreements covered by the future convention were not supposed to be limited by any kind of specific criteria for a number of reasons. On the one hand, if only certain categories of leases were within the scope of the Convention, parties to the relevant contracts would inevitably attempt to exploit the criteria used to draw a distinction between the two categories. On the other hand, the AWG, which represented the aviation industry, held a strong view that all leases should be covered by the future Convention for reasons of its own. First, the Convention remedies were expected to apply equally to all types of leasing transactions. Second, it was important to avoid complex characterisation with a view to enhancing predictability in the application of the Convention. Third, the application of priority rules established by the Convention would be unclear unless all leases were included in its scope.[84] Fourth, in an asset (as opposed to debtor-based) register filing of all types of leases was a practical solution to the above problems.[85] Fifth, even a distinction of finance leases based on whether or not the lessor was an authorised financial institution (as a possible differentiating factor) would not always work: in some jurisdictions such authorisation was not required, whereas in the area of aviation finance most high-value leasing transactions were carried out by special purpose vehicles.[86]

The Study Group concluded that the only workable way of distinguishing between types of leases could be based on the concept of the minimum term of the lease and, thus, the basic definition of 'leasing agreement' (which incorporated a three-year duration requirement) would remain unchanged, but exceptions could, in principle, be established for certain industries (eg for aircraft).[87] The concern was that the terms of the (then) current draft permitted the lessee even under a one-day lease to give good title to any third party, provided that the lessor's interest had not been registered under the Convention.[88]

[82] Unidroit, *Study LXXII – Doc. 21 (1995)* 7.
[83] Unidroit, *Study LXXII – Doc. 22 (1996)* 2.
[84] The development of the Convention's priority rules is discussed in section 6.2.
[85] The development of the Convention's registration system is discussed in section 6.3.
[86] Unidroit, *Study LXXII – Doc. 27 (1996)* 19.
[87] ibid 18.
[88] See Article 19(3) in Unidroit, *Study LXXII – Doc. 24 (1996).*

Following the third session of the UNIDROIT Study Group in 1997 the mandatory minimum term of a lease agreement (provisionally of a three-year duration) was deleted from the text of the Convention and replaced with a proviso that a minimum term may be set out in the corresponding protocol to the same.[89] This proviso, however, was soon removed after the fourth session of the Study Group held later in the same year, thus abolishing the last remaining limitation on the types of leases covered by the Convention.[90] With the exception of a number of minimal technical corrections,[91] the resulting broad concept of 'leasing agreement' was later adopted in the final text of the Convention.[92]

2.3. Proposing a Solution: The Concept of International Interest

This section focuses on the origins of the concept of 'international interest', which emerged as an alternative to an international system of recognition of foreign security interests. The Study Group expressed its preference towards a new international financing vehicle quite early, but the concept of 'autonomous' international interest, as reflected in the final text of the Convention, emerged significantly later in the development process.

2.3.1. International Interest as Alternative to Recognition

Although both the initial Study prepared by Ronald Cuming in 1989[93] and the responses to the Questionnaire of the UNIDROIT Secretariat[94] clearly favoured the idea of setting up an international system of recognition of domestic security interests, the proposal to establish an entirely new type of security interest appeared as early as in 1988, when Georges Droz, Secretary-General of the Hague Conference on Private International Law, suggested that the attention should be focused on the creation of 'a new security interest which would facilitate international relations'.[95] In 1991 Droz reiterated his idea, noting that 'the problem existed not only of recognition of security interests': domestic laws of different countries were extremely diverse and afforded them different degrees of priority. As a result, the establishment of an 'entirely new security interest' would have the advantage of

[89] See Appendix: Definitions (c) in Unidroit, *Study LXXII – Doc. 35 (1997)*.
[90] See Article 1(i) in Unidroit, *Study LXXII – Doc. 37 (1997)*.
[91] cf Article 1(n) in Unidroit, *Study LXXII – Doc. 39 (1998)*.
[92] See Article 1(q) of the CTC.
[93] See Appendix A in Unidroit, *Study LXXII – Doc. 1 (1989)* iii.
[94] As noted in section 2.2.3 the vast majority of respondents (44) supported recognition, whereas only 14 sought an entirely different financing vehicle – see Unidroit, *Study LXXII – Doc. 3 (1991)* 10.
[95] Unidroit, *Governing Council C.D. 67 – Doc. 18 (1988)* 56.

mitigating the conflict of laws problems.[96] It became apparent that whatever direction the UNIDROIT project would take, it had to deal with this diversity is some way, whether by adopting a functional approach (which would essentially require the future Convention to include the appropriate criteria to identify the qualifying security interests), by listing all types of security interests subject to recognition, or otherwise.

In 1992, the REWG considered two alternative directions for the future Convention. One involved recognition of domestic security interests validly created under the laws of the state of nationality registration of the equipment (*lex registri*) or under the law of the state in which the debtor has its place of business (*lex debitoris*), where both such states were parties to the treaty. Under this option, the characteristics of the security interests subject to recognition would be specified in the future Convention, rather than in domestic law.[97] The other option, which at the time was not considered essential for the success of the new instrument, involved the creation of a new 'international security interest' recognised in all states parties to the future Convention and registrable in an international registration system. This interest would possess three key characteristics: (i) it would be a right *in rem*; (ii) it would give its holder the right to follow the equipment into the hands of third parties, subject to applicable priority rules; and (iii) it would give the secured party a right to payment from the proceeds of disposition of the equipment in preference to other creditors, subject to applicable priority rules.[98]

Neither of the two options left to applicable law the criteria with which the relevant interest had to comply: the future Convention was expected to list these criteria directly. However, despite this similarity, the consequences of the two approaches would not be similar. In case of establishment of an 'international security interest' the validity (or invalidity) of the relevant interest under domestic law would have no bearing on the validity of the same under the Convention: as a result, there would be no pressure to account for the different concepts of 'security interest' existing in domestic laws. In contrast, a system of recognition, in order to be effective, had to cover a variety of financing devices used in national legal systems, ensuring that even transactions not considered as security agreements under the laws of some states would still fall under the treaty – as the recognition depends first and foremost on the validity of the relevant interest under the domestic law.[99]

Transition to the idea of an 'international security interest' occurred during the first session of the UNIDROIT Study Group in 1993,[100] which for the first time established the elements required to create such interest: (i) agreement in writing to create security, signed by or on behalf of the debtor and containing

[96] Unidroit, *Governing Council C.D. (70) 22 (1991)* 61.
[97] Unidroit, *Study LXXII – Doc. 5 (1992)* 5.
[98] ibid 4.
[99] Unidroit, *Security Interests Study Group 1st Session Misc. 5 (1993)* 1.
[100] Unidroit, *Study LXXII – Doc. 7 (1993)* 4.

a description of the relevant asset, and (ii) registration.[101] In 1994 the REWG added a third element: 'value'[102] and provisionally decided that all three elements could be provided in any order, with priority going back to the time of filing in the register.[103] In addition, in order to accommodate the concerns of jurisdictions outside North America which did not recognise the functional approach, it was decided to refer to the new international security interest in a more neutral manner, by omitting the word 'security'.[104]

In 1994, the Drafting Group produced the first set of draft articles of the future Convention, which was based on the decisions adopted by the Study Group and the REWG.[105] This draft distinguished between two different concepts: 'interest' and 'international interest'. The former was defined as 'an interest arising under a security agreement or a title reservation agreement', whereas the latter was established as a result of registration of an 'interest' in accordance with the draft Convention.[106] Although this draft aimed to reflect the earlier decision that registration should be one of the elements necessary to create an international interest,[107] the legal nature of an unregistered 'interest' was far from clear. Four possible explanations can be brought forward.

First, the 'interest' in this case identifies the domestic security interest arising by virtue of applicable law. Second, it could refer to the security interest which the relevant agreement *purported* to create (ie without regard to the applicable law). Third, it could be seen as a mere fiction established in the draft for the sole purpose of identifying that 'something' which could subsequently be registered with the result of creating an 'international interest'. Fourth, it could as well be an entirely new type of security interest created by virtue of the draft Convention. The first of the above explanations is problematic, as it would ultimately make the 'international interest' dependent on the validity of the relevant interest under the domestic law. The second and third options seem plausible, but do not strictly follow from the draft text, according to which the 'interest' should 'arise' (ie come into existence) from the relevant agreement. The fourth explanation seems the most conceptually sound but implies that the draft Convention creates two different kinds of interests completely independent from domestic law, only one of which is 'international'.

The second draft prepared in 1995 adopted a different approach. This time, the fact of registration no longer transformed some abstract 'interest' into an 'international interest' but was only necessary to ensure priority as against third parties (absent registration the draft Convention would have effect only as between the

[101] ibid 5.
[102] This requirement, probably inspired by Article 9 of the UCC, was not used subsequently.
[103] Unidroit, *Study LXXII - Doc. 12 (1994)* 6.
[104] ibid 5.
[105] Unidroit, *Study LXXII - Doc. 13 (1994).*
[106] Article 1(2)(b) and 1(2)(c) in ibid.
[107] In this draft the other elements identified by the Study Group and the REWG as mandatory were considered as requirements for registration: see Article 3 in ibid.

parties to the underlying agreements).[108] Registration ceased being a condition for the creation of an 'international interest' – the latter arose automatically once the three criteria listed in Article 3(1) were met: (i) an agreement in writing signed by or on behalf of the parties; (ii) a description of the equipment in the agreement sufficient to enable it to be identified; and (iii) debtor, lessor or seller (respectively) having 'rights' in the equipment.[109]

Later in 1995, the First Draft Subcommittee provisionally agreed to abolish the idea that an 'international interest' was created under the draft Convention: instead, it was decided to convert the corresponding provisions of Article 3(1) into conditions for the application of the draft Convention itself.[110] Effectively, this change meant that the draft Convention would simply apply to the interests complying with the requirements of the (then) current Article 3(1). This decision was problematic, however, as it obscured one of the principal mechanics of the document, namely the origination of the 'international interest'. As long as such interest was created by the draft Convention itself, the latter had to make it clear at which point the 'international interest' came into existence. Otherwise, confusion with domestic security interests arising under the applicable law would be unavoidable.

Following the deliberations of the First Draft Subcommittee, the Drafting Group produced a revised text, which incorporated significant changes. First, it included a new Article 1(1), which was modelled on Article 2 of the Convention for the European Patent for the Common Market[111] and introduced, for the first time, the concept of *autonomous* 'international interest'.[112] Second, the conditions necessary for the constitution of the 'international interest' previously listed in Article 3(1)[113] were revised (by adding a requirement to state the secured obligation, in case of a security agreement) and attributed an entirely different function: in the new draft they became conditions for the application of the draft Convention rules on remedies, registration, priorities and transfer of international interests.[114] However, as a result of this change the draft Convention lost all the requirements for the creation of the 'international interest', which made it impossible to identify the moment in time when such interest arose in the first place. Given the autonomous nature of the latter, one could assume that it emerged at the same time as the relevant (security, title reservation or leasing) agreement was concluded – whether or not the same agreement gave rise to any other (domestic) interest by virtue of application of any national system of law. In other words, under the new Article 1(2) alone, the international interest would arise under the relevant agreement even if such

[108] Unidroit, *Study LXXII – Doc. 18 (1995)* 3.
[109] See Article 3(1) and 3(2) in ibid.
[110] Unidroit, *Study LXXII – Doc. 21 (1995)* 7.
[111] Convention for the European Patent for the Common Market (Community Patent Convention) and Implementing Regulations [1989] OJ L 401/10.
[112] Unidroit, *Study LXXII – Doc. 22 (1996)* 1.
[113] Unidroit, *Study LXXII – Doc. 18 (1995).*
[114] See Article 6 in Unidroit, *Study LXXII – Doc. 22 (1996).*

agreement did not identify the relevant asset or if the chargor, seller or lessor did not have sufficient rights in the same.[115]

However, such conclusion would be at odds with the newly adopted definition of 'prospective international interest' in Article 4,[116] the purpose of which was to provide for a situation when the party under the relevant agreement (ie the chargor, seller or lessor) was lacking the necessary authority (ie corresponding rights) in the equipment at the time of the agreement to encumber (under the security agreement), sell (under the title reservation agreement) or lease (under the leasing agreement) the relevant asset. Such party, as a result of the combined effect of Articles 14, 17 and 19(5),[117] would be in a position to register its 'prospective international interest' so that, upon the chargor, seller or lessor obtaining the necessary rights in the asset, priority would run from the date of such registration. The very concept of 'prospective international interest' was based on the assumption that in order for the (full) 'international interest' to arise it was not sufficient to enter into the corresponding (security, title reservation or leasing) agreement: as a minimum, the relevant party had to have appropriate rights in the asset. As a result, the concept of 'prospective international interest' established in the draft Convention came in direct conflict with Article 1, which did not envisage *any* requirements for the constitution of an 'international interest' other than the existence of a particular agreement, whereas Article 6 merely listed the conditions necessary for the application of certain provisions of the draft Convention, without affecting the constitution of the 'international interest' as such.

2.3.2. Autonomous Character of International Interest; Relationship between an International Interest and Interests Created under National Laws

The emergence of the concept of *autonomous* 'international interest' deserves a separate mention, first, because it did not follow logically from the discussions held within the UNIDROIT Study Group, and second, because initially it created a great deal of confusion.

In 1995 members of the First Draft Subcommittee agreed on two different options to ensure the validity of the international interest against the debtor's trustee in bankruptcy and unsecured creditors: (i) registration in the international register established by the draft Convention, or (ii) perfection of the same in accordance with the perfection requirements of the applicable law determined

[115] This odd result might as well be merely a theoretical problem as in both cases none of the key provisions of the draft Convention on remedies, registration or priorities would apply by virtue of Article 6.

[116] See Article 4(b) in Unidroit, *Study LXXII – Doc. 22 (1996).*

[117] See Articles 14, 17 and 19(5) in ibid.

by the conflict of laws rules of the bankruptcy or attachment forum.[118] This approach did not separate an international interest from its counterpart arising out of national law, since it was *one and the same* interest registrable under the draft Convention but also capable of being perfected under national law. This duality, although attractive as a concept, created complications for the legal nature of the international interest, which was basically assimilated with the relevant national law counterpart. On the one hand, the international interest was supposed to be registrable in accordance with the applicable law. On the other hand, domestic laws did not (and could not, unless explicitly overridden by the Convention to that end) provide for the perfection of some kind of *sui generis* interest created by the Convention, even assuming that the Convention would purport to create one (which was not the case at the time). It follows that the 'international interest', as identified by the First Draft Subcommittee, was none other than a *domestic* interest capable of being registered under the Convention.

Nonetheless, the Drafting Group, which later met to incorporate the decisions taken by the First Draft Subcommittee, came up with the concept of 'autonomous' international interest,[119] which was incompatible with the duality of registration and perfection agreed by the latter. Indeed, the *autonomous* international interest was finally detached from its national law counterpart and neither affected it, nor depended on its validity. This elegant solution was not, however, endorsed by all members of the Study Group: in 1996 Charles Mooney and Thomas Whalen prepared a memorandum requesting that the approach which had been agreed by the First Draft Subcommittee be reinstated. Two arguments were put forward.[120] On the one hand, it was submitted that 'there [was] nothing inconsistent about the Convention recognising that the same agreement may create an interest that is enforceable under two different regimes'.[121] On the other, it was believed that the Convention's priority rules in Article 19(4) would subordinate any interest not registered as an international interest to a trustee in bankruptcy.[122] Neither of the two assertions is valid, however.

First, while it was of course technically possible to establish a system in which the same interest was enforceable under domestic law as well as under an international regime, such system would involve either (i) the perfection (or other type of validation) of an international interest created by the Convention in the national legal systems of states, or (ii) the registration of national interests as international interests in the international registry. The former option is unduly intrusive into national law, especially given the availability of the second option. Conversely, the latter makes registration in the international register dependent on the validity of

[118] Unidroit, *Study LXXII – Doc. 21 (1995)* 7.
[119] See Article 1(1) in Unidroit, *Study LXXII – Doc. 22 (1996)*.
[120] Essentially the same arguments were reiterated by the same later in 1997: see Unidroit, *Study LXXII – Doc. 32 Add. 3 (1997)* 2.
[121] Unidroit, *Study LXXII – Doc. 26 Add. 1 (1996)* 7.
[122] ibid.

the domestic interest under the applicable law: otherwise there is simply no interest to register (since the international interest and the domestic interest are one and the same, one does not exist without the other). But this would run counter to another important feature of the dual registration system supported by Mooney and Whalen: 'if the chargee, seller or buyer [*sic*] is concerned that the interest will be ineffective under local law, it can ensure effectiveness by making an international registration'.[123]

The only working scenario in which the validity of the international interest could be assured regardless of the validity of the corresponding interest under domestic law would, by implication, involve international registration of some freestanding concept detached from the national interest and, as far as practicable, from national laws generally. It is conceivable that such freestanding concept could take several forms: (i) an entirely new interest regulated by the Convention; (ii) an interest which the relevant agreement purported to create (ie a fiction arising by reference to the terms of the agreement alone, independently of any domestic law); or (iii) an agreement of the parties to create the relevant interest. Although the complete exclusion of national laws from the equation would probably be impossible (as the very existence of an agreement would depend on domestic law, unless regulated by the Convention as well), all of these options would allow the invalidity of the domestic interest to be disregarded. But assimilation of the latter with the international interest, which was inherent in the decision of the First Draft Subcommittee, would preclude such result.

Second, the priority rule disputed by Mooney and Whalen had already been prepared with the 'autonomous' character of the international interest in mind and was not concerned with effects of bankruptcy on domestic security interests in the first place.[124] The confusion can probably be explained by the fact that in their analysis of this provision the commentators relied on the idea that the international interest and the domestic security interest were essentially a single whole.

The matter of constitution of an international interest was debated during the second session of the UNIDROIT Study Group held in 1996. One of the concerns regarding the very concept of 'creation' of international interests in the context of sellers and lessors was that the interests of these two groups did not technically 'arise' out of such agreements. Nevertheless, the Study Group decided that the term 'creation' was justified: the intention behind the text of Article 1(1) was to provide for automatic, simultaneous creation of an international interest upon the entry into the relevant agreements.[125] The resulting international interest would be 'autonomous' in the sense that it 'would be treated as a sui generis right in rem with its own distinctive characteristics that derived from the future Convention and not from national systems of law'.[126] The key function of the term 'autonomous' was to

[123] ibid.
[124] See Article 19(4) in Unidroit, *Study LXXII - Doc. 24 (1996).*
[125] Unidroit, *Study LXXII - Doc. 27 (1996)* 11.
[126] ibid.

avoid any assimilation of the international interest with any other interest, right or authority, however defined, arising under national law: the international interest would arise under the qualifying agreement automatically and *in parallel* with any domestic interest, or, if the application of domestic law does not result in the creation of any national interest at all, regardless of the absence of any such domestic interest. Despite the high importance attributable to the 'autonomous' nature of an international interest, the Study Group considered that the text of Article 1(1) did not convey the intended purpose well enough and requested amendment.[127]

The draft which emerged following the second session of the UNIDROIT Study Group completely excluded the explicit reference to the 'autonomous' character of an international interest, without any substitute wording to take up its place.[128] The same draft corrected the inconsistency noted earlier in this section in connection with the concept of 'prospective international interest' introduced[129] by the Drafting Group: the four criteria applicable to the relevant agreements (written form, rights of the chargor, seller or lessor in the equipment, description of asset and identification of the secured obligation), previously formulated merely as conditions for the application of the draft Convention rules on remedies, registration, priorities and transfer of international interests,[130] were this time reinstated (with certain technical amendments) as requirements for the *creation* of international interests.[131] As a result, the earlier presumption about automatic creation of the international interest regardless of the relevant formalities (which was valid for the previous draft) could not be applied to the new text: in order for the international interest to emerge at all, each of the four requirements had to be satisfied first. This change warrants another look at the concept of 'prospective international interest'.

As noted previously,[132] the original purpose behind the idea of 'prospective international interest' was to permit registration of what may be referred to as 'international interests in the making' (or, in the words of the chairman of the UNIDROIT Study Group, 'international interests in negotiation')[133] in situations when the relevant party (the chargor, seller or lessor) was lacking the necessary authority (ie corresponding rights) in the equipment at the time of conclusion of the corresponding agreement. In its second session the UNIDROIT Study Group revised this concept and agreed a new approach substantially similar to that utilised in Article 9 of the UCC: (i) the draft Convention was to permit registration

[127] The second sentence of Article 1(1) stated: 'The international interest shall be of an autonomous character and shall have effect throughout the territories of Contracting States'. See Unidroit, *Study LXXII – Doc. 24 (1996).*

[128] See Article 1(1) in Unidroit, *Study LXXII – Doc. 30 (1996).*

[129] See n 116 and the relevant discussion.

[130] See Article 6 in Unidroit, *Study LXXII – Doc. 22 (1996)*; see also Article 6 in Unidroit, *Study LXXII – Doc. 24 (1996).*

[131] See Article 7 in Unidroit, *Study LXXII – Doc. 30 (1996).*

[132] See n 116 and the relevant discussion.

[133] Unidroit, *Study LXXII – Doc. 40 (1998)* 10.

of incomplete international interests which did not satisfy all the corresponding requirements; (ii) the different elements necessary for the creation of the international interest were to be capable of being satisfied in any order; and (iii) once all such elements were in place thereby constituting a full international interest, priority would be determined by reference to the date of initial filing.[134] This new approach was expected to exclude the need for a concept of 'prospective international interest', references to which were indeed removed in the following draft,[135] but soon reintroduced to ensure that priority of the fully constituted international interest would run from the moment of registration of the prospective international interest.[136] The Drafting Group expanded the relevant definition to cover situations when *any* of the elements required for the constitution of an international interest (and not just rights in the relevant asset) were missing, essentially describing the 'prospective international interest' by reference to the intent to eventually create a complete international interest.[137]

The above discussions and revisions, with technical and drafting improvements, shaped the autonomous concept of 'international interest' reflected in the final text of the Convention. Interestingly, all subsequent attempts to reintroduce the word 'autonomous' back into the body of the Convention failed.[138] This can at least partly explain why the relationship between an international interest and its national law counterparts generated so much confusion throughout the development of the CTC.[139]

2.4. Evolution of the Concept of Internationality

At the core of the concept of 'internationality' lies a presumption that the development of an international convention is only justified when matters regulated by the future instrument involve some form of foreign element, and that a convention should not apply to legal relationships considered genuinely 'internal' or 'domestic' from the national law perspective. The idea of a mandatory test of internationality emerged at an early stage of development of the CTC and remained pertinent throughout all stages of development of the instrument and its protocols. Multiple concepts and combinations of different factors were considered at various stages

[134] Unidroit, *Study LXXII – Doc. 27 (1996)* 17.

[135] See Appendix IV to ibid.

[136] See Articles 19, 27 and Appendix to Unidroit, *Study LXXII – Doc. 30 (1996).*

[137] ibid.

[138] Examples include Article 1(1) in Unidroit, *Study LXXII – Doc. 22 (1996)*; Article 1(1) in Unidroit, *Study LXXII – Doc. 24 (1996)*; Article 2(4) in Unidroit, *Study LXXII – Doc. 39 (1998)*; Attachment to Unidroit, *Study LXXII – Doc. 45 / Study LXXIID – Doc. 6 (1998).*

[139] See the comments from the French Association of Banks, Professor Klein and Professor Stoufflet in Unidroit, *Study LXXII – Doc. 36 (1997)* 45, 51; comments from the Federal German Association of Banks in Unidroit, *Study LXXII – Doc. 36 Add. 1 (1997)* 1; comments by Isabel Collaco in Unidroit, *Study LXXII – Doc. 40 (1998)* 27.

(including actual movement of assets, physical location of assets, location of parties and physical characteristics of assets). This section analyses the evolution of the test of internationality during the development of the Cape Town Convention.

2.4.1. Emergence of the Test of 'Internationality'

The Canadian Proposal[140] underlying the UNIDROIT's decision to initiate a feasibility study relating to the future Convention in 1988 was prepared on the assumption that an international treaty would be justified because 'security interests in mobile equipment may involve international elements', such as cross-border dealings between parties or movement of equipment used as collateral from one state to another.[141] As noted in section 2.3.1 above, at the early stages it was not quite clear which direction the development of the future treaty would take: recognition of domestic security interests or the creation of an entirely new international financing vehicle for mobile equipment.[142]

While both options required some indication as to when the future Convention would apply, this concern was particularly relevant in the latter scenario. A new, convention-regulated financing device was not expected to completely displace domestic rules governing security interests in movables: 'it [was] clear that the Convention [was] to apply only to security agreements that give rise to or have the potential to give rise to situations which require *international* regulation'.[143] In other words, the new treaty would create a legal regime operating in parallel with the existing domestic regulation. However, in order for this regime to be effective, the future Convention would have to contain clear rules permitting the parties engaged in financing transactions to determine *ex ante* which system of rules should apply: the new treaty or domestic laws. These concerns became increasingly relevant after the formal transition to the concept of freestanding Convention-regulated regimen for international interests.[144] In the words of one of the commentators, 'meeting the test of internationality while preventing the protections of the convention from being nullified by municipal law [was] perhaps the *most* difficult issue' in development of the future treaty.[145]

The most obvious method of delineating the scope of the Convention regulating international security interests in *mobile* equipment was based on the nature of the equipment in question. This nature could be determined by reference to a number of factors. First, certain types of assets, such as satellites, were seen as essentially international given their unique area of operation (outer space). Second, physical

[140] See n 1.
[141] ibid.
[142] See, eg, Unidroit, *Study LXXII – Doc. 3 (1991)* 10; Unidroit, *Study LXXII – Doc. 5 (1992)* 4.
[143] Unidroit, *Security Interests Study Group 1st Session Misc. 5 (1993)* 1 (emphasis added).
[144] Unidroit, *Study LXXII – Doc. 7 (1993)* 4.
[145] Unidroit, *Study LXXII – Doc. 9 (1994)* 12–13 (emphasis added).

characteristics of equipment, such as the ability to ordinarily cross national borders could indicate a greater need for international regulation. Third, high unit value of the equipment alone could be considered as sufficient to invoke the international regime to protect the holders of interests in such equipment.[146]

In 1993, the Study Group examined two alternative approaches to the test of 'internationality'. According to the first, the future Convention was to apply to security interests in all types of 'mobile equipment' (ie by reference to the physical characteristics of the asset), regardless of whether or not any international element was involved, and even in a purely domestic situation.[147] The second, favoured by the majority, involved bifurcation in the application of the Convention provisions depending on the existence or absence of an international factor: the application of the treaty *ab initio* would depend solely on the physical characteristics of the equipment (ie whether or not the equipment was of a kind normally moving between states), whereas the substantive rules would only come into play once the equipment has actually crossed national borders and a dispute emerged in the new jurisdiction. Prior to relocation of the relevant asset the rules of applicable domestic law would govern all matters relating to remedies or priority. This more conservative approach gathered greater support in view of perceived difficulties in persuading governments to accept an international convention governing transactions which had 'no international element other than that they involve mobile equipment that is capable of being moved from one State to another'.[148]

The separation suggested by the Study Group thus created two different concepts: 'potential internationality' (essentially limited to a simple 'mobility' test), necessary for the application of the future Convention to the relevant international interest immediately upon its creation, and 'actual internationality', required for the application of its priority and remedy rules. The requirement of a second (active) internationality, however, created uncertainty and complexity. First, lenders advancing funds secured by an international interest in essentially mobile assets could be discouraged from providing financing as their priority position (or available remedies) would change depending on the location of the asset controlled by the debtor: in such cases creditors would be inclined to limit the debtor's right to remove the asset from the jurisdiction. Naturally, debtors would prefer the freedom to use the asset without such restrictions.[149] Second, certain assets could frequently change the applicable regime, by shuttling between the 'home' state and other jurisdictions, which would create monitoring issues and further increase complexity.[150] Very soon, multiple prospective solutions emerged aiming to address these difficulties.

[146] See Unidroit, *Security Interests Study Group 1st Session Misc. 5 (1993)* 2.
[147] Unidroit, *Study LXXII – Doc. 8 (1993)* 18.
[148] ibid.
[149] See Unidroit, *Study LXXII – Doc. 6 Add. 2 (1993)* 1; Unidroit, *Study LXXII – Doc. 10 (1994)* 2.
[150] See United Nations, *Report of the Secretary-General: Study on Security Interests (A/CN.9/131) (1978)* 210; Unidroit, *Study LXXII – Doc. 9 (1994)* 1.

In 1994 Charles Mooney proposed an alternative test to determine the types of situations which could be considered 'purely domestic' and thus warranted exclusion from the scope of the future Convention. According to the suggested approach, the Convention's registration and priority rules were not applicable to a scenario whereby (i) the debtor created a security interest in accordance with the law of a contracting state while located in that state, and (ii) the debtor had its place of business in that state. The future Convention would be triggered only when the equipment actually moved to another state or the interest was registered in the international registry established by the future Convention.[151] This test narrowed the list of 'purely domestic' situations by excluding interests registered under the treaty even when the asset did not move outside the relevant jurisdiction: as long as both the debtor and the secured party voluntarily chose the Convention regime and gave notice to the world, the decision to apply the treaty would apply in full. The solution had two key benefits: first, it reflected the key commercial concept of party autonomy; second, it would greatly enhance predictability, giving financiers the opportunity to avail themselves of the Convention protections from day one in cases when the laws of the *situs* did not provide enough assurance to the creditor.[152] The downside of this approach was that any third party wishing to protect itself would inevitably have to check the international registry for existing registration (and register its own interest first) even in a purely domestic scenario, although this concern is obviously less acute in commercial financing involving sophisticated parties.

A different solution was suggested by Jan-Hendrik Roever, who proposed two alternative criteria of internationality: (i) internationality of transaction, and (ii) location of places of business of the parties in different countries.[153] The second alternative was conceptually similar to the test of 'mobility' applied by the Study Group in the sense that it did not guarantee that the equipment would eventually move between states, and can thus be considered another type of 'potential internationality'.

Ronald Cuming, using several case scenarios, proposed a different test, which involved a subjective element – namely ascertaining the actual *intention* of the parties to the relevant security agreement. In his view, the enforcement rules of the future Convention were supposed to apply, even if the equipment remained within the same jurisdiction, in situations when the circumstances of the case evidenced the intention of the parties to the security agreement to use the equipment primarily outside the country of its original *situs*. In contrast, the Convention's protections were not supposed to be available to the secured party in a similar situation if the intention of the parties was to use the equipment primarily within the same country, disregarding occasional instances of use in other states.[154] The apparent

[151] Unidroit, *Study LXXII – Doc. 10 (1994)* 2–3.
[152] ibid 3.
[153] Unidroit, *Study LXXII – Doc. 11 (1994)* 6.
[154] Unidroit, *Study LXXII – Doc. 8 (1993)* 29.

difficulty associated with this approach was its lack of predictability, as any attempt to apply it would necessarily involve an element of court discretion.

A fourth, and more radical solution, was suggested by The Boeing Company: 'given the futility of separating domestic from international aircraft finance transactions, the convention would apply even in a purely domestic context'.[155]

In view of expressed concerns, the First Draft Subcommittee significantly expanded the list of 'non-domestic' situations which made possible the application of the Convention's priority and remedy rules.[156] Two new scenarios giving rise to the Convention's protections were envisaged, in addition to the actual movement of the equipment: (i) a situation when at the time of conclusion of the security agreement both parties had their places of business in different states, and (ii) a situation when the security agreement expressly provided that the relevant equipment would move between different states.[157] The latter scenario differed significantly from the solution suggested by Cuming earlier[158] in that the subjective element (ascertaining the actual intention of the parties) was replaced with reference to the express terms of the contract for the purposes of enhanced predictability. This important change created the only opportunity for a secured party located in the same country as the debtor to guarantee its priority over foreign creditors in a situation when the equipment did not move outside its *situs* at all: absent this proviso the draft Convention would create a rather unwelcome mechanism clearly favouring foreign creditors to the prejudice of domestic creditors (as the latter would not be in a position to protect their priority vis-à-vis competing creditors located abroad).

The report of the First Draft Subcommittee[159] does not make it clear whether, in order to satisfy the internationality requirement, the equipment needed only to cross national borders or was also required not to return back into the country of its initial *situs*. Nonetheless, the first set of draft articles adopted the latter, more restrictive approach: the situation was considered 'non-domestic' only when at the time of the proceedings the equipment ended up in a state different from the *situs* of such equipment at the time of conclusion of the agreement.[160] The result of this approach was that (in a situation when neither of the other two internationality criteria applied) even an aircraft regularly travelling two times a day between two bordering countries (and remaining in each state for an equal amount of time), one of which was the country of its original *situs* at the time of the security agreement, would satisfy the internationality requirement necessary for the application of Convention's protections only fifty percent of the time.

[155] Unidroit, *Security Interests Study Group Sub-committee 1st Session Misc. 3 Add. (1994)* 2.

[156] This decision was later reflected in the first set of draft articles of the Convention – see Article 4 in Unidroit, *Study LXXII – Doc. 13 (1994).*

[157] Unidroit, *Study LXXII – Doc. 12 (1994)* 4.

[158] See n 154.

[159] See n 157.

[160] See Article 4(2)(c) in Unidroit, *Study LXXII – Doc. 13 (1994).*

Overall, the internationality requirement in the first set of draft articles remained rather strong, despite the revisions proposed by the First Draft Subcommittee. The only effective way for the financier to control the fulfilment of the test of internationality (and, as a result, obtain the Convention's protections) was through the terms of the relevant agreement.

2.4.2. Decline of Internationality

This position was reversed during the second session of the First Draft Subcommittee, which considered Article 4 of the draft treaty (which listed the 'non-domestic' criteria) obsolete in the light of the inherently 'international' character of mobile equipment.[161] This decision was expected to provide greater certainty for third parties, which would be in a position to determine *ex ante*, simply by looking at the type of equipment, whether or not it might be subject to the effects of the Convention, without the need to know the place of business of the parties to the relevant financing arrangements. In addition, the financiers located in the same country as the debtor would no longer have to rely on the express terms of the agreement[162] to guarantee the application of the Convention's protections in order to protect themselves against competing interests of foreign creditors, who automatically satisfied the international requirement (as established in the previous draft) by virtue of their location in another country.[163]

At the same time, the First Draft Subcommittee was not yet prepared to abandon the idea that purely domestic transactions were to be excluded. It was felt that governments would have a particularly strong interest in the application of their own domestic laws in a situation when: (i) both the secured party and the debtor were carrying on business in the same state; (ii) the equipment never left that state; and (iii) enforcement proceedings were instituted in that same state. It was agreed that in this situation the Convention's remedy provisions would not apply, but only between the parties to the relevant agreement: the Convention itself would continue to be effective in relations involving third parties.[164]

Two important observations must be made. First, the very logic of the Convention's internationality rules was thus reversed: while Article 4 by default prevented the application of Convention's provisions (unless one of the three exceptions applied, signalling that the issue was 'non-domestic'), under the new approach the internationality requirement would be satisfied automatically, subject only to the 'domestic transaction' rules. Second, the First Draft Subcommittee considered a special exemption from the 'domestic transaction' rule (essentially constituting an exception to an exception), which would permit the Convention protections to

[161] Unidroit, *Study LXXII – Doc. 15 (1995)* 6.
[162] See Article 4(2)(b) in Unidroit, *Study LXXII – Doc. 13 (1994).*
[163] See Article 4(2)(a) in ibid.
[164] See paragraph 9(xvi) Unidroit, *Study LXXII – Doc. 15 (1995)* 6–7.

apply in a purely domestic scenario with respect to particularly high-cost assets (like aircraft and ships): it was feared that without access to the Convention's remedies financiers in countries with unsophisticated secured financing laws would be left without adequate protection.[165]

Before the Drafting Group had an opportunity to implement the above changes, UNIDROIT received from the AWG a memorandum strongly suggesting the abolition of any internationality requirement whatsoever in respect of aircraft due to the fact that aviation financing transactions were per se international. Four reasons were given for such proposal: (i) the high mobility of aircraft; (ii) the high complexity of aircraft financing; (iii) the need for commercial certainty and predictability; and (iv) the need to eliminate prejudice towards domestic financiers who could find themselves unable to tap into the Convention regime.[166]

Perhaps as the result of the position taken by the aviation industry, the next draft set of articles of the future Convention[167] did not contain *any* rules concerning internationality, particularly with respect to the 'domestic transaction' exceptions agreed by the First Draft Subcommittee. Nevertheless, the discussions concerning the test of internationality did not stop, establishing two main lines of thought. The first was expressed by the increasingly active aviation industry represented by the AWG and IATA (International Air Transport Association), which supported the idea of total abolition of the test of internationality in relation to aircraft equipment, essentially on the basis of the earlier assertion that aircraft equipment was per se international.[168] The second suggested a more cautious approach, stressing the need to account for the possible reluctance of governments to relinquish the application of their domestic laws to essentially internal transactions, even if the latter covered mobile equipment.[169]

The revised drafts[170] of the future Convention prepared by the Drafting Group in the run-up to the second session of the Study Group in 1996 followed the approach of the second draft and did not contain any specific rules on internationality. The Study Group eventually confirmed the status quo, without any reference to the 'purely domestic' exception: 'it should be sufficient that the equipment was mobile as defined in Article 2 of the Convention, because essentially this meant equipment that by its nature moved regularly from one country to another'.[171] The resulting draft reflected this position and also contained no specific rules concerning internationality.[172]

[165] ibid 7.
[166] Unidroit, *Study LXXII – Doc. 16 (1995)* 7.
[167] Unidroit, *Study LXXII – Doc. 18 (1995).*
[168] Unidroit, *Study LXXII – Doc. 32 Add. 2 (1997)* 8.
[169] See Unidroit, *Study LXXII – Doc. 17 (1995)* 9; Unidroit, *International Interests Study Group Sub-committee 3rd Session Misc. 3 (1995).*
[170] See Unidroit, *Study LXXII – Doc. 22 (1996)*; Unidroit, *Study LXXII – Doc. 24 (1996).*
[171] Unidroit, *Study LXXII – Doc. 27 (1996)* 7.
[172] Unidroit, *Study LXXII – Doc. 30 (1996).*

2.4.3. Declarations on Purely Domestic Transactions

The matter of internationality was revisited in the 1997 draft of the CTC, which was supplemented by a new Article W permitting states to make a declaration that they would not apply the Convention in relation to a 'purely domestic transaction'.[173] As was later explained by the chairman of the Study Group, this new provision was introduced to deal with a case of eg 'a train in one State running round a circle in such a way that it would never leave that State's boundaries'.[174] In other words, a purely domestic transaction was one in which 'there was never any movement across … national frontiers'.[175] At the time the idea of a 'domestic' exception was not, strictly speaking, novel: as noted previously,[176] in 1995 the First Draft Subcommittee considered the same issue and came up with a three-pronged test.[177] Nonetheless, the new provision did not establish any particular criteria that had to be satisfied in order to constitute a 'purely domestic transaction': the decision was left to the governmental experts, despite several proposals to abolish this concept altogether.[178]

Limited progress was achieved during First[179] and Second[180] Joint Sessions[181] and no attempt to identify purely domestic transactions (which were renamed to 'purely internal transactions') was made. Instead, at the end of the Second Joint Session the Drafting Committee[182] proposed an alternative draft of Article V, which essentially left the matter of identifying such transactions in the hands of contracting states, as the latter were given the authority not only to declare that the Convention would not apply to a purely internal transaction, but also to specify the types of transactions falling under this category.[183] Such a broad provision carried with it the danger that states, in the absence of clear criteria defined in the Convention, would use it as a loophole to exclude whole classes of transactions, regardless of whether or not they were truly devoid of a genuine international element.

[173] Unidroit, *Study LXXII – Doc. 37 (1997).*

[174] Unidroit, *Study LXXII – Doc. 40 (1998)* 26.

[175] ibid.

[176] See text to n 164.

[177] See Unidroit, *Study LXXII – Doc. 15 (1995)* 6.

[178] See Unidroit, *Study LXXII – Doc. 43 / Study LXXIID – Doc. 4 (1998)* 6; Unidroit, *Study LXXII – Doc. 49 / Study LXXIID – Doc. 9 (1999)* 2.

[179] Unidroit, *Unidroit CGE/Int.Int./Report ICAO Ref. LSC/ME-Report (1999)* 17.

[180] See paragraph 5:37 in Unidroit, *ICAO Ref. LSC/ME/2-Report Unidroit CGE/Int.Int./2-Report (1999).*

[181] In this book, the terms 'First Joint Session', 'Second Joint Session' and 'Third Joint Session' refer to the three consecutive sessions of governmental experts held in 1999 and 2000 in the run-up to the Cape Town Diplomatic Conference to adopt the Convention and the Aircraft Protocol.

[182] In this book, mentions of the 'Drafting Committee' should be read as references to the specific drafting committee operating at the time in question under the auspices of the relevant session of governmental experts or during the diplomatic conference (as the context requires): see section 8.2.2.

[183] See Article V of Attachment F in Unidroit, *ICAO Ref. LSC/ME/2-Report Unidroit CGE/Int.Int./2-Report (1999).*

The problem of internationality was one of the most difficult issues during the Third Joint Session held in 2000.[184] The discussion was opened by the proposal of the French delegation, which aimed to reintroduce the test of internationality in a very strong form.[185] The idea was to alter in several ways the list of requirements in Article 3 that had to be met before the Convention could apply. The initial criteria (as drafted prior to the application of the new proposal) had been very lenient: it was sufficient if (i) the obligor was situated in a contracting state, or (alternatively) (ii) the equipment subject to an international interest had a connection with a contracting state. The proposed changes were substantial. First, at the time of the agreement creating or providing for an international interest, both parties had to have their places of business in different countries, such countries being contracting states.[186] Second, both legs of the test (ie location of the parties and connection of the equipment to a contracting state) were to become cumulative (rather than alternative). The level of disagreement was such that it was decided to convene a special working group to examine the relevant provisions in more detail and provide recommendations. Eventually three principles were formulated.[187]

First, a transaction was deemed 'purely internal' if at the time of the agreement (i) the creditor and debtor were located in the same contracting state, and (ii) the relevant object was registered or situated in that contracting state. Second, contracting states could make a declaration preventing the application of the Convention to purely internal transactions, in which case, however, parties to an agreement would still be able to invoke the Convention by agreement. Third, parties to an agreement covered by the above declaration would have the right to give notice to the international registry of the relevant national interest, in which case the Convention priority rules would apply.

While the second principle did not gather enough support, the first and the third of them formed the basis of the revised concept of internationality, which had the following characteristics. First, the test of internationality was met if the relevant (security, title reservation or leasing) agreement related to the types of equipment to which the Convention applied. Second, states were permitted to make declarations in respect of internal transactions,[188] but could not freely determine which transactions were considered 'internal'.[189] Third, the test to determine what constitutes an 'internal transaction' involved two elements: (i) location of

[184] See Unidroit, *Unidroit CGE/Int.Int./3-Report ICAO Ref. LSC/ME/3-Report (2000).*

[185] Unidroit, *Unidroit CGE/Int.Int./3-WP/17 ICAO Ref. LSC/ME/3-WP/17 12/03/00 (2000).*

[186] In this respect, the proposal was modelled after Article 1(1) of the CISG; Article 2 of the 1988 UNIDROIT Convention on International Factoring (adopted 28 May 1988, entered into force 1 May 1995) 2323 UNTS 373 and Article 4 of the 1995 United Nations Convention on Independent Guarantees and Stand-by Letters of Credit (adopted 11 December 1995, entered into force 1 January 2000) 2169 UNTS 163.

[187] See Unidroit, *Unidroit CGE/Int.Int./3-WP/27 Corr. ICAO Ref. LSC/ME/3-WP/27 27/03/00 (2000).*

[188] See Article S(1) Attachment C Appendix I in Unidroit, *Unidroit CGE/Int.Int./3-Report ICAO Ref. LSC/ME/3-Report (2000).*

[189] See Article 1(q) Attachment C Appendix I in ibid.

both parties to the agreement in the same contracting state, and (ii) location of the relevant object in the same contracting state, each at the time of conclusion of the transaction.[190] Fourth, declarations made by contracting states with respect to internal transactions did not prevent the application of certain provisions of the Convention (including rules on priority) to such transactions.[191]

The issue of internal transactions was subsequently discussed during the Cape Town Diplomatic Conference. These discussions added two principal changes. First, the ability of contracting states to make a declaration on internal transactions was limited to situations when such contracting states had in place the registration machinery by which notices of national interests could be transmitted to the international registry.[192] This change resulted from the fact that a declaration on internal transactions by a contracting state effectively made it impossible for the relevant parties to register an international interest under the Convention and thus it was considered prudent to require some assurance that parties to internal transactions would be in a position to protect their priority position should the need arise. This echoed the earlier concerns about the need to avoid jeopardising the position of domestic financiers.[193] Second, although contracting states were not in a position to redefine what constituted an 'internal transaction', it was agreed that they should nevertheless be given the opportunity to choose whether to exclude the application of the Convention to all such transactions or only with respect to certain types of equipment.[194] This was a departure from the 'all or nothing' approach, which emerged at the conclusion of the Third Joint Session.

Nonetheless, the added flexibility of this provision has not been utilised by states until now: each of the existing declarations under Article 50(1) of the CTC excluded the application of the Convention to all internal transactions in their entirety.[195] Furthermore, the possibility of limiting the list of objects to which the internal transaction exception applies could not override the aforementioned 'gateway' requirement that interests under all internal transactions should be registered in the relevant national registries. As a result, objects for which no domestic registration systems were in place could not be excluded even pursuant to a

[190] ibid.
[191] See Article S(2) Attachment C Appendix I in ibid.
[192] See Article 1(n) of the CTC.
[193] See n 157 and the relevant discussion in section 2.4.1.
[194] See Article 50(1) of the CTC.
[195] See paragraph 4 in Unidroit, 'Declarations Lodged by The People's Republic of China (PRC) under the Cape Town Convention at the Time of the Deposit of its Instrument of Ratification' www.unidroit.org/status-2001capetown?id=463; paragraph 3 in Unidroit, 'Declarations Lodged by the United Mexican States under the Cape Town Convention at the Time of the Deposit of its Instrument of Accession' www.unidroit.org/status-2001capetown?id=476; paragraph 3 in Unidroit, 'Declarations Lodged by the Republic of Panama under the Cape Town Convention at the Time of the Deposit of its Instrument of Ratification' www.unidroit.org/status-2001capetown?id=484; paragraph (iv) in Unidroit, 'Declarations Lodged by the Republic of Turkey under the Cape Town Convention at the Time of the Deposit of its Instrument of Ratification' www.unidroit.org/status-2001capetown?id=492; paragraph 1 in Unidroit, 'Declarations Lodged by Ukraine under the Cape Town Convention at the Time of the Deposit of its Instrument of Accession' www.unidroit.org/status-2001capetown?id=493.

declaration under Article 50(1) of the CTC. The lack of local registration systems for rolling stock made this concern particularly relevant for the rail industry[196] and later resulted in the implementation of an alternative test for 'internal transactions' based solely on the physical characteristics of the asset, to which the requirements of mandatory national registration did not apply. This new test was based on a single factor: whether or not the object was *only* capable, in its normal course of use, of being operated on a single railway system within the contracting state concerned.[197] Interestingly, a similar 'immobility' test was not reproduced in the newly adopted MAC Protocol, even though the assets covered by the latter may be even less mobile compared to rolling stock.[198]

[196] See footnote 58 in Unidroit, *Study LXXIIH – Doc. 8 (2003)* 52.
[197] See Article XXIX(2) of the Rail Protocol.
[198] See section 3.5 below.

3

Selecting the Asset Types Covered by the Convention

3.1. Overview

This chapter focuses on the key element defining the scope of the Cape Town Convention, the concept of 'mobile equipment'. Seeking the most appropriate formula to restrict the application of the CTC to a limited and clearly identified group of mobile assets was 'the most intriguing question of the whole exercise' that determined the outcome of many other issues.[1]

Section 3.2 covers the genesis of the scope-defining notion of mobile equipment and explains the transition to a protocol-driven structure that largely eliminated the need to clearly define the scope of the CTC ex ante. The chapter then addresses the key challenges associated with identifying Convention assets by analysing – and drawing a stark contrast – between the success history of aircraft objects (in section 3.3) and the exclusion of ships from the scope of the treaty (section 3.4), despite many objective similarities. Finally, section 3.5 focuses on the most recent expansion of the CTC in 2019 to cover a new category of assets – mining, agricultural and construction equipment – and examines the difficulties this expansion has revealed.

3.2. Evolution of the Concept of Mobile Equipment

As noted in section 2.2.1 above,[2] the Canadian Proposal acted as a catalyst for the development of the CTC and at first did not envisage any instrument for the suggested harmonisation other than an international convention. It concluded, however, that the new instrument should have a limited scope: 'Such a project should be narrow in scope and should be undertaken only if it can be demonstrated that there is a commercial need for further international regulation in this area'.[3] It was thus suggested that the new convention should be limited to security interests in 'mobile equipment' – but no definition or explanation of the term was provided.

[1] Unidroit, *Study LXXII – Doc. 11 (1994)* 5.
[2] See n 1 in section 2.2.1.
[3] ibid.

The Study prepared by Ronald Cuming as a follow-up to the Canadian Proposal was based on a hypothetical scenario in which 'valuable mobile equipment' subject to a security interest created in one country was moved across national borders to another state.[4] Nonetheless, no attempt to define 'mobile equipment' was considered feasible at the time:

> Should a decision be taken to prepare a draft convention, it will be a matter for the participants in that undertaking to determine on the basis of empirical information what types of movables should be included in the definition.[5]

The early attempts to determine the defining criteria of 'mobile equipment' can be tracked all the way back to Cuming's Questionnaire (circulated in 1990). First, in the Questionnaire, designed to test his preliminary conclusions and assumptions, Cuming occasionally referred to movables 'of a kind *generally* moved from one State to another'[6] suggesting a certain degree of frequency of movement of equipment subject to the future convention. Second, following the analysis of responses to the Questionnaire, Cuming stressed that the term 'mobile equipment' was not by itself a generic reference to a particular type of goods – it was only meant to 'describe the *use* to which the goods [were] being put by the debtor'.[7] In other words, movables held as consumer goods, rather than equipment, were to be excluded.

These two factors formed the basis of two parallel processes in determining the subject matter of the future convention: (i) defining the generic concept of 'mobile equipment', and (ii) examining various specific types of mobile equipment. These are considered in sections 3.2.1 and 3.2.2, respectively.

3.2.1. Generic Concept of Mobile Equipment

Both the REWG in 1992 and the Study Group in 1993 essentially reproduced the two criteria identified by Cuming: mobile equipment had to be (i) of a kind normally moving from one state to another in the ordinary course of business, and (ii) held by the debtor for business use (as opposed to consumer goods or inventory).[8] Both legs of the test, however, created practical difficulties in satisfying the main objective identified by the REWG, namely that 'the equipment should be identifiable from the terms of the security agreement as being of a kind governed by the Convention'.[9] In other words, parties to an agreement creating a security interest, as well as any third party needed an easy way of determining

[4] Unidroit, *Study LXXII – Doc. 1 (1989)* 4.
[5] ibid 5.
[6] Unidroit, *Study LXXII – Doc. 2 (1989)* 8 (emphasis added).
[7] Unidroit, *Study LXXII – Doc. 4 (1992)* 2 (emphasis added).
[8] See Unidroit, *Study LXXII – Doc. 5 (1992)* 3; Unidroit, *Study LXXII – Doc. 7 (1993)* 4.
[9] Unidroit, *Study LXXII – Doc. 5 (1992)* 3.

whether the asset in question was covered by the new instrument or not, particularly in the light of an early decision to incorporate directly into the Convention priority rules regulating the priority of convention-specific security interests and any other *in rem* security interests (other than non-consensual interests).[10]

The 'mobility' test, as formulated by the REWG and the Study Group, did not depend on the actual movement of the asset in question: what mattered was whether the *type* of equipment was generally moved across national borders. One obvious difficulty here was the lack of clarity as to the minimum frequency of movement required to satisfy the test. The other problem lay in the variance generated by its application in countries of different sizes: in Liechtenstein almost any movable asset would probably satisfy the above test of 'mobility', whereas in Russia even airplanes would not always meet the criterion (especially in the case of medium and short-range models).

The 'business use' test had two distinct problems as well. On the one hand, it excluded from the scope of the future convention certain very high value assets used for non-business purposes, such as personal aircraft and pleasure boats.[11] On the other, the purpose for which many assets were used would not be apparent for any third party and could change with time, so that some kind of characterisation rule would be necessary to ensure that a subsequent change in the use of the asset would not jeopardise the validity of the international interest and the priority position of the financier.[12]

Even the combination of both tests did not result in a workable solution, as certain (relatively) small value assets, such as cars, small trucks and minor construction equipment ended up within the scope of the future Convention. This would impose on any potential financier in these items the burden of making searches in the international registry system envisaged at the early stage of development of the CTC.[13] To address the above issues, several alternative solutions were proposed.

The first was suggested by Cuming and took the form of an additional requirement – a test of 'self-propulsion'. The logic was simple: equipment capable of self-propulsion would ensure that only items of significant value are covered by the new convention. The problem with this proposal, however, was that some very valuable equipment that was not capable of self-propulsion (such as containers, drilling equipment and railway rolling stock) would be excluded.[14] In addition, this test did not really solve the issues with some of the (relatively) low-cost equipment, such as cars and small trucks.

The second prospective solution revolved around specifying a minimum (threshold) cost of equipment, such as USD 50,000, as proposed by Thomas Whalen in 1994.[15] This approach offered a meaningful way of limiting the scope

[10] ibid 6.
[11] Unidroit, *Study LXXII – Doc. 8 (1993)* 3.
[12] ibid 4.
[13] Unidroit, *Study LXXII – Doc. 5 (1992)* 5.
[14] Unidroit, *Study LXXII – Doc. 8 (1993)* 5.
[15] Unidroit, *Study LXXII – Doc. 9 (1994)* 5.

of the future convention, but required a reliable and publicly available source of pricing information for all eligible assets (such as the manufacturer's original price).[16] Unfortunately, the solution was highly problematic: it could induce pressure on manufacturers to increase the prices of certain items to ensure that they are covered by the new convention, especially if the treaty offered enhanced creditor protection mechanisms.

The deficiencies surrounding the early attempts to define 'mobile equipment' suggested that a more flexible approach to selecting the object of the new treaty might be necessary. A possible solution, suggested by Cuming in 1993, included not only the tests of mobility, business use and self-propulsion, but also a set of caveats, either expanding (eg in the case of high value consumer goods) or narrowing (eg in the case of low-cost trucks) the scope of the future convention.[17]

Interestingly, the first draft articles of the Convention did not reflect the new proposals.[18] In that draft, the concept of 'mobile equipment' revolved around the tests of 'mobility' and 'business use',[19] but with one exception: the draft articles provisionally applied to 'pleasure craft'.[20] The challenges underlying the concept of 'mobile equipment', however, remained largely unanswered.

Two changes were proposed by the First Draft Subcommittee in 1994. First, the 'mobility' test was to be amended to refer to equipment normally 'used' in different countries (as opposed to equipment normally 'moved' across borders).[21] This change had two reasons. On the one hand, it allowed better differentiation between equipment and inventory (as the latter was not supposed to be covered by the Convention). On the other hand, it excluded assets intended to be moved to some fixed destination in another country, never to be moved again. Second, the Study Group for the first time agreed to draw up a list of assets falling within the scope of the Convention.[22] Although no decision was made as to whether the list would be exclusive or merely by way of example, this was a serious departure from the previous approach, which was built around the general concept of 'mobile equipment'.

As a reflection of the above decisions of the First Draft Subcommittee, the revised draft articles of the Convention incorporated two alternative (and mutually exclusive) approaches to defining its object: (i) a closed list of assets, and (ii) a combination of a general concept of 'mobile equipment' and a non-exhaustive list of eligible assets.[23] Both options were problematic. The former lacked flexibility

[16] ibid.

[17] Unidroit, *Study LXXII – Doc. 8 (1993)* 5.

[18] See Article 1(1), Article 1(2)(a) and Article 1(3) in Unidroit, *Study LXXII – Doc. 13 (1994)* 1.

[19] This formula emerged from the agreement of the First Draft Subcommittee to implement a 'broad approach to the definition of mobile equipment … with specific exclusions rather than defining mobile equipment in terms of a limited list'. See Unidroit, *Study LXXII – Doc. 12 (1994)* 4.

[20] The term 'pleasure craft' was included in square brackets. See Article 1(3) in Unidroit, *Study LXXII – Doc. 13 (1994)* 2.

[21] Unidroit, *Study LXXII – Doc. 15 (1995)* 4.

[22] ibid.

[23] See two alternative wordings of Article 2 in Unidroit, *Study LXXII – Doc. 18 (1995)* 5.

on several levels. On the one hand, some categories of equipment (eg oil rigs or agricultural equipment) were not uniform and included both mobile and immobile assets. As a result, an attempt to include these categories in the scope of the Convention would make the list of assets overly inclusive (and vice versa). On the other hand, failure to include some categories of equipment (for whatever reason) in the scope of the treaty would make it difficult, if not impossible, to change the decision after its adoption. The second option offered only limited certainty (somewhat mitigated by adding a non-exhaustive list of eligible equipment in the definition).

Strictly speaking, any attempt to define the scope of the future treaty by reference to some general concept, such as 'mobile equipment', generated uncertainty as to whether certain unspecified or unforeseen categories of assets were 'in' or 'out'. At a policy level, a decision had to be made based on the overall preference for greater certainty, on the one hand, or flexibility, on the other. Such a decision was made during the third meeting of the First Draft Subcommittee in 1995: the vote in favour of a *closed list* of assets covered by the convention was unanimous.[24]

This new approach, reflected in the next draft set of articles of the new Convention,[25] reduced the term 'mobile equipment' to a mere label used in the name of the treaty, with no substantive value. In order to determine whether the Convention applies, parties no longer had to be concerned about an asset's mobility or the purposes for which it was used: it was sufficient that the asset belonged to one of the categories listed in the draft Convention. The change of direction, however, brought with it not only enhanced clarity – it reduced the scope of the new treaty and, by extension, its potential economic impact. Nevertheless, the greater certainty resulting from the transition to a closed list of assets trumped other concerns in the light of the decision to implement an international public notice system (in the form of an international registry) and the corresponding need to ensure that third parties were in a position to know in advance which objects were governed by the new convention.[26]

Although the concept of 'mobile equipment' was replaced by a closed list of assets governed by the Convention, ultimately it did not lose all of its relevance. Having limited the scope of the treaty to specific groups of objects, the developers of the CTC had to ensure that the Convention would remain open to adjustment to cover other groups of assets should such need arise in the future. To address the problem of lack of flexibility, the First Draft Subcommittee considered introducing rapid amendment procedures already implemented in existing international conventions.[27] A similar provision in the Convention was seen as a workable

[24] Unidroit, *Study LXXII – Doc. 21 (1995)* 6.

[25] See Article 2 in Unidroit, *Study LXXII – Doc. 22 (1996)*.

[26] Unidroit, *Study LXXII – Doc. 27 (1996)* 16.

[27] See Article XVIII of the International Convention on Civil Liability for Oil Pollution Damage (adopted 29 November 1969, entered into force 19 June 1975) 973 UNTS 3, which envisages the convening of an ad hoc conference for the purposes of amending the treaty at the request of no less than one-third of contracting states. See also Article 45 of the Convention on the Establishment of an

solution: the developers could initially focus only on those assets for which there was immediate industry and governmental interest, whereas the treaty could be amended in the future by way of a simplified procedure, as necessary.[28] At the same time, it remained unclear how to ensure that the overall scope of the Convention is not diluted by various adjustments, creating uncertainty. It became clear that the concept of 'mobile equipment' would have to be retained in some form, this time not as the main criterion of the Convention's applicability, but rather as a residual category preventing unlimited expansion of the latter.

The essential characteristics of 'mobile equipment' as a *residual* category took significant time to crystallise. The earliest draft of the corresponding provision was prepared by the Drafting Group in 1997 and incorporated only two main characteristics: (i) unique identification ('is uniquely identifiable'),[29] and (ii) actual mobility ('habitually moves from one State to another in the ordinary course of business').[30] However, this new draft went much further than just listing the relevant criteria: the developers decided to switch to a dual structure based on the main convention and a set of asset-specific protocols.[31] This change made the application of the Convention to any type of asset (ie those named in the text of the treaty as well as those forming part of the residual category) dependent on the existence and entry into force of a specific protocol and practically eliminated uncertainty created by the open-ended nature of the residual category of 'mobile equipment'.[32] As a result, third parties would not have to rely on the generic description of 'mobile equipment' listed among other asset types – eventually only the existence (or absence) of a protocol determined the applicability of the new treaty to any object whatsoever. This fundamental change of approach greatly reduced pressure on the developers in formulating the criteria of the residual category, which lost its definitive nature and now acted merely as guidance. Despite this, the concept of 'mobile equipment' was subject to the same scrutiny by the commentators as before.[33] Some reviewers noted the need to refer to assets of 'high value' only[34]

International Fund for Compensation for Oil Pollution Damage (adopted 18 December 1971, entered into force 16 October 1978) 1110 UNTS 57, which has a similar provision.

[28] See Unidroit, *Study LXXII – Doc. 27 (1996)* 16.

[29] The matter of unique identification was a key requirement for the operation of an asset-based international registry and had a different impact on the various types of mobile equipment: while the identification of aircraft objects was relatively straightforward (as a reference to the serial number, manufacturer's name and model designation was sufficient at all times), other asset types were not so homogeneous and required additional workaround solutions (see, eg, Article XIV of the Rail Protocol and Article XXX of the Space Protocol).

[30] See Article 2(1)(i) in Unidroit, *Study LXXII – Drafting Group Fourth Session (1997).*

[31] The reasons behind this change and the corresponding challenges are discussed in ch 4.

[32] Article 2(2) states that the Convention 'shall not come into force as regards any category of object until there is in force a Protocol relating to such category'.

[33] This might, to some extent, be the result of certain confusion among commentators as to whether the new concept of 'mobile equipment' was actually a residual category or merely an additional test used to qualify the asset types already expressly listed in the draft Convention. See, eg, paragraph 42 and paragraph 46 in Unidroit, *Study LXXII – Doc. 36 (1997)* 12.

[34] See paragraph 42 in ibid.

and even suggested introducing a certain minimum threshold value of eligible objects.[35] Others recommended focusing on objects 'used for business or professional purposes' only.[36]

In late 1997, the Study Group revised the scope of the draft Convention once more, taking a different approach to the concept of 'mobile equipment'. First, the test of mobility was no longer limited to the residual category of equipment – it applied even to the asset categories that were listed in the Convention itself. Second, the actual mobility test ('habitually moves from one State to another in the ordinary course of business') was slightly relaxed by reference to the intent to engage in regular movement of assets ('which is to be regularly moved'), rather than their actual movement, although it is not quite clear whether the object would fail to meet the test if later no movement in fact took place.[37] This lack of certainty was noted by the Steering and Revisions Committee ('the SRC')[38] in 1998 and, as a result, the test of mobility was finally deleted from the text of the Convention entirely.[39] Whether or not an asset actually moved across borders (or beyond any national jurisdiction, in the case of objects located in space) was deemed irrelevant: the 'typically mobile character' of each of the relevant categories listed in the draft Convention was sufficient to bring them within its scope.[40]

While it was true that the asset types enumerated in the text of the treaty could be seen as essentially mobile by nature (and that, as a result, an extra mobility requirement might be unnecessary), the decision to remove the test of mobility in its entirety had a serious impact on the residual category of mobile equipment, which was reduced to a mere reference to 'other categories of uniquely identifiable object'.[41] As a result, the draft Convention lost virtually all of the safeguards against potentially unlimited expansion of its scope in the future, except for the requirement that eligible assets should be subject to unique identification.[42]

This loss of the mobility requirement was not, however, seen as an impediment by the governmental experts during the First Joint Session. Furthermore, the fact that the Convention would not apply to any asset category without a dedicated protocol was considered a sufficient guarantee of legal certainty – as a result, the list of various asset types governed by the draft Convention was completely removed from its text.[43] Thanks to this change, the residual category of mobile equipment, which had previously been reduced to a single test of unique identification,

[35] See Unidroit, *Study LXXII – Doc. 36 Add. 1 (1997)* 1.
[36] See paragraph 43 in Unidroit, *Study LXXII – Doc. 36 (1997)* 12.
[37] See Article 3 in Unidroit, *Study LXXII – Doc. 39 (1998).*
[38] The role of the SRC is discussed in section 4.3 (n 60 and the relevant discussion) and section 8.2.1.
[39] See paragraph 19 and paragraph 22 in Unidroit, *Study LXXII – Doc. 41 (1998)* 12.
[40] See paragraph 19 in ibid.
[41] See paragraph 22 in ibid.
[42] This is best illustrated by the revised Article 3 (as read in conjunction with Article U) in Unidroit, *Study LXXII – Doc. 42 (1998).*
[43] Unidroit, *Unidroit CGE/Int.Int./Report ICAO Ref. LSC/ME-Report (1999)* 7.

effectively became the *only*[44] restriction on the types of objects regulated by the new treaty.[45] The exclusion of the list of eligible assets from the draft Convention was approved by the Second Joint Session, subject to the consensus decision to somewhat limit the scope by reference to objects of 'high value' only. However, the location and wording of this new (high cost) criterion was left to the determination of the Drafting Committee, which, nonetheless, did not make any changes to the substantive criteria of mobile equipment in Article 2(2),[46] keeping the only reference to 'high value' equipment in the preamble.[47] As a result, at that stage the draft Convention remained potentially open to *any* types of movable objects, from cars to personal computers.

The resulting possibility of almost indefinite expansion of the scope of the new convention created a lot of debate during the Third Joint Session. The French government stressed the need to restore the list of assets regulated by the Convention to avoid extending its scope to mobile equipment 'of lesser importance', noting that the reference to 'high value' had no 'real legal value' due to the fact that it was located in the preamble.[48] In addition, UNCITRAL, which contemplated the adoption of a new treaty regulating assignment of receivables, insisted on the reintroduction of a list of eligible assets to ensure that the UNIDROIT convention would not be concerned with other, non-high value objects, thereby eliminating the potential for overlap between the two instruments.[49] In UNCITRAL's view, any uncertainty, including the residual category of 'any uniquely identifiable equipment', should have been eliminated to avoid conflict with its own treaty.

To reconcile the existing draft with the above proposals, the UNIDROIT Secretariat suggested an alternative approach, which was quite similar to the earlier drafts of the Convention: a list of particular asset types governed by the treaty accompanied by a residual concept of mobile equipment restricting any further extension of scope.[50] While this approach was not new, the proposed characteristics of objects potentially falling into the catch-all clause appeared much more restrictive. To be eligible for inclusion in the scope of the treaty, the assets would not have to be merely uniquely identifiable – only 'high value capital infrastructure equipment' would qualify.[51] The UNIDROIT proposal was accepted by the governmental experts with certain minor adjustments: the list of assets was

[44] One may argue that another safeguard was incorporated in the preamble of the draft Convention, which spoke of 'the need to acquire and use *high value* mobile equipment' (emphasis added), but the legal effects of the preamble remained very limited (as evidenced by Article 6 of Attachment D (Appendix I) in ibid) and did not directly affect the categories of objects to which the draft Convention applied.

[45] See Article 2(2) of Attachment D (Appendix I) in ibid.

[46] See Article 2(2) of Attachment F (Appendix I) in Unidroit, *ICAO Ref. LSC/ME/2-Report Unidroit CGE/Int.Int./2-Report (1999).*

[47] See Preamble of Attachment F (Appendix I) in ibid.

[48] Unidroit, *Unidroit CGE/Int.Int./3-WP/4 ICAO Ref. LSC/ME/3-WP/4 (2000)* 4.

[49] Unidroit, *Unidroit CGE/Int.Int./3-WP/10 ICAO Ref. LSC/ME/3-WP/10 (2000)* 2.

[50] Unidroit, *Unidroit CGE/Int.Int./3-WP/14 ICAO Ref. LSC/ME/3-WP/14 (2000)* 2.

[51] ibid.

reduced to airframes, aircraft engines, helicopters, railway rolling stock and space property, while the residual category was qualified by the word 'mobile' and moved to a separate article.[52] The resulting draft (in particular Article 2 and Article U)[53] reflected these changes, except for the UNIDROIT Secretariat's reference to objects relating to 'capital infrastructure'. Thus, the scope of any future expansion of the Convention was limited to assets simultaneously possessing three characteristics: (i) mobility; (ii) high value; and (iii) unique identification. This three-prong test is now reflected in the final text[54] of the CTC.[55]

Despite the extensive discussion and difficulties surrounding each criterion, the Convention eventually got rid of *any* attempt to define in greater detail the residual category of 'mobile equipment', which, contrary to the overall spirit of the treaty, intentionally retains an element of uncertainty.[56] On the one hand, this seems justified, given the need to explore the possibilities for expanding the scope of the CTC in the future. On the other, the vagueness of the relevant criteria (especially the one of 'high value') may pave the way to the inclusion of peculiar groups of assets in the future, such as high-end portable computers (since these are mobile by nature, have unique serial numbers and may cost as much as an automobile). This is the result of transition to the dual (convention/protocol) structure and, in particular, Article 49(1), which makes the application of the Convention to any group of assets dependent on the existence and entry into force of a specific protocol. Eventually, the existence or absence of market demand and the interests of various stakeholders will determine what new asset types may be covered by the CTC – the Convention has simply left its door open.

3.2.2. Specific Types of Equipment

The three asset types reflected in the final text of Article 2(3) of the CTC represent only a fraction of the various categories of equipment originally considered by the developers. The first attempt to identify objects fitting the new convention – Cuming's Questionnaire – revealed numerous options: trucks, automobiles, railway rolling stock, construction equipment, earth-moving equipment, industrial

[52] Unidroit, *Unidroit CGE/Int.Int./3-Report ICAO Ref. LSC/ME/3-Report (2000)* 8.

[53] See Attachment C (Appendix I) in ibid.

[54] The difficulties surrounding the selection of particular asset types and, in particular, the wording of Article 2(3) of the CTC, are discussed in section 3.2.2.

[55] See Article 2(3) and Article 51(1) of the CTC.

[56] One could argue that the residual category of 'mobile equipment' was retained merely to convey the basic idea behind the asset types covered by the Convention, devoid of any independent legal significance. This is certainly true for the three categories listed in Article 2(3) of the CTC. As for the other types of mobile equipment, this residual category serves a 'gatekeeping' function under Article 51(1) of the Convention concerning the possibility of adoption of new protocols. This residual test remains an autonomous Convention-regulated concept not based on any domestic classification of the relevant assets. In the context of the MAC Protocol, however, this conclusion is put to the real test in the light of the problem of land-associated objects: see text to n 121 in section 7.3.

machinery, oil drilling equipment, agricultural equipment, ships, vessels and floating equipment, aircraft, containers, computer equipment, graphic arts equipment, telecommunication equipment, recreation vehicles and trailers.[57] However, the difficulties in formulating a single workable definition of 'mobile equipment' mentioned in the previous section called for a more flexible approach: certain important assets (eg pleasure craft) satisfied some (high value, mobility), but not all (no business use) of the relevant criteria (and thus should have been included by express reference); others (eg ships) satisfied all criteria, but for other reasons[58] had to be excluded (also by express reference).

Although the first set of draft articles of the Convention did not list any specific asset categories,[59] proposals to forego generality in favour of increased certainty appeared rather quickly.[60] In response to these proposals, the First Draft Subcommittee initially considered incorporating a list of eligible assets directly into the Convention,[61] seeking inspiration from the responses to Cuming's Questionnaire (which, as noted in the previous paragraph, identified a wide variety of asset types) and later unanimously agreed to switch to a closed list formula.[62]

Despite the numerous available options and types of equipment identified by Cuming, all the subsequent drafts[63] leading up to the governmental expert stage retained the same categories of mobile equipment: aviation assets (aircraft, engines and, later, helicopters), ships, oil rigs, containers, railway rolling stock and space assets (satellites, later replaced with 'space property'). There is limited documentary evidence as to the exact reasons for the early exclusion of other types of mobile equipment, however several important observations should be made. First, lower cost items, such as computer equipment, arguably did not possess sufficient value to be covered by the convention:[64] at its third session in 1995, the First Draft Subcommittee agreed to consider 'possible techniques for limiting the application

[57] See Unidroit, *Study LXXII - Doc. 4 (1992)* 3.

[58] The exclusion of ships is discussed in section 3.4.

[59] See Article 1(2)(a) and Article 1(3) in Unidroit, *Study LXXII - Doc. 13 (1994).*

[60] In his comments Thomas Whalen noted that the existing definition was 'too general' and should be further limited by reference to types of equipment. See Unidroit, *Study LXXII - Doc. 14 Add 1 (1994)* 1. Rolf Herber, in turn, stressed the need for the industry to know which particular asset types could potentially be subject to the new convention in order to determine whether or not to consult the public notice (registration) system to be created by the treaty. See ibid 2.

[61] Unidroit, *Study LXXII - Doc. 15 (1995)* 4.

[62] Unidroit, *Study LXXII - Doc. 21 (1995)* 6.

[63] See Article 2(1) in Unidroit, *Study LXXII - Doc. 22 (1996)*; Article 2(1) in Unidroit, *Study LXXII - Doc. 24 (1996)*; Article 2(1) of Appendix IV in Unidroit, *Study LXXII - Doc. 27 (1996)*; Article 2(1) in Unidroit, *Study LXXII - Doc. 30 (1996)*; Article 2(1) in Unidroit, *Study LXXII - Drafting Group Fourth Session (1997)*; Article 2(1) in Unidroit, *Study LXXII - Doc. 35 (1997)*; Article 2(1) in Unidroit, *Study LXXII - Doc. 37 (1997)*; Article 3(1) in Unidroit, *Study LXXII - Doc. 39 (1998)*; Article 3(1) in Unidroit, *Study LXXII - Doc. 41 (1998)*; Article 3(1) in Unidroit, *Study LXXII - Doc. 42 (1998).*

[64] The idea that eligible assets should be of sufficiently high value was considered one of the baseline concepts in identifying the object of the CTC throughout the whole development process. See Unidroit, *Study LXXII - Doc. 8 (1993)* 4; Unidroit, *Study LXXII - Doc. 9 (1994)* 5; Unidroit, *Study LXXII - Doc. 12 (1994)* 4; Unidroit, *Study LXXII - Doc. 16 (1995)* 3.

of the proposed Convention to big – ticket [*sic*] items'.[65] Second, certain assets, such as cars and trucks, created difficult characterisation issues, as it was very hard to draw a distinction between vehicles used as equipment (ie in business not for resale) and vehicles used as consumer goods.[66] Third, construction and other similar equipment incapable of self-propulsion possessed questionable international mobility: while these assets were indeed moved across national borders, quite often this was done only to deliver them to a stationary operating area, never to be moved again to another country.[67]

In the light of these legitimate concerns, the inclusion of oil rigs and containers seemed problematic. On the one hand, certain oil rigs share the limited mobility characteristics of construction equipment (as they are not moved to a new location). On the other hand, containers come in different forms and sizes, and it is not always clear whether a certain item is of sufficiently high value. To address these difficulties, the next drafts qualified both types of assets with additional criteria: mobility for oil rigs ('oil rigs not intended to be permanently immobilised') and minimum size for containers ('containers with a cubic capacity of not less than x').[68]

During the review of various asset types at its second meeting in 1996 the Study Group re-examined the feasibility of expanding the list of eligible equipment, considering a variety of options, from lorries and omnibuses to air-cushion vehicles and computers.[69] At that time the draft Convention remained still open for expansion by way of adding additional types of equipment to the definitive list, subject only to the satisfaction of three criteria:[70] (i) high value; (ii) mobility (frequent use on a cross-border basis); and (iii) unique identification required for the functioning of the new international registry.[71] Yet, perhaps more importantly, the Study Group acknowledged the need to consult the relevant industries in order to make an informed decision. This practical solution both imposed pressure on the various stakeholders in the corresponding sectors (as well as developers of the CTC) and acted as a maturity test for the industries in question. Those failing to demonstrate the immediate demand for inclusion of the relevant group of assets would have to rely on the draft Convention's rapid amendment provisions.[72]

[65] Unidroit, *Study LXXII – Doc. 21 (1995)* 6.

[66] Unidroit, *Study LXXII – Doc. 4 (1992)* 2.

[67] A clear preference for essentially movable assets follows from the decision of the First Draft Subcommittee to refer to equipment 'used' in several jurisdictions as opposed to equipment 'moved' across national borders – see Unidroit, *Study LXXII – Doc. 15 (1995)* 4. However, see section 3.5.

[68] See Article 2(1)(d) and Article 2(1)(e) in Unidroit, *Study LXXII – Doc. 22 (1996)*. See also Article 2(1)(d) and Article 2(1)(e) in Unidroit, *Study LXXII – Doc. 24 (1996)*. Later the relevant qualification criteria were moved to the definitions section: see, eg, Part III(a) and Part III(c) of Appendix in Unidroit, *Study LXXII – Doc. 30 (1996)*.

[69] Unidroit, *Study LXXII – Doc. 27 (1996)* 15.

[70] ibid 16.

[71] The challenges relating to the establishment and operation of the international registry are discussed in section 6.3.

[72] Unidroit, *Study LXXII – Doc. 27 (1996)* 16. See also Article 2(2) in Unidroit, *Study LXXII – Doc. 24 (1996)*.

The window of opportunity to expand the list of eligible types of mobile equipment was closing.

In early 1997 the Study Group decided[73] to switch to a dual (convention/protocol) structure.[74] The new approach recognised the specific characteristics and financing needs of the parties to asset finance transactions involving different types of mobile equipment and was based on the notion that the future Convention would come into force with respect to those types of assets for which there would be in force a separate protocol.[75] As a result, the problem of securing industry support became even more acute, since preparation of specific protocols required input from various stakeholders involved in financing transactions. This pragmatic approach allowed the developers to focus on assets in sectors where the industry was both ready and willing not only to use the Convention, but also to apply the necessary pressure on the governments during adoption and implementation.

This was not, however, the only reason to seek the support within the relevant business circles. First, only the industry could provide the appropriate definition of each type of mobile equipment (as was demonstrated by the difficulties in differentiating airframes from aircraft engines – see section 3.3 below). Second, it could help introduce certain additional criteria (such as weight or capacity) limiting the scope of the new convention to objects of high value.[76] Third, the industry was best placed to suggest the appropriate mode of asset identification required for the operation of an asset-based (as opposed to debtor-based) registry.[77] Fourth, it could propose additional rules specific to a particular category of mobile equipment.[78]

As a result of the above developments, by the start of the governmental expert stage an interesting status quo emerged with respect to the list of asset types covered by the draft Convention. On the one hand, it was clear that industry involvement was the decisive factor in determining which objects should be governed by the new treaty for reasons identified in the previous paragraph. On the other hand, the list of eligible assets remained open-ended due to the rapid amendment mechanics incorporated into the text based on the residual category of mobile equipment discussed in section 3.2.1.[79] This eased the pressure on the relevant industries, keeping the treaty open for future expansion. On top of this, the draft Convention only applied to those asset groups for which there was in force a corresponding protocol.[80] This factor acted both ways: it demanded industry involvement, but

[73] See Introductory Note in Unidroit, *Study LXXIID – Doc. 1 (1998)* 1.

[74] The reasons behind transition to the umbrella structure and the corresponding challenges are examined in ch 4.

[75] This change was first reflected in Article 2(2) of Unidroit, *Study LXXII – Drafting Group Fourth Session (1997)*.

[76] Reliance on *objective* criteria for limiting the categories of eligible equipment eliminated the risk of price manipulation and artificial inflation for the purposes of subjecting the assets to the protections established by the draft Convention.

[77] See section 6.3.

[78] Unidroit, *Study LXXII – Doc. 40 (1998)* 6.

[79] See Article 3(i) and Article W in Unidroit, *Study LXXII – Doc. 42 (1998)*.

[80] See Article U in ibid.

at the same time made the list of specific types of assets enumerated in the text of the convention indicative, rather than definitive. The resulting construct made the effects of any shrinking or expansion to the list of eligible assets practically irrelevant from the legal perspective: eventually the protocol would determine which objects are covered. Therefore, the changes that followed during the governmental expert stage were largely driven by political, procedural and technical concerns, rather than strictly legal considerations.

Against this background, the decision to get rid of the list of specific assets adopted during the First Joint Session[81] does not look so surprising: according to the UNIDROIT Secretariat, the only reason for this was 'delegations' preference for a more concise and hence more elegant drafting'.[82] Another concern against enumerating eligible assets was voiced at the Third Joint Session: during adoption, accession or ratification the list could be seen by governments as a 'political promise' to ensure the application of the Convention to all types of objects named in it. Likewise, the reincorporation of the list during the Third Joint Session was a result of a political compromise to alleviate the concerns expressed by UNCITRAL, which was working on a draft convention on assignment in receivables financing.[83] In order to avoid potential clash of the two instruments, UNIDROIT favoured the idea of specific exclusion from the UNCITRAL's document of assignments of receivables that may overlap with the provisions of the draft Convention.[84] Despite the fact that UNCITRAL itself admitted the absence of purely *legal* concerns (after all, only a working protocol could allow the Convention to apply to any kind of mobile equipment), both UNCITRAL and UNIDROIT favoured the reintroduction of a list of specific assets as a matter of policy, namely for the sake of added clarity.[85] The resulting consensus achieved by the delegates of the Third Joint Session consisted of a coherent three-part structure: (i) a closed list of assets (aircraft objects, railway rolling stock and space property);[86] (ii) a proviso stating that the Convention applies only to those types of equipment for which there is in force a protocol;[87] and (iii) a simplified procedure for the adoption of new protocols to the Convention.[88]

The matter of listing different categories of equipment, surprisingly, generated a lot of debate during the final stage of development of the CTC, during the 2001 Cape Town Diplomatic Conference. While there was virtually no disagreement as to the open-ended nature of the list of eligible assets and the pivotal role of

[81] Unidroit, *Unidroit CGE/Int.Int./Report ICAO Ref. LSC/ME-Report (1999)* 7. See also Article 2(2) of Appendix I in ibid.

[82] Unidroit, *Unidroit CGE/Int.Int./3-WP/14 ICAO Ref. LSC/ME/3-WP/14 (2000)* 1.

[83] See n 49.

[84] See Appendix to Unidroit, *Unidroit CGE/Int.Int./3-WP/14 ICAO Ref. LSC/ME/3-WP/14 (2000)*.

[85] See Unidroit, *Unidroit CGE/Int.Int./3-WP/10 ICAO Ref. LSC/ME/3-WP/10 (2000)* 2 and Unidroit, *Unidroit CGE/Int.Int./3-WP/14 ICAO Ref. LSC/ME/3-WP/14 (2000)* 2.

[86] See Article 2(3) of Appendix I to Attachment C in Unidroit, *Unidroit CGE/Int.Int./3-Report ICAO Ref. LSC/ME/3-Report (2000)*.

[87] See Article R of Appendix I to Attachment C in ibid.

[88] See Article U of Appendix I to Attachment C in ibid.

protocols in defining the scope of the Convention, questions remained about the best textual implementation of this approach. The proposals suggested various alternatives, from complete removal of the list of different types of equipment to re-opening the list again. However, two main factors decided the eventual outcome of the discussion: one policy matter and one matter of drafting. The first was formulated by the Rail Working Group,[89] which stressed the need to retain in the text of the Convention itself express references to those types of equipment which were backed by the industries already working on their corresponding protocols (namely, the rail and space industries).[90] Removal of the relevant assets from the CTC could be seen as a bad message to the various stakeholders that could hinder the progress made up to that moment. The second issue (a matter of drafting) was resolved thanks to the proposal of the UK representative, who suggested a minimalist, yet effective, approach to combining the three key elements identified in the preceding paragraph, namely a list of assets, the primacy of protocols and a mechanism for the adoption of new protocols. The latter was supplemented with a proviso stating that whenever a new protocol in respect of equipment not listed in the Convention was adopted, the Convention would, as a whole, apply to such equipment. This provision was considered desirable, as the closed list of eligible assets, taken separately, created the impression of limiting the scope of the CTC only to those three categories of equipment.[91]

In retrospect, the listing of specific types of assets (which can be grouped into three categories: aircraft objects, railway rolling stock and space assets) in the text of the CTC did not achieve much in terms of substance – but it provided UNCITRAL,[92] governments, as well as the rail and space industries with a degree of certainty that was needed at the final stage to achieve the adoption of the draft Convention and to preserve the momentum in developing new protocols. The challenges surrounding the key asset categories covered by the adopted protocols were unique and cannot all be addressed in this book. For this reason, the following sections focus on issues specific to three types of mobile equipment: (i) aircraft objects (as the only type of equipment covered by a protocol currently in force); (ii) ships (as the type of equipment perfectly matching the Convention criteria, but at the same time not covered by a protocol); and (iii) mining, agricultural

[89] The Rail Working Group is a rail industry association established to represent the position of the rail industry relating to adoption and implementation of a dedicated protocol on railway rolling stock. It enjoyed the status of observer during the Cape Town Diplomatic Conference to adopt the Convention and the Aircraft Protocol and during the Luxembourg Diplomatic Conference to adopt the Rail Protocol.

[90] The Convention was adopted during the Cape Town Diplomatic Conference alongside a single protocol only – the Aircraft Protocol. The Rail and Space Protocols were adopted later, in 2007 and 2012, respectively.

[91] This solution can be found in Article 51(5) of the CTC.

[92] In addition to a closed list of assets with respect to which the Convention – pursuant to Article 45 *bis* – prevails over the United Nations Convention on the Assignment of Receivables in International Trade (adopted 12 December 2001), Article 51(6) of the CTC expressly states that for any other types of mobile equipment the CTC will *only* have similar priority if it is provided for in the corresponding protocol.

and construction equipment (as the first (and so far the only) type of assets not expressly mentioned in the CTC).

3.3. Aircraft

The Aircraft Protocol was the only protocol ready for adoption alongside the CTC in 2001, perhaps suggesting that the issues surrounding this category of assets were less pronounced, compared to others. This is true only to a certain extent. On the one hand, aircraft easily satisfied the criteria of high cost and mobility[93] and operated within a consolidated industry that took an early interest in the UNIDROIT's project to develop an international convention on international interests in mobile equipment.[94] On the other hand, aircraft equipment created unique challenges for the developers of the CTC – they are addressed further in this section.

3.3.1. Pre-CTC International Rules Affecting Aircraft Finance

Existing international regulation in the area of aviation finance created the first notable difficulty for the UNIDROIT project to develop the Convention. The idea that the *lex situs*[95] approach is inappropriate for security interests over aircraft had already been recognised and reflected in the 1948 Geneva Convention, which provided for the international recognition of 'mortgages, hypotheques and similar rights in aircraft … created as security for payment of an indebtedness' when such rights were constituted in accordance with the law of the state of registration[96] of the aircraft at the time of their creation and 'regularly recorded in a public record' of the state of registration of the aircraft.[97] The 1948 Geneva Convention

[93] See, eg, Unidroit, *Study LXXII – Doc. 1 (1989)* 16.

[94] Among the respondents to Cuming's Questionnaire in 1990 were both the aircraft manufacturers (Airbus Industrie, France) and the aircraft operators (Air Portugal, Portugal; Air New Zealand Limited, New Zealand). The Boeing Company joined the discussions in 1994: see Unidroit, *Security Interests Study Group Sub-committee 1st Session Misc. 3 (1994)*. The Boeing Company and Airbus Industrie subsequently established an international working group (AWG) to produce a representative industry view on the future Convention, which also included leasing companies, engine manufacturers and banks: see Unidroit, *Study LXXII – Doc. 16 (1995)* 1.

[95] For a more detailed discussion of the various connecting factors in the context of mobile equipment see section 2.2.1.

[96] Registration of aircraft is governed by the Convention on International Civil Aviation (adopted 7 December 1944, entered into force 4 April 1947) 15 UNTS 295 (the 'Chicago Convention'), which does not permit simultaneous registration of aircraft in more than one state: see Article 18 of the Chicago Convention.

[97] Article I(1)(d) of the 1948 Geneva Convention.

essentially addressed the *lex situs* problem and, from this perspective alone, the UNIDROIT project did not look particularly attractive.[98]

Nevertheless, the aviation industry, represented by the AWG, took a broader view of the aircraft financing mechanisms and the risks associated with them: the new UNIDROIT convention was considered as an opportunity to change the existing international regime by addressing its deficiencies. First, the 1948 Geneva Convention was mostly a conflict of laws instrument, the effectiveness of which for financiers ultimately depended on the different national laws regulating the matters of creation, perfection[99] and priority:[100] if such national laws were weak or non-existent, the value of the recognition mechanics established by this treaty diminished greatly. Furthermore, the state of registration of aircraft was free to deny the recording of any security rights that could not be constituted under its domestic law.[101] Second, the absence of a working system of recording security interests in the state of registration of aircraft made their recognition impossible.[102] Third, the 1948 Geneva Convention treated aircraft engines on a par with any other spare parts[103] and imposed onerous requirements for the recognition of security rights in them: they had to be not only identified as being subject to a security right, but also stored in a specific location at all times.[104] These requirements were seen by the industry as 'unrealistic' in the light of their high cost and established operating practices whereby engines were frequently removed from the airframe and replaced with spare engines from an engine 'pool'.[105] Fourth, the 1948 Geneva Convention had no clear provision on the treatment of lease assignments and other contract rights, which were widely used in aviation finance practice.[106] Fifth, it did not address the risks of secured creditors in case of bankruptcy of the party providing security. Overall, in broad terms, the 1948 Geneva Convention created a degree of legal certainty by specifying which law governs the security interests over aircraft (*lex registri*), but did almost nothing in terms of enhancing that law.[107]

Other aviation conventions did not promote aircraft financing either. The Chicago Convention, whilst in force in most states across the globe, did not

[98] Although the 1948 Geneva Convention was not (and is still not) ratified by a number of key jurisdictions (such as Canada, India, Indonesia, Japan, Russia and the United Kingdom), by 1989 it had come into force in 53 states. Against this background, the prospects of greater success of an entirely new international treaty at the time were questionable at best.

[99] According to Article I(1)(i), the security rights must be constituted according to the law of the state in which the aircraft is registered.

[100] Article II(2) states that the effects of security rights recognised under the treaty are determined in accordance with the laws of the state in which these rights are recorded.

[101] Article II(3) of the 1948 Geneva Convention.

[102] Article I(1)(ii) of the 1948 Geneva Convention.

[103] See Article X(4) of the 1948 Geneva Convention.

[104] Article X(1) of the 1948 Geneva Convention.

[105] Unidroit, *Study LXXII - Doc. 16 (1995)* 19.

[106] ibid 15.

[107] For a more comprehensive account of the criticism of the 1948 Geneva Convention and the circumstances of its adoption see Donal Hanley, 'The Relationship between the Geneva and Cape Town Conventions' (2015) 4 *Cape Town Convention Journal* 103, 106.

allow simultaneous registration of an aircraft in more than one jurisdiction, but permitted transfers of registration between states.[108] Both the initial registration and the transfer of registration, however, were governed by the domestic laws of the relevant country,[109] which left in the hands of contracting states a significant degree of discretion. Consequently, the domestic laws could have a serious bearing on the ability of the secured party to immobilise the aircraft by restricting its de-registration (eg by requiring the consent of the airline/other party).[110] Another treaty, the 1933 Rome Convention,[111] restricted the ability of the secured party to seize the aircraft 'actually put in service on a regular line of public transportation and indispensable reserve aircraft', as well as aircraft 'assigned to the transportation of persons or property for hire, when it is ready to depart for such transportation' (except where the attachment involves a debt incurred for the trip and that trip is the one which the aircraft is about to make).[112]

Against this background, it does not seem surprising that the aviation industry showed an interest in the UNIDROIT project, seeing it as an opportunity to set a certain minimum level of protection of the secured party in aircraft finance transactions that was not possible under the existing combination of international and domestic rules. In its first submission to UNIDROIT the AWG expressly stated that, in its view, 'the value of the proposed convention [was] directly related to the extent to which its terms ... result in an increase in the availability of credit, and/or a reduction in the cost of such credit, to owners/operators of aircraft equipment'.[113] This highly practical approach later resulted in the significant expansion of scope of the Convention to cover matters beyond recognition of foreign security interests, basic remedies and priorities. Yet more importantly for this section, the aviation industry saw the UNIDROIT convention as a new opportunity to change the existing rules – and was willing to support the idea in anticipation of significant financial gains.[114]

3.3.2. Aircraft Engines

Despite the active involvement of the industry, the development of an appropriate definition of 'aircraft' in the context of the draft Convention was not a simple

[108] Article 18 of the Chicago Convention.
[109] Article 19 of the Chicago Convention.
[110] Unidroit, *Study LXXII – Doc. 16 (1995)* 31.
[111] Convention for the Unification of Certain Rules Relating to the Precautionary Attachment of Aircraft (adopted 25 May 1933, entered into force 12 January 1937) 192 LNTS 289 (the 'Rome Convention').
[112] Articles 3(1)(b) and 3(1)(c) of the Rome Convention.
[113] Unidroit, *Study LXXII – Doc. 16 (1995)* 5.
[114] The matter of economic benefit analysis is addressed in greater detail in section 7.2.2, whereas the effects of the involvement of various industries in the development of the CTC are discussed in section 8.4.

task. In its first formal submission to UNIDROIT the AWG avoided any attempts to come up with the relevant definition,[115] but noted the distinct characteristics of aircraft engines (also undefined at the time)[116] as parts of an aircraft that warranted special treatment (contrary to their classification as any other spare parts of an aircraft in the 1948 Geneva Convention).[117] First, engines themselves formed an extremely valuable asset category: the proportion of their value to the overall value of an aircraft was ranging between 15 per cent to 20 per cent, with the acquisition costs of new jet engines varying between USD 2.5 million and USD 10 million.[118] Second, engines were subject to special engine pooling arrangements whereby they were removed from the airframes and replaced with other engines taken from a pool – a practice implemented for operational purposes, often in violation of contractual prohibitions.[119] These pooling arrangements were not uniform: some contemplated a transfer of title over a dismantled engine to the corresponding pool, while others did not (subject to the applicable domestic contract and accessions laws).[120] Third, national laws differed greatly when determining whether an attachment to an asset becomes a part of that asset.[121] Fourth, the interests of engine financiers could differ from the interests of other aircraft financiers, since engines could be subject to separate security arrangements that did not cover the aircraft as a whole.[122]

Together these factors raised two key policy concerns. On the one hand, it became clear that engines formed a distinct group of aviation assets that needed to be covered by the future Convention, even though their actual function did not differ from that of other spare parts. At the time, the specific nature of aircraft engines was recognised not only by the financiers and their clients: the recently adopted Financial Leasing Convention treated the engines as separate from the aircraft (as a whole) for the purposes of determining the applicable law regulating the public notice requirements.[123] On the other hand, the engine pooling arrangements and differing national laws on accession of parts to the main asset came in direct conflict with the 'title tracking approach'[124] advocated by the AWG, whereby

115 See footnote 5 in Unidroit, *Study LXXII – Doc. 16 (1995)* 3.

116 See footnote 43 in ibid 19.

117 Article X(4) of the 1948 Geneva Convention.

118 See footnote 44 in Unidroit, *Study LXXII – Doc. 16 (1995)* 19.

119 ibid.

120 See footnote 45 in ibid.

121 For example, in Germany the act of installation of an engine on an aircraft effectively resulted in the transfer of ownership over the engine to the aircraft owner: see Annex 3 in ibid 42.

122 ibid 19.

123 See Article 7(3)(b) and Article 7(3)(c) of the Financial Leasing Convention. However, the express reference to aircraft engines in the Financial Leasing Convention was a last-minute change introduced only at the adoption stage: the final draft prepared in the run-up to the Diplomatic Conference in Ottawa mentioned 'all other [mobile] equipment [normally used in more than one State]' generally: see draft Article 5(3)(a) and 5(3)(b), as well as paragraphs 95 and 96 in Unidroit, *Study LIX – Doc. 48 (1987)* 52–53.

124 It should be noted that the 'title tracking approach' suggested by the AWG was not limited to recording only security interests against a specific engine: the proposed registration system was expected to cover title transfers as well.

a financier holds an interest in a specific engine, regardless of its physical location, installation on or detachment from any airframe.[125]

Given the lack of an internationally accepted standard in engine financing and the widely differing national laws on accession, and in order to collate the views of the engine manufacturers and financiers, the AWG convened a small aircraft engine subgroup (the 'Engines Subgroup') consisting of representatives of Rolls Royce, GE Aircraft Engines, the International Lease Finance Corporation, Snecma and Pratt & Whitney. Having acknowledged its potential drawbacks (such as the increased administrative burden resulting from the need to work out appropriate engine-specific contractual restrictions), the Engines Subgroup unanimously approved the title tracking approach: the enhanced clarity resulting from such a system would 'far outweigh' any increased costs, whereas the mechanisms established by the new convention would set a market standard in the (engine financing) area where there had been none.[126] At the same time, the costs associated with the title tracking system were seen as prohibitive for any other category of aircraft parts other than engines: 'the number of types of parts, let alone the number of all parts, would be too great to manage'.[127]

The recommendations of the AWG concerning the separation of aircraft engines were reflected in the revised draft articles of the Convention prepared in 1995, which covered both 'aircraft' and 'aircraft engines'. However, since the industry had not proposed a clear definition for either category, the two terms created uncertainty: the former was broader and could absorb the latter entirely. This problem was promptly addressed by the AWG in its second memorandum to UNIDROIT, which avoided overlapping terms by suggesting that 'airframe' should replace 'aircraft' as the base term.[128] The resulting bifurcation of 'aircraft' into 'airframes' and 'aircraft engines' was retained in the final text of the CTC.[129] This change made it unnecessary to use the term 'aircraft' in the text of the Convention. Nevertheless, the Aircraft Protocol has retained this word primarily[130] in the context of aircraft registration and de-registration[131] – a process

[125] Unidroit, *Study LXXII – Doc. 16 (1995)* 19. The 'title *tracking* approach' was considered a more appropriate alternative to a 'title *transfer*' system, whereby engines are legally viewed as part of an airframe to which they are attached.

[126] See Annex 3 to ibid 42.

[127] ibid 43.

[128] Unidroit, *Study LXXII – Doc. 23 (1996)* 9.

[129] Article 2(3)(a) of the CTC.

[130] For a detailed summary of the various applications of the term see paragraph 5.3 in Goode, *Convention on International Interests in Mobile Equipment and Protocol thereto on Matters Specific to Aircraft Equipment: Official Commentary* (4th edn, International Institute for the Unification of Private Law (UNIDROIT) 2019) 483–84. The term is rarely used for purposes not connected with aircraft registration: examples include Articles XXIII/XXIV regulating the conflicts between the CTC and other aviation treaties, as well as Article XIV(3), which preserves the rights and interests in an aircraft engine 'upon installation on or removal from an aircraft'.

[131] De-registration is an aircraft-specific remedy available to the financier under Article IX of the Aircraft Protocol that is used to 'ground' an aircraft and effectively prevent its exploitation by the operator.

of terminating the nationality registration under the Chicago Convention, which applies to 'aircraft' as a whole.[132]

3.3.3. Helicopters and Helicopter Engines

The Aircraft Protocol treats helicopters as 'aircraft', on a par with airframes with installed aircraft engines.[133] This is quite clear from the classification of aircraft in Annex 7 to the Chicago Convention: all rotorcraft (let alone helicopters) are, by definition, a sub-category of 'aircraft'[134] and are registrable as such (as to nationality) in the corresponding state registries. By the same logic (namely that any helicopter is an aircraft *ipso facto*), one might expect helicopter engines to be another form of 'aircraft object' under the Convention, particularly in the light of the very broad definition of 'aircraft engines'.[135] The Official Commentary supports this approach, explaining that a helicopter engine is indeed an 'aircraft engine', but only 'prior to installation or after removal and before reinstallation'.[136] Upon installation on a helicopter an engine ceases to be an 'aircraft engine' within the meaning of the CTC and the Aircraft Protocol, becomes an accessory of the helicopter and 'while so installed is not capable of being the subject of a separate international interest under the Convention'.[137] This conclusion is a result of the threefold classification of 'aircraft objects', which oddly puts a complete aircraft (helicopter) on a par with elements of construction of an aircraft (airframes and aircraft engines).

This classification is unfortunate, since the ability of an engine financier to protect itself by taking an international interest over a helicopter engine turns on the fact of separation of such engine from the helicopter frame. Naturally, it is possible to create an international interest over a helicopter engine *prior* to its installation. The Official Commentary also suggests a helpful workaround solution in the form of 'prospective international interest' over an installed helicopter engine that would automatically create a 'full' international interest *after* its detachment. Both solutions are cumbersome, since in the event of a dispute they would likely require an engine financier to provide evidence that the engine had indeed been separated from the helicopter frame at the time of creation of an

[132] In other words, aircraft engines, unlike aircraft taken as a whole, do not have a nationality based on registration under the Chicago Convention.

[133] Article I(2)(a) of the Aircraft Protocol.

[134] Annex 7 to the Chicago Convention is cited not only for the purposes of suggesting an authoritative classification of aircraft: the definition of 'aircraft' in the Aircraft Protocol (Article I(2)(a)) is based on (but is not limited to) the corresponding definition in the Chicago Convention: '"aircraft" means aircraft *as defined for the purposes of the Chicago Convention* which are either airframes with aircraft engines installed thereon or helicopters' (emphasis added).

[135] See Article I(2)(b) of the Aircraft Protocol.

[136] See paragraph 3.9 in Goode, *Convention on International Interests in Mobile Equipment and Protocol thereto on Matters Specific to Aircraft Equipment: Official Commentary* (4th edn, International Institute for the Unification of Private Law (UNIDROIT) 2019) 204–05.

[137] ibid 206.

international interest. Yet, so long as an engine *remains installed* on the helicopter, the Convention and the Aircraft Protocol do not give an engine financier the tools to protect its priority by taking an international interest over the engine.

The otherwise elegant bifurcation of aircraft, for the purposes of the Convention, into separate aircraft objects (airframes and engines), each of which can be subject to a separate international interest, simply does not work for a complete helicopter. In the case of aircraft other than helicopters such separation means that, in order to create security over the *whole* aircraft, the international interest would have to be created separately in respect of each of its frame and engines. The same approach, however, would not work in the context of helicopters: in terms of the CTC and the Aircraft Protocol, there is no difference between an international interest over a helicopter with or without engines installed on it, since the 'aircraft object' here remains unchanged – a helicopter (with any spare parts, including engines, attached to it).

The documentary history does not provide a clear evidence of the reasons behind the odd treatment of 'helicopters' in the Aircraft Protocol.

In its initial submission to UNIDROIT in 1995 the AWG made it clear that the future convention on international interests in mobile equipment would have to treat aircraft engines differently from the other types of spare parts, but refrained from suggesting a definition for 'aircraft engines'[138] or even 'aircraft'.[139] Unfortunately, it is not at all clear what types of aircraft are discussed in the AWG paper: aeroplanes only or other types of aircraft as well (eg airships, rotorcraft, ornithopters). The fact that no attempt was made to define the term suggests that this matter required additional consideration by the AWG.

In 1996, the AWG prepared its second memorandum, which proposed for the first time a 'bifurcation of aircraft into airframes and aircraft engines', whereby 'the appropriate base definition … should be "airframe" rather than aircraft'.[140] The focus of the AWG at the time was on developing a definition for both terms that would, first, limit the scope of the Convention to objects that are more expensive, advanced and 'commercial' and, second, be objective by nature. As a result, 'airframes' were defined by reference to their capacity to transport passengers (or cargo)[141] and 'aircraft engines' – by reference to the corresponding propulsion power and technology.[142] Neither definition was restricted by references to a particular sub-category of aircraft (eg aeroplanes) and, theoretically, any airframe or engine meeting the corresponding physical characteristics would qualify. The only other limitation was based on the purpose for which the assets were used (objects used for military, customs or police purposes were excluded).

[138] See footnote 43 in Unidroit, *Study LXXII – Doc. 16 (1995)* 19.
[139] See footnote 5 in ibid 3.
[140] Unidroit, *Study LXXII – Doc. 23 (1996)* 8.
[141] See paragraph (4) in Annexure to Annex 1 in ibid.
[142] See paragraph (2) in Annexure to Annex 1 in ibid.

The same memorandum by the AWG also contained the first ever proposal to add 'helicopters' as a separate category of objects within the Convention. Several points should be stressed here. First, helicopters were not specifically considered by the AWG when it was contemplating the bifurcation of 'aircraft' into airframes and engines, as is clear from the caveat made by the AWG: 'we reserve at this stage on the questions of whether and to what extent the recommendations of the aviation working group ought to apply with equal force to helicopters'.[143] Second, the inclusion of 'helicopters' was – at the time – provisional in nature, since the term remained in square brackets.[144] Third, the term 'helicopters' was added without a corresponding definition.[145]

The first mention of 'helicopters' as a separate category within the text of the draft Convention was added by the Drafting Group during its session held on 13 and 15 April 1996, which coincided with the second meeting of the Study Group.[146] Just as in the second memorandum of the AWG, no definition of the term was provided.[147] As a result, helicopters were in an awkward position: apparently, the aviation industry had some thoughts about this asset category, and yet there was no clarity about how to proceed with this knowledge. More importantly, there seemed to be no guidance on how to distinguish helicopters from all other aircraft (to which the bifurcation into airframes and aircraft engines applied equally and seemed to create no objections). Perhaps as a result of this odd status quo, a peculiar drafting change occurred in October 1996: the Drafting Group separated all definitions in the draft Convention into three parts: 'definitions common to all categories of object', 'definitions exclusive to aircraft property' and 'other definitions'.[148] Both 'airframes' and 'aircraft engines' formed the second part (aircraft-specific definitions), while 'helicopters' (still undefined) were swept into the third group, alongside 'containers', 'oil rigs', 'railway rolling stock', 'registered ships' and 'satellites'.[149]

Following the transition to a dual convention/protocol structure,[150] all the asset-specific definitions were moved to the relevant protocols: 'there was agreement that the Protocol was the best place for defining the different categories of assets encompassed by the future Convention'.[151] As a result, the definition of 'helicopters' was introduced only in the draft Aircraft Protocol prepared by the Aircraft Protocol Group.[152] This definition formed the third element of the threefold classification of 'aircraft objects' that exists in the final text,[153] but was rather different

[143] ibid 23.
[144] See footnote 18, as well as paragraph (3) in Annexure to Annex 1 in ibid 8.
[145] See paragraph (14) in Annexure to Annex 1 in ibid.
[146] See Article 2(1)(c) in Appendix IV to Unidroit, *Study LXXII – Doc. 27 (1996).*
[147] See paragraph (i) in Part I of the 'Appendix' to Appendix IV in ibid.
[148] See Appendix in Unidroit, *Study LXXII – Doc. 30 (1996)* 23–25.
[149] ibid.
[150] See ch 4.
[151] Unidroit, *Study LXXII – Doc. 35 (1997)* 4.
[152] See Article 1(2)(l) in Unidroit, *Study LXXIID – Doc. 1 (1998)* 5.
[153] Article I(2)(c) of the Aircraft Protocol.

from the other two (airframes and aircraft engines) in the sense that it referred to an actual flying machine, rather than its elements of construction. Unlike airframes and aircraft engines, only helicopters were given a non-circular definition, ie a definition that does not use the defined term as part of itself.[154] This definition reproduced, almost word for word, the definition of 'helicopter' in Annex 7 to the Chicago Convention and added certain threshold physical characteristics, such as minimum carrying capacity.[155]

While it is clear that the authors of the definition of 'helicopter' relied on the text of Annex 7 to the Chicago Convention, it is puzzling why no attempt to reconcile all three 'aircraft objects' was made in the light of the well-developed terminology found in that document. The key problem with the term 'helicopter' used in parallel with 'airframes' and 'aircraft objects' is that the former represents a specific *type of aircraft* characterised by the technology used to support it in the air, whereas the latter two are merely elements of construction of aircraft. Annex 7 to the Chicago Convention divides all aircraft into two groups: those which are 'lighter-than-air'[156] and those which are 'heavier-than-air'.[157] Both groups are then sub-divided further into categories, depending on whether the aircraft is power-driven or not. Even if the AWG, which proposed the bifurcation of aircraft into airframes and aircraft engines, only considered power-driven aircraft (thus excluding balloons, gliders and kites), there is still a substantial variety of aircraft with airframes and engines that could potentially qualify under the Convention (assuming they meet the minimum requirements of carrying capacity or power, respectively): airships, aeroplanes, ornithopters and rotorcraft (gyroplanes and helicopters). The lack of any specificity relating to the types of aircraft of which the qualifying airframes and aircraft engines form part makes the inclusion of 'helicopters' as standalone 'aircraft objects' redundant. On the one hand, there is no evidence that 'aircraft engines' were never intended to include helicopter engines: in 1997, the Russian Federation Aviation Working Group[158] came up with a proposal to classify helicopter engines as a standalone category of aircraft objects,[159] but this idea never made it into any of the drafts, let alone the final text of the Convention. On the other hand, there is no documentary evidence suggesting that 'airframes' were never intended to include helicopter airframes (especially given that helicopter airframes are still 'airframes' in every sense of the word).

[154] 'Airframes' and 'aircraft engines' were essentially defined, respectively, as airframes and aircraft engines meeting certain physical characteristics: see Article 1(2)(d) and Article 1(2)(b) in Unidroit, *Study LXXIID – Doc. 1 (1998)* 3–4.

[155] The only change was in the form of replacing the word 'aircraft' with the word 'machine', presumably made due to the fact that the draft Aircraft Protocol had already incorporated the term 'aircraft' in the sense that was narrower than that used in Annex 7 to the Chicago Convention.

[156] These are defined as aircraft 'supported chiefly by [their] buoyancy in the air' (eg balloons).

[157] These are defined as aircraft 'deriving [their] lift in flight chiefly from aerodynamic forces' (eg aeroplanes).

[158] A group of domestic producers and carriers formed in Russia under the aegis of the national chamber of industry and commerce positioning itself (at the time) as a counterpart to the AWG.

[159] Unidroit, *Study LXXII – Doc. 31 (1997)* 1.

The odd classification of 'helicopters' as 'aircraft objects' was later discussed by the governmental experts during the Third Joint Session: a proposal was made to reconsider the latter definition, since 'helicopters constituted both aircraft and aircraft objects'.[160] Unfortunately, this proposal was never reflected in any of the subsequent drafts. The odd categorisation created confusion among the participants: one delegation, noting that helicopters were a subset of the broader category of 'aircraft' under the Chicago Convention, proposed 'broadening the list of categories of equipment to include "aircraft" as a whole'.[161] The suggestion was dismissed, as the draft Convention 'was concerned with the financing of aircraft objects and … airframes and aircraft engines [were] … subject to … separate security'.[162] Unfortunately, the discussion did not transition to a more conceptual level, which would no doubt reveal the internal inconsistencies among the three types of 'aircraft objects'.

The above historical analysis does not give a conclusive explanation of the reasons behind the classification of 'helicopters' as standalone 'aircraft objects'. If nothing else, it shows that the problems surrounding the threefold structure of the latter term were not given sufficient attention at the development stage. The absence of detailed recorded conceptual and comparative analysis of each group of 'aircraft objects', the constant focus on the bifurcation of aircraft into airframes and engines, as well as the late inclusion of 'helicopters' in the form of an ill-explained add-on to an otherwise well-functioning classification have produced a result that is both illogical and inherently inconsistent. Article I(2)(c) is in need of revision once the opportunity presents itself, such as in case of a review conference convened pursuant to Article XXXVI(2) of the Aircraft Protocol. Of course, it is highly doubtful that a review conference would be convened solely for the purpose of addressing this particular issue (particularly in the absence of clear pressure from the relevant financing circles), but attracting attention to this issue may end up at least clarifying the actual reasons behind the unfortunate drafting of Article I(2)(c). After all, these actual reasons might have been quite convincing – but if that is the case, they should be brought to light.

3.4. Ships

The history of development of the CTC provisions relating to ships is filled with obscurity and uncertainty. The UNIDROIT initiative to develop an international treaty regulating security interests in mobile equipment produced a very different outcome within the maritime sector, compared to its aviation counterpart: ships ended up being completely excluded from the scope of the Convention. This seems

[160] Unidroit, *Unidroit CGE/Int.Int./3-Report ICAO Ref. LSC/ME/3-Report (2000)* 7.
[161] See paragraph 56 in ibid 8.
[162] ibid.

all the more puzzling, since ships – just like aircraft – should easily satisfy any requirements of high cost and mobility: the former are objects of very high value, often cross national borders and can operate beyond national sovereign jurisdiction on the high seas. What went wrong and why were the results so different for the maritime industry?

3.4.1. Pre-CTC International Rules Affecting Ship Finance

As in the case of aircraft, the main initial challenge for the application of the draft Convention in the area of maritime financing was created by the existing international regulation. The deficiencies of *lex situs* had already been recognised and reflected in a number of international instruments. The 1926 Brussels Convention[163] provided for the recognition of all 'mortgages, hypothecations, and other similar charges upon vessels', whenever these were (i) 'duly effected in accordance with the law of the contracting state to which the vessel belongs', and (ii) 'registered in a public register either at the port of the vessel's registry or a central office'.[164] The 1967 Brussels Convention similarly treated as 'enforceable' those mortgages and 'hypotheques' over sea-going vessels which were 'effected and registered in accordance with the law of the State where the vessel [was] registered'[165] (while adding a whole array of other requirements, such as the need to disclose the amount secured).[166] Both instruments, however, enjoyed limited success and did not apply in major shipping countries.[167]

A similar approach was utilised in the 1965 Geneva Convention, which provides that 'rights of ownership, usufruct or mortgage entered in a register of one of the Contracting Parties shall be recognised in the territory of the other Contracting Parties'.[168] However, the application of this treaty was also very limited: by 1989 it had been adopted only in five states: Austria, France, Luxembourg, Netherlands and Switzerland.

As a result, at the start of development of the Cape Town Convention the international regulation of security interests over vessels of various types was somewhat similar to that which applied to aircraft. The *lex situs* connecting factor was deemed clearly inconsistent with the interests of legal certainty and replaced

[163] In this book the author uses the translation taken from the Treaty Information Bulletin No. 19, 1931, of the Department of State of the United States of America, as reproduced in Unidroit, *Security Interests Study Group 1st Session Misc. 3 (1993).*

[164] Article 1 of the 1926 Brussels Convention.

[165] Article 1(a) of the 1967 Brussels Convention.

[166] See Article 1(b) and 1(c) of the 1967 Brussels Convention.

[167] By 1989 only 23 states had been bound by the 1926 Brussels Convention, while the 1967 Brussels Convention had been adopted by five, and ratified by just three, countries (Denmark, Norway and Sweden).

[168] Article 5 of Protocol No. 1 Concerning Rights *in rem* in Inland Navigation Vessels to the 1965 Geneva Convention.

with *lex registri*[169] in a number of international instruments. On the other hand, the shipping conventions struggled to achieve the level of acceptance of the 1948 Geneva Convention, which had applied in 53 states by 1989. The most successful treaty (at the time) regulating security over vessels, the 1926 Brussels Convention, was in need of revision and modernisation,[170] and its 1967 successor had failed to achieve that. The prospects of further unification in the area of security interests over vessels on the basis of pre-existing international instruments seemed questionable, and one might expect that the shipping industry would be genuinely interested in the UNIDROIT initiative – and be mistaken.

3.4.2. Exclusion of Ships from the Scope of the CTC

The first argument in favour of excluding ships from the scope of the future Cape Town Convention surfaced at the very start of the project: in June 1990 Danmarks Rederiforening (Danish Shipowners' Association) submitted a letter to UNIDROIT which stated that the two Brussels Conventions of 1926 and 1967 had been under review by IMO and UNCTAD for a couple of years, a new draft treaty had been prepared on the basis of such review and, consequently, ships (as well as mobile platforms) should be excluded from the scope of the new UNIDROIT convention. In early 1992 the first formal group of experts convened to assess the UNIDROIT project (the REWG) acknowledged the existence of this parallel project by IMO and UNCTAD as a 'strong argument for excluding ships'[171] – a year later the same point was reiterated during the first session of the Study Group by the observer representing the International Maritime Committee (CMI).[172]

At the time, the discussions concerning ships shared two common characteristics. First, rather surprisingly, there is no record of any substantive analysis of the provisions of the IMO/UNCTAD convention in the context of the UNIDROIT project. Of the two treaties, the one prepared by IMO/UNCTAD[173] came out first: its final text was adopted on 6 May 1993 during the Diplomatic Conference in Geneva and was ready for review (at that time the UNIDROIT project was still at an early stage – it would take more than a year for the first basic set of draft articles

[169] But see n 17 in section 2.2.1.

[170] While endorsing the *lex registri* approach, the 1926 Brussels Convention did little else to harmonise the international regime for the creation and effectiveness of ship mortgages and hypothecations: it left the registration requirements to be regulated by national laws, adopted a hands-off approach to the effects of valid (and recognised) mortgages and hypothecations created under domestic law and did not regulate priority as between various consensual security interests *inter se* (while stating that they rank below maritime liens). For a more detailed discussion of the deficiencies of the two Brussels conventions, see Ole Böger, 'The Cape Town Convention and Proprietary Security over Ships' (2014) 19 *Uniform Law Review* 24, 41.

[171] Unidroit, *Study LXXII – Doc. 5 (1992)* 3.

[172] Unidroit, *Study LXXII – Doc. 7 (1993)* 4.

[173] International Convention on Maritime Liens and Mortgages (adopted 6 May 1993, entered into force 5 September 2004) 2276 UNTS 39 (the '1993 Geneva Convention').

of the CTC to emerge in the first place). As a result, the overall appropriateness of the 1993 Geneva Convention for the shipping industry as a whole, and the ship financiers in particular, was not scrutinised by the UNIDROIT working groups or those commentators who advocated a total hands-off approach.[174] Second, neither UNIDROIT, nor the CMI – at least officially – excluded the opportunity for reopening the discussion about ships once the UNIDROIT project crystallised into a more definitive draft. To this end the Study Group 'decided to defer consideration of the matter until such time as it had a clearer idea of the kind of rules that were emerging',[175] while the CMI acknowledged that 'there was a possibility that ships might ultimately benefit from inclusion in the projected Unidroit Convention if they could be shown to fit into the system created thereunder'.[176] Furthermore, the UNIDROIT treaty was even considered as a potentially helpful addition to the recent 1993 Geneva Convention: the former could be drafted in a such a way that would exclude its application to registered ships (as these had already been covered by the latter), and instead target non-registered ships, as well as containers and other maritime equipment.[177]

Overall, the prospects of extending the scope of the draft CTC to ships did not seem entirely unrealistic initially: in the end, it was perfectly reasonable to wait until the UNIDROIT convention takes shape before any conclusive decision could be made. This optimistic conclusion is supported by the comments of Rolf Herber, representative of the CMI, who approached the matter from the end user's viewpoint: the future UNIDROIT convention could actually make it *beneficial* for ship financiers to 'enter … rights into an additional register under the proposed Unidroit Convention in order to extend their recognition'.[178] According to Herber,[179] such a scenario was actually possible, provided that 'the charge on the vessel as such would not be changed by the Convention, but only the scope of its recognition'.[180] In other words, another treaty which would strengthen the

[174] In its comments submitted in early 1993 (shortly before the adoption of the 1993 Geneva Convention) the German Federal Ministry of Justice simply concluded that 'in view of both the existing international Conventions for the unification of certain rules relating to maritime liens and mortgages and the additional prospective Convention on this subject, there did not seem to be any need for any further international regulation in this field': see Unidroit, *Study LXXII – Doc. 6 Add. (1993)* 2. One cannot help but wonder why the same comments – but in respect of aircraft – conversely deemed it 'necessary … to check carefully as to what extent [the 1948 Geneva Convention] was inadequate', especially considering that at the time the aviation convention had almost twice as many ratifications and accessions as both of the 1926 and 1967 Brussels Conventions combined. However outdated the 1948 Geneva Convention might have been at the time (see section 3.3 above), it is hard to figure out the reason why the system of international regulation of security interests over ships, built around three conventions on maritime liens and mortgages (one of which had very limited application and the others were not even in force) was to be accepted at face value.

[175] Unidroit, *Study LXXII – Doc. 7 (1993)* 4.

[176] Unidroit, *Study LXXIIB – Doc. 1 (1995)* 11.

[177] Unidroit, *Study LXXII – Doc. 14 Add 1 (1994)* 2.

[178] ibid.

[179] These comments were submitted by Rolf Herber in his personal capacity, and 'did not represent the considered opinion of the CMI': see footnote 1 in ibid 1.

[180] ibid 2.

position of financiers, while preserving the existing system of security interests in registered ships revolving around maritime liens and mortgages, would in principle be acceptable.

Such open-minded approach seemed to be a reasonable compromise: it effectively gave UNIDROIT every opportunity to develop a new treaty that could ultimately be accepted by the shipping industry if tangible benefits for ship financiers were shown to stem from it. For this reason, the drafting of the CTC remained open-ended, permitting ships to be included in its scope, either impliedly[181] or by express reference.[182]

In 1996, following the second session of the Study Group, it became clear that the UNIDROIT initiative had evolved into a rather ambitious undertaking aimed at establishing a new international regime for international interests in mobile equipment – interests that were *sui generis* in nature, completely detached from their domestic law counterparts[183] and thus in no way interfering with the validity of the latter. This regime would regulate not only the effects of international interests between parties to the relevant transaction *inter se* (ie remedies of the creditor), but also the effects of an international interest as against third parties (ie priorities). Herber's hypothetical scenario whereby the UNIDROIT instrument would preserve the existing system of security interests, while strengthening the position of the creditor, was slowly being realised. The time was ripe to re-examine the case of ships.

After the initial opposition from shipping circles it was imperative for UNIDROIT either to reverse the position of the CMI or to obtain support from the industry itself. To that end UNIDROIT invited the CMI to 'organise a working group … to submit a representative shipping industry view on the desirable content of the proposed Convention as the same related to shipping'.[184] The example, which had been set by the aviation industry in the form of the AWG, was still fresh, and there is little doubt that a favourable reaction from the industry could sway the CMI and provide the much-needed support for the UNIDROIT initiative. But more importantly, only feedback from the industry itself could adequately address what seems to be the key concern expressed by Herber back in 1994, namely 'whether it could be of benefit to creditors of maritime mortgages to enter these rights into an additional register under the proposed … Convention'.[185]

Unfortunately, the possibility of a constructive dialogue with the shipping industry was made virtually impossible by the international organisations standing behind the 1993 Geneva Convention. In July 1996 Secretaries-General of

[181] See Article 1(2)(a) referring to any 'equipment of a kind normally moved from one State to another in the course of business' in Unidroit, *Study LXXII – Doc. 13 (1994)*.

[182] In subsequent drafts ships were included in the text in square brackets, ie on a provisional basis. See Article 1(2)(c) in Unidroit, *Study LXXII – Doc. 18 (1995)*; Article 2(1)(c) in Unidroit, *Study LXXII – Doc. 22 (1996)*; Article 2(1)(c) in Unidroit, *Study LXXII – Doc. 24 (1996)*.

[183] See section 2.3.2 above.

[184] Unidroit, *Study LXXII – Doc. 27 (1996)* 13.

[185] Unidroit, *Study LXXII – Doc. 14 Add 1 (1994)* 2.

UNCTAD and IMO submitted two separate, yet similar,[186] letters to UNIDROIT requesting that ships be excluded from the Convention. The arguments given in both letters were essentially the same. First, the new UNIDROIT Convention was considered a potential source of conflict with the recently adopted 1993 Geneva Convention. Second, international maritime law was seen as a distinctive *corpus juris* developed by specialised international organisations.[187] Both arguments were driven by the clear intention to preserve the status quo in the maritime industry, to the exclusion of other valid concerns. On the one hand, at the time it was already clear that the international interest created by the Convention would be of *sui generis* nature and thus detached from any national law counterparts, significantly reducing the possibility of overlaps with the other international treaties. On the other hand, the pressure to exclude ships regardless of any meaningful discussion and analysis of the scope, structure and implications of the UNIDROIT instrument within the shipping industry – given that the latter could end up being the main beneficiary of the Convention – was likely to generate substantial opportunity costs. The absence of such discussion and analysis is perhaps the best explanation for the UNIDROIT's decision at that stage not to exclude ships from the scope of the Convention, albeit provisionally: the standpoint of the CMI, and Rolf Herber specifically, up to that point seemed more constructive and left room for further discussion about the fate of ships.[188]

This optimism, however, soon dissipated, as the CMI itself called for the exclusion of ships from the scope of the Convention in 1997. Interestingly, the CMI also attempted to defend the status quo in ship financing, by concluding that 'present national regimes [had] proved satisfactory for the necessities of the shipowning countries'.[189] There can be little doubt that this conclusion was not based on the actual satisfaction with the coexistence of widely differing national regimes – instead, it was an acknowledgment that the previous attempts to harmonise maritime law had failed and therefore 'achieved only a part of the aim to unify'.[190]

Perhaps the most troubling aspect of this conclusion lies in the lack of conceptual analysis of the draft Convention, which did not in reality attempt to unify the very different domestic laws governing national security over movable assets:[191] in 1997 the draft treaty was clearly aiming to establish and regulate an entirely new, international, type of interest that would be separate from its domestic law counterparts.[192]

[186] The timing, brevity, argumentation of both letters, as well as the coordinated effort of the two organisations to produce the 1993 Geneva Convention strongly suggest a degree of coordination between IMO and UNCTAD at that stage.

[187] See Appendices I and II in Unidroit, *Study LXXII – Doc. 29 (1996)*.

[188] See n 178 and the corresponding discussion.

[189] Unidroit, *Study LXXII – Doc. 36 (1997)* 11.

[190] ibid.

[191] See sections 2.2.2 and 2.2.3 discussing the various unification options.

[192] See section 2.3.2.

While it is conceivable that previous unsuccessful unification attempts in maritime law may have discouraged the corresponding international organisations and even end users of such law, this does not explain why such negative experiences might have affected the Convention – a treaty specifically drafted to avoid wholesale international harmonisation of domestic legal regimes. The argument of the CMI was thus somewhat similar to those formulated by IMO and UNCTAD: the means of reaching the destination (ie the argumentation against the UNIDROIT instrument) appeared less important than the destination itself (ie preserving the status quo in international maritime law).

The decision to switch to an umbrella structure of the Convention[193] helped ease the tension generated by the shipping circles: at least on paper the CMI acknowledged that it might be 'possible at a later stage to extend the Convention to apply to registered ships if and when the necessity [was] felt in shipping circles'.[194] Until recently, little had been done to actually assess whether such a necessity might exist.[195] It is, however, perhaps symbolic that it was the CMI which took the first steps in this direction: in 2015 it established an International Working Group to consider the existing financing security practices in various states to form an opinion 'as to whether anything has changed since the Cape Town Convention in 2001'.[196] It remains to be seen whether the signs of a renewed interest of the shipping circles towards the CTC will lead to any tangible results, but history suggests it is highly unlikely that a shipping protocol would ever emerge without the full support of the industry.[197]

3.5. Mining, Agricultural and Construction Equipment

The adoption of the Space Protocol in 2012 completed the initial agenda envisaged in the text of Article 2(3) of the CTC to cover three groups of assets: aircraft objects, railway rolling stock and space assets. Since these categories are the only ones expressly referred to in the Convention, any further expansion of the scope of the latter means that 'latecomers' to the CTC family of protocols will first have to pass the residual 'gateway' tests established in Article 51(1) in relation to eligible equipment: (i) high value; (ii) mobility; and (iii) unique identifiability. As was

[193] See ch 4.
[194] Unidroit, *Study LXXII - Doc. 36 (1997)* 11.
[195] Despite the very limited signals coming from the shipping industry, a recent academic study has concluded that the preparation of a shipping protocol 'could be an enormously valuable contribution to the law of proprietary security over ships worldwide'. See Ole Böger, 'The Case for a New Protocol to the Cape Town Convention Covering Security over Ships' (2016) 5 *Cape Town Convention Journal* 73, 101.
[196] CMI, *CMI Yearbook 2015* 428.
[197] The relevance of industry support is discussed in greater detail in section 8.4.

noted in section 3.2.1, each leg of this test was intentionally left vague to keep the CTC open for future expansion. Mining, agricultural and construction equipment comprises the first asset category to which the requirements of Article 51(1) have been applied in practice: the MAC Protocol was adopted in Pretoria on 22 November 2019.

Interestingly, the idea of addressing mining, agricultural and construction equipment in the Convention emerged long before the adoption of the first protocol in 2001. At its second session in 1996, the Study Group considered 'construction machinery' and 'tunnel-digging equipment' among other asset types.[198] In 1997 Mooney and Whalen recommended the inclusion of 'both construction equipment and agricultural equipment' to the list of eligible objects.[199] Similarly, Electricite de France proposed to add cranes and construction equipment to the list.[200]

The level of support in favour of regulating these asset types, however, was not high enough to warrant a place among the potential lists of eligible equipment in any of the drafts of the CTC (unlike ships, oil rigs and even containers).[201] On the one hand, this signals an overall lower level of support coming from the relevant industries at the time (although the same can be said about the maritime industry). On the other hand, the physical characteristics of the assets covered by the MAC Protocol challenge the very concept of 'mobile equipment' and each of the three eligibility criteria established by the Convention. In doing so, they test the limits of the scope envisaged by the CTC system and affect the possibility of future expansion via new protocols.

The major difficulty is presented by the 'mobility' requirement: while potentially movable, the relevant assets (eg earth-moving equipment) may never cross national borders. At first glance, this argument does not seem particularly problematic. First, the Convention has abolished the test of 'internationality' and applies to domestic transactions (subject to declarations under Article 50(1) of the CTC).[202] Second, the cross-border operation of most equipment is not determined by its physical characteristics in many situations and may be driven by a number of accidental factors (such as the size of the relevant country): in larger states aircraft are often operated on domestic routes, never crossing any borders.[203]

Overall, there is no question that mining, agricultural and construction equipment is able to cross national borders. However, there is a difference between the

[198] See paragraphs 24–25 in Unidroit, *Study LXXII – Doc. 27 (1996)* 15.

[199] See paragraph 31 in Unidroit, *Study LXXII – Doc. 36 (1997)* 10.

[200] See paragraph 41 in ibid.

[201] See, eg, Article 1(2) in Unidroit, *Study LXXII – Doc. 18 (1995)* 5; Article 2(1) in Unidroit, *Study LXXII – Doc. 22 (1996)*; Article 2(1) in Unidroit, *Study LXXII – Doc. 30 (1996)* 9–10; Article 2(1) in Unidroit, *Study LXXII – Doc. 35 (1997)*.

[202] See section 2.4.3.

[203] In addition, according to a recent observation of the UNIDROIT Secretariat, over 50% of registrations performed in the international registry established under the Aircraft Protocol 'were for assets that were not internationally mobile in their operation'. See paragraph 53 in Unidroit, *Study 72k – SG3 – Doc. 5 (2015)* 8.

asset's 'transportability', on the one hand, and its operational mobility. In the end, most things on the planet could be moved with the right technology: even the colossal Statue of Liberty crossed the ocean to reach New York in 1885. The question is thus: when do we say 'enough' and draw a line that should not be crossed? Is it enough that the asset is merely 'transportable' to another location (as in the case of the famous monument)? These questions are especially relevant in the context of those types of mining, agricultural and construction equipment, which remain entirely stationary during their operation (eg cranes).

What seemed like a distant problem back in 2001, when the Convention was adopted, suddenly became a very serious issue with little prospect of satisfactory resolution. At its third session held in 2015, the study group established by UNIDROIT to prepare the draft MAC Protocol considered a number of alternative approaches to the satisfaction of the mobility criterion. Unfortunately, most of the proposed solutions eventually implied a replacement of the idea of mobility with the concept of 'internationality', whereby the former test was satisfied so long as the underlying financing transaction was international in nature or the object was exported to another state.[204] In doing so, members of the study group were effectively substituting one of the key eligibility requirements linked to the physical characteristics of an asset (mobility) with a long-abolished concept relying on the structure of the underlying transaction and factual circumstances of a particular situation (internationality), perhaps forgetting about the main reason for its abandonment: the need to achieve greater certainty and to give third parties the ability to know from the nature of the object *alone* whether or not it is subject to the Convention rules.[205] In other words, there is a big difference between asking whether an object has actually moved across national borders and asking whether such object is of a kind that can be moved internationally. The answer to the first question depends on the circumstances of each particular situation. The answer to the second depends on the characteristics of the asset.

Overall, the mobility problem proved too difficult to handle and the study group resorted to the same solution as it had previously envisaged to tackle the 'high value' criterion, namely the Harmonized Commodity Description and Coding System (the 'Harmonized System') developed by the WCO to achieve uniform classification of commodities in international trade and covering over 98 per cent of all international trade.[206] This solution identified eligible equipment not on the basis of its physical characteristics as such, but by reference to the corresponding code of the Harmonized System annexed to the MAC Protocol.

The new approach had the potential to address more than one problem, if utilised correctly. First, it could eliminate the need to come up with additional

[204] See paragraphs 54 and 60 in ibid 8–9.
[205] See section 2.4.2.
[206] See paragraph 6 in Unidroit, *Study 72k – CGE1 – Doc. 4 (2017)* 3.

criteria to filter out low-cost items.[207] Second, it could be used to cover all three (mining, agricultural and construction) groups of assets, without the need to develop special criteria for each category. The underlying difficulties however, were also self-evident: (i) the relevant codes had to be carefully selected (as assets not covered by them would be left out); (ii) some codes could be used to identify more than one category of equipment[208] and thus could create problems in states applying the MAC Protocol to some, but not all, of such categories; and (iii) an externally administered system of codes would be subject to changes, which the draft protocol would have to address.

These largely technical issues were mostly resolved at the first session of governmental experts in March 2017.[209] However, following adoption of the MAC Protocol in 2019, the complexity of the Harmonized System remains a serious challenge: it uses a variety of codes containing different numbers of digits (the longer the code, the more specific it becomes), which could confuse governments.[210] The asset selection criteria in the MAC Protocol are much more technical (compared to other protocols) and may cause difficulties at the implementation stage. Nevertheless, the Harmonized System appears to be an efficient solution.

The attractiveness of this system is easily explained from the point of view of increased certainty generated by the use of specific codes: if the HS classification is the only criterion for identifying eligible equipment, then the test is objective, does not depend on transaction mechanics and, with the right codes, could be sufficiently specific. If the requirements of 'high value' and 'mobility' are seen as *prerequisites* necessary to provide private parties with clear guidance as to what assets are covered by the protocol, then the Harmonized System indeed does the trick by jumping over these undefined terms straight to the list of assets.

At the same time, the tests in Article 51(1) have another important, 'gatekeeping' function: they preserve the integrity of the CTC system aimed at promoting asset financing of equipment enshrined in its Preamble. From this perspective,

[207] The high-cost requirement has to be 'built into' the code selection. At the same time, the MAC Protocol incorporates codes covering objects of relatively low value (eg HS code 843221 covers harrows used for soil cultivation that could cost, according to the UNIDROIT documentation, as low as USD 10,000). See section 21 in Unidroit, *Study 72k – CGE1 – Doc. 5 corr (2017)* 10.

[208] eg HS code 842919 covers certain multiple purpose bulldozers and angledozers (graders, levellers, scrapers, mechanical shovels, excavators, shovel loaders, tamping machines and road rollers).

[209] See the revised drafts of Article II(3) and Article XXXII in Appendix III to Unidroit, *Study 72k – CGE1 – Report (2017)* 28, 43–44.

[210] This was the case during the first session of governmental experts in March 2017, when the South African delegate expressed serious concerns about including the first HS code mentioned in Annex 1 to the draft MAC Protocol. The objection stemmed from the description of the relevant code, which included, among other things, fire extinguishers and spray guns. It was later explained by other delegations, that the different codes vary in their specificity, shorter codes being more general and longer codes being more specific. Apparently, the confusion came from the fact that the actual codes in the annexes to the MAC Protocol were using six-digit codes (which included higher value items), whereas the textual descriptions (provided for clarity) were borrowed from the more general four digit codes (which could indeed incorporate less expensive items).

the Harmonized System appears to be a convenient workaround for the test of 'mobility' in cases when stationary equipment is captured by the selected HS codes. In this case, the use of numbers (coupled with a supportive official commentary confirming that all the necessary boxes have been ticked) looks much more plausible than an odd attempt to define something that never moves as 'mobile'. A quick look at the pre-selected equipment categories shows that certain stationary equipment is indeed covered by the MAC Protocol: examples include HS code 847432 (machines for mixing mineral substances with bitumen) and HS code 847982 (mixing, kneading, crushing, grinding, screening, sifting, homogenizing, emulsifying or stirring machines).[211]

One could argue that not all equipment covered by the other protocols is mobile per se: indeed, airframes do not move without their engines attached. But the above HS codes do not represent high value *parts* of a larger asset (of which there are many examples in the MAC Protocol):[212] they represent the complete final equipment that is entirely stationary. In this respect, this protocol goes beyond the other three by covering assets that do not move at all during operation. In a sense, the MAC Protocol has substituted the 'mobility' criterion with 'transportability' (akin to that displayed by the Statue of Liberty).[213] Yet, in practical terms, there is nothing wrong with expanding the scope of the Convention to cover any high cost 'transportable' equipment, so long as in doing so the MAC Protocol promotes asset financing.

[211] See Annex 3 to the MAC Protocol.

[212] See, eg, HS code 843210 covering a variety of ploughs.

[213] Issues concerning the appropriateness of the selected HS codes to meet all the 'gateway' criteria were raised multiple times during the governmental expert session in March 2017: see paragraphs 85–87, 159–61 in Unidroit, *Study 72k – CGE1 – Report (2017)* 10, 17–18.

4

Choosing an Appropriate Structure for the Convention

4.1. Overview

The current structure of the CTC comprises the Convention itself and four protocols: the Aircraft Protocol, the Rail Protocol, the Space Protocol and the MAC Protocol.[1] The protocols amend, supplement and override the CTC in order to adapt its provisions to each specific type of mobile equipment. This so-called 'umbrella' structure is, however, more common for business contracts, rather than commercial law treaties.[2] It was not envisaged by the developers of the Convention at the start of the project and emerged at a later stage. This chapter explains the origins of such change and analyses the challenges that led to the adoption of the umbrella structure.

Section 4.2 shows that the transformation occurred because the aviation industry, spearheaded by the Aviation Working Group, proceeded at a much higher pace compared to all other prospective beneficiaries of the Cape Town Convention. Section 4.3 then argues that – despite the pressure from the interested parties – the decision to switch to the umbrella structure was in itself an achievement that helped to prevent conversion of the CTC into an aviation sector treaty while preserving the continuity of the Convention's key provisions and at the same time providing other industries with time and flexibility to develop own protocols at their own pace. The adoption of the fourth protocol in November 2019 is the direct result of this transition.

[1] At the time of writing only the Aircraft Protocol is in force.

[2] International over-the-counter derivative transactions (ie those which are not concluded on an exchange) are often based on the templates promulgated by the International Swaps and Derivatives Association (ISDA), which comprise the Master Agreement and a corresponding Schedule: the former sets out the basic provisions, while the latter adds party-specific or jurisdiction-specific details (such as additional representations by the weaker party or provisions required to meet various transaction execution formalities). A similar practice applies in international repo transactions (ie transactions for the sale of an asset, such as securities, with an obligation to repurchase such asset in the future) that follow the Global Master Repurchase Agreement template developed by the International Capital Market Association (ICMA), and in bullion transactions concluded using the standard form International Bullion Master Agreement drafted by the London Bullion Market Association (LBMA).

4.2. Transition to Asset-Specific Regulation

While the first draft set of articles of the CTC prepared in 1994 did not include any provisions specific to any category of financiers,[3] the feedback received from the AWG[4] in 1995 reflected not only a high interest of the aviation industry towards the Convention, but also the industry's expectation that the new treaty would reflect its specific needs through an 'increase in the availability of credit, and/or reduction in the cost of such credit, to owners/operators of aircraft equipment'.[5] Many of the changes proposed by the AWG, however, went far beyond the scope of the first draft.

First, the future Convention was to treat aircraft engines differently from other aircraft parts: any interests in engines were to be made registrable separately by reference to the manufacturer's serial number.[6] Second, the Convention was expected to permit not only the registration of international interests over aircraft and aircraft engines, but also title/ownership transfers over the same in a way that failure to do so would render such transfer voidable as against third parties who register their interests subsequently (but not as between the parties themselves).[7] Third, lease assignments were to be covered by the Convention to reflect the existing practices in aviation finance transactions.[8] Fourth, the creditor's position was to be significantly improved by establishing mandatory time limits within which courts having jurisdiction under the Convention were required to issue judgments concerning remedies, on the one hand, and by allowing the financier to deregister (and thus effectively ground) the relevant aircraft upon default by the debtor without any interference by any government or third party (eg the operating airline), on the other.[9] Fifth, the AWG called for the abolition of any requirement of 'internationality' whatsoever.[10] Sixth, state parties to the future treaty were expected to lodge with UNIDROIT a list of types of creditors whose rights would have priority over an international interest under the law of such states, in order to give prospective financiers maximum information for the purposes of calculating legal risks (as any category of preferred domestic creditors not recorded with UNIDROIT would lose its priority).[11] Seventh, the Convention was to envisage several optional provisions that states could opt into: (i) an unqualified recognition of the law chosen by the parties to a Convention-governed transaction as the law

[3] See Unidroit, *Study LXXII – Doc. 13 (1994)*.
[4] See section 3.3.
[5] Unidroit, *Study LXXII – Doc. 16 (1995)* 5.
[6] ibid 18.
[7] ibid 8.
[8] ibid 15.
[9] ibid 17.
[10] ibid 20. Cf Article 4 in Unidroit, *Study LXXII – Doc. 13 (1994)*. See also section 2.4.
[11] Unidroit, *Study LXXII – Doc. 16 (1995)* 22.

regulating the contractual interpretation and remedies,[12] and (ii) a rule requiring the debtor/lessee, in the event of insolvency proceedings, either to cure all defaults within a specified time, or to return the aircraft equipment to the financier/lessor.[13]

Overall, the level of detail and specificity found in the recommendations of the AWG made it clear that the original Convention structure – which comprised merely five articles – would require a major overhaul to accommodate the changes (if they were found desirable). Yet the primary challenge, as was rightly pointed out by Thomas Whalen in 1995, was 'the difficult task … to develop a universally acceptable Convention covering various forms of mobile equipment, the financing of which may not have reached the sophistication of aircraft financing'.[14] Despite the absence of similar reaction from other industries, the feedback of the AWG could be neither ignored, nor used to change the overall structure of the first draft without turning the draft Convention into essentially an aircraft-specific treaty. As a result, the Drafting Group decided to create (albeit provisionally) a special chapter (entitled 'Special Provisions for Aircraft and Aircraft Engines') to incorporate all matters specific to aircraft.[15] The resulting second draft of the CTC marked the beginning of separation of industry-specific provisions from the 'core' of the Convention.

While all of the AWG recommendations sought to address aircraft finance practices, only some of the suggested amendments were, strictly speaking, unique to the aviation industry.[16] Most of the proposed changes could eventually prove useful for the other industry groups – when the latter were prepared to consider the scope of the future Convention. As a result, the list of aircraft-specific rules could potentially be reduced by turning some of them into the baseline provisions of general application once it became clear that they were supported by other industries. In the absence of any guidance from the latter, the AWG was invited by UNIDROIT in 1995 to give shape to its recommendations by formulating the 'supplementary rules for aircraft and aircraft engines'.[17] The resulting feedback, surprisingly,[18] did not take the form of stand-alone supplementary rules: the AWG effectively redrafted the whole text of the Convention incorporating new provisions into the existing structure.[19] More importantly, the resulting

[12] ibid 24.
[13] ibid 26.
[14] Unidroit, *Study LXXII – Doc. 17 (1995)* 2.
[15] See Appendix to Unidroit, *Study LXXII – Doc. 18 (1995)* 2.
[16] An example would be the proposed different treatment of aircraft engines or the proposed remedy of aircraft deregistration.
[17] Unidroit, *Study LXXII – Doc. 21 (1995)* 13.
[18] The commentary of the AWG shows that, instead of literally following the request of UNIDROIT to prepare 'the text of supplementary rules', it relied on the Study Group's conclusion that some of its proposed rules 'might be found to have more general application and might to this extent assist other industry groups in their analysis of the desired scope and content of the proposed convention'. See Unidroit, *Study LXXII – Doc. 23 (1996)* 2–3.
[19] See Annex 1 (labelled 'Convention on International Interests in Mobile Equipment: Draft Aviation Text') to ibid.

'Draft Aviation Text' not only proved that the (then) current draft Convention could accommodate most of the AWG suggestions as basic (rather than aircraft-specific) provisions, but, by establishing a new template for the UNIDROIT treaty, it substantially modified the agenda for any subsequent discussions of the draft Convention and provided other industries with a clear, albeit lengthy, account of the aviation industry needs. Out of 32 articles comprising the Draft Aviation Text only one was limited to matters specific to aircraft – which included different treatment of engines, the unique remedy in the form of deregistration of aircraft upon default of the debtor and the relationship of the draft Convention with the other aviation treaties.[20]

Despite the proactive stance of the aviation industry, the UNIDROIT Study Group was not quick to incorporate the amendments suggested by the AWG, particularly in the light of limited feedback from other industries: the two subsequent drafts of the Convention prepared in 1996 retained a placeholder (empty) chapter labelled, respectively, 'Special Provisions for Aircraft and Aircraft Engines'[21] and 'Special Provisions for Aircraft Property'.[22] At the time, there was no argument as to the possibility of seamless incorporation of the AWG provisions into the body of the UNIDROIT text: Roy Goode, chairman of the Study Group, specifically addressed the issue by drawing up a revised structure of the future Convention 'with a view to seeing how the … draft might look after incorporation of key elements of the draft aviation text'.[23] The resulting structure proved workable and had no significant impact on the basic structure.

Against this background, a scenario whereby a *single* international convention would be able to cover international interests in various types of mobile equipment at once did not seem entirely unrealistic – all that was needed was to ensure which proposals of the AWG would be acceptable for other industries (and if they were, the asset-specific provisions could be limited to a single article, as was demonstrated by the Draft Aviation Text). Nevertheless, as discussions continued, more and more evidence emerged suggesting that mechanisms to promote aviation financing proposed by the AWG might generate opposition from the other industries.

The first point of contention concerned the extension of the scope of the future Convention to outright sales, ie transactions whereby title passes to the purchaser at once without any form of reservation of title by the seller (as opposed to retention of title agreements). The intent of the aviation industry was clear: the registration of sales in addition to an already comprehensive array of transactions having the function of security (security agreements in the narrow sense, leases and reservation of title agreements) would not only simplify any priority rules by eliminating contests between purchasers and/or their creditors and the holders of

[20] See Article 23 in Annex 1 to ibid.
[21] See Chapter VIII in Unidroit, *Study LXXII – Doc. 24 (1996).*
[22] See Chapter VIII in Appendix IV to Unidroit, *Study LXXII – Doc. 27 (1996).*
[23] See Appendix III in ibid.

interests in aircraft objects – they would facilitate the market for used engines and aircraft[24] and even eliminate the problem of characterisation of agreements into outright sales or title retention contracts. Furthermore, the practice of registering title transfers over aircraft had already been widely used in a substantial number of jurisdictions.[25]

At the same time, the manner in which this concept was incorporated into the Draft Aviation Text was somewhat inelegant: the AWG document effectively labelled the right of ownership as yet another type of 'international interest' (on a par with the interests of a chargor under a security agreement, seller under a title reservation agreement and lessor under a leasing agreement), disregarding the fact that an 'international interest' is, *ipso facto*, an *in rem* right having the function of security (which of course cannot be said about the title passing under an outright sale agreement).[26] Yet, while the drafting problem could no doubt be resolved at a later stage, the AWG proposal appeared so radical that the aviation industry effectively had to defend its idea not only against potential dissent from the other industries (which had not at the time expressed their views on the matter), but also against members of the Study Group itself, some of whom reserved their position 'until they had time to appreciate the full implications of this proposal'.[27] In the absence of any expression of interest towards extending the scope of the Convention to outright sales, the Drafting Group subsequently chose not to rectify the deficiencies in the Draft Aviation Text and simply moved the draft provision on outright sales to the chapter concerning aircraft-specific provisions.[28]

The second challenge was even more fundamental: no other industry had managed to come up with a truly representative group to act as its 'voice' in the course of development of the Convention. As a result, the occasional signs of support in favour of including one or another asset category[29] into the scope of the UNIDROIT instrument remained inconclusive and unsystematic. After all, any

[24] According to the AWG's own calculations performed in 1995, roughly a quarter of newly financed aircraft were subsequently refinanced, with yearly financing of used aircraft equipment estimated at approximately USD 12.5 billion. See footnote 17 in Unidroit, *Study LXXII – Doc. 16 (1995)* 8.

[25] According to the AWG, the following jurisdictions either permitted, or required such registrations: Argentina, Austria, Belgium, Brazil, Chile, China, Colombia, Costa Rica, Denmark, Egypt, France, Germany, Greece, Guatemala, Iceland, Israel, Italy, Japan, Luxembourg, Mexico, Netherlands, New Zealand, Peru, the Philippines, Poland, Portugal, South Africa, Spain, Sweden, Switzerland, Taiwan, Turkey, UAE, the United States, Uruguay, Venezuela. See footnote 19 in ibid 9.

[26] See Article 1(3)(e) in Annex 1 to Unidroit, *Study LXXII – Doc. 23 (1996)*, which defines an 'international interest' as 'an interest … transferred by a transferor under a transfer document', and paragraph 48 in Annexure to ibid, whereby a 'transfer document' is defined as 'an agreement (other than a title reservation agreement) … by or in which one person … sells … property to another person … and that is expressed to fully divest the transferor of its interest in the property'.

[27] Unidroit, *Study LXXII – Doc. 27 (1996)* 12.

[28] See paragraph 16 in Unidroit, *Study LXXII – Doc. 30 (1996)* 4. See also draft Chapter X in Revised Draft Articles of a Future Unidroit Convention on International Interests in Mobile Equipment in ibid.

[29] This was the case with, eg, omnibuses, construction machinery and large lorries supported by Germany, or the enthusiasm in the United States to include pleasure yachts, or even the proposal of the UNIDROIT Secretariat to extend the scope of the Convention to air-cushion vehicles. See Unidroit, *Study LXXII – Doc. 27 (1996)* 15.

extension of scope to a different industry was not simply a technical matter: if nothing else, the new treaty was expected to give registered international interests priority over *any* unregistered interests, thus generating pressure to register in all situations out of fear of losing priority.[30]

The third difficulty concerned a very ambitious proposal by the AWG to fix in the Convention absolute time limits for any judicial proceedings relating to the enforcement of Convention remedies: court actions relating to the ability of a holder of an international interest to take possession of the charged property following a default by the debtor were to be completed within five working days after their commencement, whereas court actions relating to 'any other claim or right' were to be completed within 30 days after their initiation (in either case proceedings were to be commenced within three working days after lodging 'an initiating document' with the relevant authorities).[31] Although the record of the Study Group deliberations on this matter in April 1996 shows an overall positive reaction of the members to the AWG proposal, the very idea of imposing a hard cap on the duration of court proceedings appeared extremely difficult to stomach. Instead of supporting the AWG approach in its original form, the Study Group agreed that 'in practice the chargee's single most effective weapon in the type of circumstance contemplated was the ability to obtain *interim injunctive relief* to have the asset held in one place',[32] essentially substituting the AWG concept of an overall limit on the duration of court proceedings with a view that effective interim relief would be more appropriate. The fundamental difference between the two approaches is clear – the watered-down alternative of the Study Group imposed no obligation on the court to issue a final decision as to the substance of the dispute (which could effectively drag on for years). Nevertheless, in an attempt to alleviate the concerns of the aviation industry, the Study Group added two elements to the proposed interim relief mechanism. First, it would include 'the ability to have the asset held in one place under judicial supervision and control' as a form of asset immobilisation.[33] Second, it was suggested that the court would be given the power to appoint a receiver 'to realise the value of the asset as speedily as possible'.[34] Despite the 'widespread agreement' of the Study Group on this solution, the AWG representative reserved the position of the AWG, given the big transformation that had occurred to its proposal.[35]

For the purposes of this section, however, another factor is of paramount importance: in the course of the above discussions the Study Group performed an unenviable function of determining whether the concept suggested by the AWG would remain realistic not only as part of aviation-specific provisions, but also – potentially – as a baseline provision applicable to *all* asset types covered by

[30] Challenges involved in the development of the system of priorities are examined in section 6.2.
[31] See Article 13 in Annex 1 to Unidroit, *Study LXXII – Doc. 23 (1996)*.
[32] Unidroit, *Study LXXII – Doc. 27 (1996)* 41 (emphasis added).
[33] ibid 41.
[34] ibid.
[35] The development of the concept of advance relief is discussed in greater detail in section 5.3.3.

the Convention. If that were not the case, the proposal to establish a cap on the duration of judicial proceedings could have been more easily dealt with by sweeping the corresponding provision into the 'aircraft-specific' category (just as this was done in the case of outright sales). Instead, the relevant discussions of the Study Group addressed the feasibility of having an overall timing limit for obtaining relief under the Convention as a baseline provision: the Drafting Group was eventually tasked with preparing a general 'formula which would permit the chargee, seller or lessor to obtain expeditious relief in order to protect its position'.[36] As a result, the subsequent draft prepared by the Drafting Group in October 1996 – which incorporated for the first time an article on advance relief – located it among other general provisions.[37] Nonetheless, the solution (and the corresponding provision) remained merely a compromise compared to the original proposal of the AWG, acting as yet another reminder of the very far-reaching expectations of the aviation industry from the future Convention.[38]

The combined effect of all of the above factors clearly demonstrated the divide between the aviation industry and any other potential beneficiaries of the draft Convention considered at the time. The detailed and very ambitious agenda of the former had no equal – and was beginning to stall. By June 1996 the need to address this issue became so apparent that two members of the UNIDROIT Governing Council had to voice a proposal to 'deal in the first instance only with aircraft and perhaps one or two other categories, possibly leaving other types of equipment to be catered for in a *second instrument*'.[39] The existence of a draft Convention in the form of a single document was coming to an end.

4.3. Separation of the Aircraft Protocol

The actual separation of the draft Convention into separate instruments began with a letter prepared jointly by the AWG and IATA in December 1996, which proposed a two-part structure for the UNIDROIT treaty: the base/umbrella Convention setting out 'the basic legal framework applicable to all categories of equipment' and equipment-specific protocols.[40] Four observations supported this suggestion, three of which were either not new, or derived from the previous negotiation/drafting process: (i) there was a need for asset-specific rules for

[36] Unidroit, *Study LXXII – Doc. 27 (1996)* 42.

[37] See Article 15 in Revised Draft Articles of a Future Unidroit Convention on International Interests in Mobile Equipment in Unidroit, *Study LXXII – Doc. 30 (1996).*

[38] The perception of the AWG proposals as very ambitious can be perhaps best demonstrated by the Study Group's concern that the approach of the AWG 'might cause the future Convention to overreach itself by seeking to deal with all matters seen as having a bearing on the effectiveness of the international interest'. See paragraph 108 in Unidroit, *Study LXXII – Doc. 27 (1996)* 46.

[39] Unidroit, *Study LXXII – Doc. 28 (1996)* 4 (emphasis added).

[40] Unidroit, *Study LXXII – Doc. 32 (1996)* 2.

each category of equipment; (ii) other industries needed to organise themselves to contribute to the UNIDROIT project; and (iii) different industries might require different timetables to reach a consensus among themselves.[41] The fourth one was new, however, and involved the possibility to adopt and ratify the Convention on an equipment-specific basis[42] – unlike the previous discussions, this one no longer focused on the need to incorporate asset-specific provisions into the text (something that was not really disputed), but rather allowed selective application of the Convention to different objects through the interface of protocols.[43]

The proposal quickly gained support within the Study Group[44] and was formally approved at its third session in January 1997, and by the Governing Council at its 76th session in April 1997.[45] Following this decision, the President of UNIDROIT invited Jeffrey Wool, an expert consultant to the Study Group on international aviation finance matters and coordinator of the AWG, to organise a special working group to prepare the first draft protocol on aircraft equipment.[46]

The initial reaction towards the dual convention/protocol structure was almost universally favourable:[47] the possibility of sending all asset-specific provisions to separate documents gave unprecedented freedom and flexibility to accommodate the needs of different industries as and when they were ready,[48] while at the same time providing the governments with – in the words of Roy Goode – a 'menu' of protocols to choose from.[49] The Drafting Group was unanimous in its view that the protocol approach was 'essential' to make it possible to simultaneously accommodate both a free-standing instrument and asset-specific provisions:[50] protocols were seen as a 'fundamental necessity … at least in the absence of any other workable solution'.[51] Ironically, another 'workable solution' emerged very quickly – and generated much greater debate.

In February 1998, the UNIDROIT Governing Council finally had before it the results of the labour of the Study Group and the new working group for the preparation of a protocol specific to aircraft (Aircraft Protocol Group or the 'APG'): the revised draft Convention and the draft Aircraft Protocol prepared pursuant to an earlier decision to switch to the umbrella structure.[52] Despite the efforts of the rail

[41] ibid.

[42] ibid.

[43] For a more detailed discussion of the protocol system utilised by the CTC see Mark J. Sundahl, 'The Cape Town Approach: A New Method of Making International Law' (2006) 44 *Colum J Transnat'l L* 339.

[44] See Unidroit, *Study LXXII – Doc. 32 Add. 1 (1997)* 1; Unidroit, *Study LXXII – Doc. 32 Add. 3 (1997)* 2.

[45] See Introductory Note in Unidroit, *Study LXXIID – Doc. 1 (1998)* 1.

[46] ibid.

[47] For a somewhat critical view of the protocol system (although more in terms of technical issues, rather than the substance) see paragraph 50 in Unidroit, *Study LXXII – Doc. 36 (1997)* 14–15.

[48] See Unidroit, *Study LXXII – Doc. 35 (1997)* 5. See also paragraph 49 in Unidroit, *Study LXXII – Doc. 36 (1997)* 14.

[49] Unidroit, *Study LXXII – Doc. 40 (1998)* 7.

[50] See paragraph 13 in Unidroit, *Study LXXII – Doc. 35 (1997)* 13.

[51] See paragraph 18 in ibid 4–5.

[52] See n 46 and the corresponding discussion.

and space industries, no other draft protocol was ready at the time, as 'work on the preparation of these texts had commenced later than work on the aircraft equipment protocol and had not … attracted quite the same degree of support from industry'.[53] Consequently, the main point of the agenda was to review the draft Convention and the draft Aircraft Protocol and determine whether the documents were ready to be submitted to governmental experts for finalisation.[54]

A new concern was first voiced by the French member of the UNIDROIT Governing Council, Jean-Pierre Plantard, who observed that the provisions of the draft Aircraft Protocol 'frequently contradicted or varied the terms of the preliminary draft Convention via a series of exceptions and cross-references' and thus wondered whether 'a clearer result might not be obtained by drawing up several *different Conventions* rather than one framework Convention and several different Protocols'.[55] Several standalone conventions would be 'easier to read and understand' and still reflect the earlier decision to separate asset-specific provisions. Therefore, the question as to whether asset-specific provisions should be moved into a different document lost its relevance and was superseded by a more pressing concern: how best to achieve this separation.

The ease of comprehension was not the only difficulty created by the dual convention/protocol structure. Of much greater importance was the need to secure the broad acceptance of the new instruments among various states: a look from a 'purely strategic point of view'[56] suggested that an aircraft-only convention would be easier to promote, while the conceptual sacrifices would be easier to swallow if limited to only one type of equipment (both at the cost of the overall ambition of the project to cover other types of movable assets).[57]

Objections to the suggested structure based on a series of standalone treaties were essentially two-fold. First, the complexity and lack of coordination[58] between the existing documents was, at its core, a problem of style, which could be resolved by moving certain provisions of the draft Aircraft Protocol to the main Convention. Second, and more importantly, abandoning the protocol-based

[53] Unidroit, *Study LXXII – Doc. 40 (1998)* 3.

[54] ibid 1.

[55] ibid 19 (emphasis added).

[56] ibid 21.

[57] Examples of conceptual challenges included the limited availability of self-help remedies in civil law jurisdictions, equal treatment of 'true leases' and leases having the function of security (see section 2.2.4.i) and the concern that civil law countries 'were not familiar with the chattel mortgage concept' (see commentary by Anne Marie Trahan in ibid 21).

[58] The Aircraft Protocol Group, which had prepared the draft Aircraft Protocol, did not mirror the membership of the UNIDROIT Study Group working on the baseline Convention, and was formed of aviation experts: Ludwig Weber (Director of the ICAO Legal Bureau), Lorne Clark (General Counsel and Corporate Secretary of IATA) and Jeffrey Wool (Partner at Perkins Coie, coordinator of the AWG and expert consultant to the Study Group on international aviation finance). As a result of lack of coordination, the draft Aircraft Protocol emerged so detailed that the number of articles in it (47) surpassed that of the main draft Convention (45, counting all draft final provisions). Cf Unidroit, *Study LXXIID – Doc. 1 (1998)* and Unidroit, *Study LXXII – Doc. 37 (1997)*.

approach would deprive the UNIDROIT project of its unifying factor and require either a separate convention of general provisions somehow incorporated in each equipment-specific convention, or a series of conventions essentially repeating the general provisions in their texts.[59]

Whilst the Governing Council adopted no immediate conclusion as to the most appropriate structure of the future Convention, a decision was made to address at least one of the key issues identified during the discussion: the lack of coordination between the draft Convention and the draft Aircraft Protocol. A special working group (the Steering and Revisions Committee) was formed to refine both drafts by, first, relocating the protocol provisions of general application to the draft Convention, and, second, aligning the instruments as to both style and methodology.[60]

The SRC, which convened later the same year, performed mostly a technical role of reconciling the two instruments and did not regard itself as competent to decide upon the final structure of the UNIDROIT instrument.[61] The latter was considered a policy problem and submitted to the governmental experts alongside three alternatives. The first one was based on the existing draft and was favoured by the SRC, which stressed its key advantage: the flexibility for different industry sectors to address their specific needs '*at such time as they were ready to do so* but *without compromising the aviation sector's desire to see the Convention in operation as regards aircraft equipment as speedily as possible*'.[62] The second option involved separate asset-specific conventions, whereas the third alternative 'at all worthy of consideration' contemplated a single treaty with a set of annexes akin to the Chicago Convention.[63]

The problem of determining the structure of the Convention was one of the first to emerge during the First Joint Session of governmental experts in 1999 – it was raised at the very start of the proceedings. While no conclusive decision about the structure emerged out of these discussions, the most notable development in this context can be attributed to the delegation of Germany, which prepared and submitted for consideration the first consolidated text of the draft Convention and the Aircraft Protocol.[64] The document, entitled 'Consolidated Version of a Preliminary Draft Unidroit Convention on International Interests in *Aircraft* Equipment' (emphasis added) was intended to change the direction of the drafting process towards creating a standalone aircraft-specific treaty, since, as the German

[59] Unidroit, *Study LXXII – Doc. 40 (1998)* 20. It is also clear that the new conventions were likely to be 'drafted by different hands', making the results less predictable: see Roy Goode, 'From Acorn to Oak Tree: the Development of the Cape Town Convention and Protocols' (2012) 17 *Uniform Law Review* 599, 604.

[60] Unidroit, *Study LXXII – Doc. 40 (1998)* 37.

[61] As a result of this revision, the number of provisions in the draft Aircraft Protocol was reduced by more than a quarter – from 47 to 34 articles.

[62] Unidroit, *Study LXXII – Doc. 41 (1998)* 28 (emphasis in the original).

[63] ibid.

[64] See Unidroit, *Unidroit CGE/Int.Int./WP/9 ICAO Ref. LSC/ME-WP/20 (1999).*

delegation noted, 'there was no guarantee that other preliminary draft Protocols would emerge'.[65] The persistence of the German delegation,[66] however, did not result in a great deal of approval, particularly in the light of submitted evidence that the work on other draft protocols was ongoing.[67] But perhaps more importantly, the consolidated text demonstrated quite well that the dual convention/protocol structure could be presented in the form of a single document, should such need arise.

When the same matter of structure of the Convention was discussed during the Second Joint Session, the possibility of having a single consolidated convention/protocol text came up more than once[68] – yet this time it was viewed not as an alternative to the umbrella structure suggested by the German delegation during the First Joint Session, but rather as an element of convenience allowing to have the best of both different structures: a stable core of Convention provisions, an expandable scope based on a series of protocols and the user-friendliness of the consolidated text. The precise moment when such text should be prepared was left open – but it was clear that the criticism of the umbrella structure of the future Convention was losing its substance. The remaining arguments were twofold: one delegation saw a problem of legitimacy in the fact that other industries would end up using a baseline treaty developed by the aviation sector;[69] another expected difficulties with ratification of a 'complex two-instrument structure'.[70] Neither of the two seems convincing, however. The first fell apart when viewed through the prism of the work that had been performed by the rail and space industries to prepare (and *ipso facto* support) separate protocols[71] and paled in comparison to the free-riding opportunity and 'broader social benefit' generated by the combined efforts of the aviation industry.[72] The second argument simply overstated the problem, which would not exist so long as the relationship between the baseline Convention and each protocol was clearly articulated.

The lack of substantive issues with the umbrella structure was later confirmed in the opening statement of the Third Joint Session by Herbert Kronke (who noted that the former 'was no longer a source of concern to States'),[73] as well as by the Public International Law Working Group[74] (which concluded that 'the

[65] See paragraph 22 in Unidroit, *Unidroit CGE/Int.Int./Report ICAO Ref. LSC/ME-Report (1999)* 6.

[66] The same delegation kept raising the issue repeatedly: see paragraphs 151 and 157 in ibid 22–23.

[67] According to the Secretary-General of UNIDROIT, draft protocols on railway rolling stock and space property were 'at an advanced stage of preparation'. In addition, OTIF, which had agreed to coordinate the consultations on the preliminary draft protocol on railway rolling stock, had submitted to UNIDROIT a letter stressing 'the importance of maintaining the dual structure of a base Convention and specific Protocols for different categories of equipment'. See paragraph 22 in ibid 6; Unidroit, *Unidroit CGE/Int.Int./WP/8 ICAO Ref. LSC/ME-WP/19 (1999)*.

[68] See paragraphs 4:2, 4:3, 4:5 in Unidroit, *ICAO Ref. LSC/ME/2-Report Unidroit CGE/Int.Int./2-Report (1999)*.

[69] See paragraph 4:4 in ibid.

[70] See paragraph 4:5 in ibid.

[71] See paragraph 4:1 in ibid.

[72] See paragraph 4:6 in ibid.

[73] See paragraph 2 in Unidroit, *Unidroit CGE/Int.Int./3-Report ICAO Ref. LSC/ME/3-Report (2000)* 1.

[74] The role of various working groups is examined in section 8.2.3.

Convention/Protocol structure contemplated by the proposed new international regimen was consistent with existing treaty law and practice').[75]

The final test of the two-instrument approach, however, took place during the Cape Town Diplomatic Conference. The two working groups developing the draft protocols on railway rolling stock and space assets reiterated their commitment to the prompt finalisation of the corresponding protocols. In its comments the Rail Working Group firmly rejected 'any idea of an "Aviation only Convention"',[76] noting, among other reasons, the high inefficiency of such approach, which would preclude the development and use by practitioners in different industries of 'a common base position and common jurisprudence'.[77] In an independent submission, OTIF not only supported the umbrella structure, but also annexed a 'Preliminary Draft Protocol on Matters Specific to Railway Rolling Stock'.[78] Similarly, the Space Working Group expressed a strong urge to uphold the dual convention/protocol approach and attached, respectively, the preliminary draft 'Protocol on Matters specific to Space Property'.[79] In the light of the above developments, delegates to the Cape Town Diplomatic Conference expressed overwhelming support[80] towards the adoption of the Convention and its protocols as separate documents (with the exception of the delegations of China and Lebanon), which culminated in the immediate adoption of the CTC and the Aircraft Protocol in November 2001 – with the Rail, Space and MAC Protocols following in 2007, 2012 and 2019, respectively.

Over the years of development, the Convention had gone a long way from attempting to integrate the Draft Aviation Text submitted by the AWG into the basic draft Convention to the separation of a single draft into a baseline treaty accompanied by a set of protocols. While the CTC and each protocol were adopted as separate documents, the usefulness of the *consolidated* versions of the corresponding texts (now found in the corresponding Official Commentaries) suggests that, perhaps in the eyes of the end user, the development of the Convention eventually turned full circle: practitioners would clearly prefer to use a single document. However, as has been shown in this chapter, the structure of an international convention as adopted may be quite different from the structure of the same instrument as utilised by the end users – the existence of a 'basic' convention has preserved the continuity of international interests across a whole range of mobile equipment (aircraft objects, railway rolling stock, space and MAC assets) and will continue to do so for any future protocols.

[75] See paragraph 9 in Unidroit, *Unidroit CGE/Int.Int./3-WP/18 ICAO Ref. LSC/ME/3-WP/18 12/03/00 (2000)* 5.

[76] Unidroit, *Diplomatic Conference to Adopt a Mobile Equipment Convention and an Aircraft Protocol: Acts and Proceedings; [Convention on International Interests in Mobile Equipment and Protocol thereto on Matters Specific to Aircraft Equipment]* (UNIDROIT 2006) 135.

[77] ibid 136.

[78] ibid 114.

[79] ibid 129.

[80] This support was expressed by the German delegation as well: see ibid 745.

5

Addressing Inter Partes Matters: Remedies and Party Autonomy

5.1. Overview

The autonomous concept of 'international interest' developed within the UNIDROIT Study Group was an elegant alternative to the recognition of various interests established under domestic laws: it envisaged the creation of a new, Convention-based type of security regardless of the existence of a national law counterpart.[1] This solution, however, had little inherent value for financiers without a dedicated machinery in place to give effect to the international interest, thus giving it purpose. As a result, the Convention gained a whole array of provisions that associate the international interest with tangible consequences, both between the parties to the relevant underlying (security, lease, title reservation) agreements (*inter partes* effects) and against third parties. These consequences, and the history of development of the corresponding provisions, are the focus of chapter five and chapter six, respectively.

This chapter addresses *inter partes* aspects of the CTC as follows. First, it briefly explains the relevance of party autonomy in the Convention. Second, it tracks the evolution of enforcement provisions under the CTC, focusing on the most challenging areas, such as applicability of remedies, advance relief and the problem of striking the right balance of interests of different parties in financing transactions.

5.2. The Role of Party Autonomy

The Convention's preamble expressly recognises the importance of party autonomy, calling it 'necessary' in asset-based financing and leasing transactions. The Official Commentary[2] and other academic literature[3] treat party autonomy as one

[1] See section 2.3.2.

[2] See paragraphs 2.23–2.25 in Goode, *Convention on International Interests in Mobile Equipment and Protocol thereto on Matters Specific to Aircraft Equipment: Official Commentary* (4th edn, International Institute for the Unification of Private Law (UNIDROIT) 2019) 23, 25.

[3] See, eg, Orkun Akseli, *International Secured Transactions Law: Facilitation of Credit and International Conventions and Instruments* (Routledge 2011) 121.

of the underlying principles of the CTC and its protocols. The reasons for the wide application of the principle of party autonomy were succinctly summarised by Roy Goode, who explained that 'contracting parties to … high-unit value transactions should in general be able to look after themselves and therefore enjoy a wide measure of freedom of contract, albeit subject to certain mandatory provisions to prevent possible abuse'.[4]

This important principle is reflected in a number of provisions of the Convention and its protocols. These provisions allow parties, by virtue of agreement among them, to: (i) agree on the use of certain remedies;[5] (ii) identify events that trigger the application of remedy provisions;[6] (iii) agree upon remedies not envisaged by the Convention;[7] including special remedies added by the protocols;[8] (iv) derogate from the Convention's remedy provisions in their relations with each other;[9] (v) derogate from the protocol provisions in their relations with each other;[10] (vi) exclude certain debtor protection mechanisms;[11] (vii) add extra creditor protection mechanisms,[12] (viii) remove certain creditor protection mechanisms,[13] (ix) change the priority of competing rights and interests between their holders;[14] (x) exclude priority-related enforcement restrictions;[15] (xi) select the courts having jurisdiction over claims brought under the CTC;[16] or (xii) determine the law governing their contractual rights and obligations.[17]

[4] Unidroit, *Study LXXII – Doc. 40 (1998)* 40.

[5] See Articles 8(1), 9(1) of the CTC. Article 13(1) only applies if the debtor has agreed to advance relief.

[6] Article 11 of the CTC.

[7] Article 12 of the CTC.

[8] Article IX(1), Article X(3) of the Aircraft Protocol, Article VIII(3) of the Rail Protocol, Articles XIX and XX(3) of the Space Protocol, Article IX(3) of the MAC Protocol.

[9] Article 15 of the CTC. Exceptions are limited and are driven largely by the need to: (i) protect the debtor against abuse of the creditor's dominant position (Article 8(3)–(6), Article 9(3)–(4), Article 13(2) of the CTC); (ii) prevent unjust enrichment by the holder of a senior interest (Article 8(6) of the CTC); and (iii) preserve integrity of domestic rules of procedure of states (Article 14 of the CTC).

[10] Article IV(3) of the Aircraft Protocol, Article III of the Rail Protocol, Article XVI of the Space Protocol, Article III of the MAC Protocol. The exceptions pursue three objectives: (i) debtor protection (Article IX(3) of the Aircraft Protocol, Article VII(3) of the Rail Protocol, Article XVII(1) of the Space Protocol, Article VIII(3) of the MAC Protocol); (ii) protection of the interests of the senior creditor (Article IX(2) of the Aircraft Protocol, Article VIII(2) of the MAC Protocol); and (iii) enhancing legal certainty by defining 'reasonable prior notice' (Article IX(4) of the Aircraft Protocol, Article VII(4) of the Rail Protocol, Article XVII(2) of the Space Protocol, Article VIII(4) of the MAC Protocol).

[11] Article X(5) of the Aircraft Protocol, Article VIII(5) of the Rail Protocol, Article XX(5) of the Space Protocol, Article IX(5) of the MAC Protocol.

[12] Article XXV(4) of the Rail Protocol.

[13] Article XXVII(9) of the Space Protocol.

[14] Article 29(5) of the CTC.

[15] Article XVII(3) of the Space Protocol. The provision does not raise a priority issue as such, as the interests are in different objects: see paragraph 5.71 in Goode, *Convention on International Interests in Mobile Equipment and Protocol thereto on Matters Specific to Space Assets: Official Commentary* (International Institute for the Unification of Private Law (UNIDROIT) 2013) 451.

[16] Article 42 of the CTC. Exceptions relate to advance relief remedies (Article 43 of the CTC) and jurisdiction to make orders against the Registrar (Article 44 of the CTC).

[17] Article VIII(2) of the Aircraft Protocol, Article VI(2) of the Rail Protocol, Article VIII(2) of the Space Protocol and Article VI(2) of the MAC Protocol. Neither provision applies by default: in each

These provisions share a common feature: their effect is entirely *inter partes*. In addition, the overwhelming majority of articles based on party autonomy relate to remedies and enforcement under the CTC and its protocols: the remaining few provisions affect priorities, jurisdiction and applicable law. The following sections focus on the remedy provisions in the Convention, which at first reflected the concept of party autonomy in its purest form (as they were available only pursuant to an agreement of the parties), but over the years were supplemented by a number of important exceptions in an attempt to achieve a fair balance of interests of various parties.

5.3. Remedies

The key role of remedy provisions in the Convention has been summarised in the Practitioner's Guide issued by the AWG:

> A core purpose of the Convention is to create greater certainty that, upon default, creditors can swiftly, but in a commercially reasonable manner, exercise their remedies to repossess, deregister and export, if applicable, and sell or otherwise realize upon aircraft objects.[18]

While this commentary refers only to aircraft objects, it provides perhaps the strongest possible evidence of the relevance of enforcement provisions, since it reflects the views of practitioners as end-users of the CTC.

5.3.1. Origins of the Enforcement Provisions in the Convention

The need to protect in the future Convention the rights of a secured party in the event of default of the debtor was first recognised by Cuming in his 1989 Study, which suggested 'either … consistent choice of law rules to determine the law governing such rights or a set of substantive rules dealing with default rights and remedies'.[19] Responses to Cuming's subsequent Questionnaire did not reveal a clear preference among the respondents in favour of either option. Twenty-six votes supported the idea of setting up dedicated rules 'to deal with inter partes rights and

case, a state must make a corresponding declaration (see Article VIII(1) of the Aircraft Protocol, Article (VI)(1) of the Rail Protocol, Article VIII(1) of the Space Protocol and Article VI(1) of the MAC Protocol).

[18] The Legal Advisory Panel of the Aviation Working Group, *Practitioners' Guide to the Cape Town Convention and The Aircraft Protocol* 109.

[19] Unidroit, *Study LXXII – Doc. 1 (1989)* 29.

remedies upon default where a security interest is being enforced in a State other than that of the State the laws of which govern the validity of the security interest being enforced'. Nineteen respondents favoured leaving *inter partes* rights to the law applicable to the validity of the security interest. Twenty-one respondents preferred to retain the distinction between substantive and procedural matters, leaving the former to the law governing the validity of the security agreement and the latter – to the law of the forum.[20] To make matters worse, Cuming later acknowledged 'some support' for an alternative that had not been suggested in his Questionnaire at all: a number of respondents preferred 'to allow the parties to the security agreement to choose the applicable law'.[21] This lack of consensus among respondents gave little guidance to the Study Group, which essentially considered two different options.[22] The first involved setting up dedicated rules on 'rights of possession and sale' (as modified by the security agreement).[23] The alternative was basically a hands-off approach to regulating all *inter partes* matters altogether: 'rights of the parties ... could be left to be dealt with by [their] agreement as controlled by the law applicable under the rules of private international law of the forum'.[24]

This lack of consensus can be explained by the lack of uniform approach to security interests at the early stage, when the idea of establishing an 'international security interest' coexisted with the concept of recognition of foreign (national) security interests.[25] The latter was associated with the problem of transposition (ie finding the closest domestic equivalent for foreign security interests), a key obstacle to enforcement acknowledged by the EBRD, which warned that 'it [was] difficult to see how the courts in one Contracting State [could] be relied on to provide proper remedies in relation to a security interest under the laws of another Contracting State'.[26] Another difficulty was associated with the problem of 'internationality':[27] according to Cuming, 'it would be necessary to avoid imposing the convention enforcement system on what would be viewed as purely domestic situations'.[28]

[20] Unidroit, *Study LXXII - Doc. 3 (1991)* 12.

[21] Unidroit, *Study LXXII - Doc. 4 (1992)* 9.

[22] This lack of consensus within the Study Group was later expressly acknowledged by Cuming in Unidroit, *Study LXXII - Doc. 8 (1993)* 28.

[23] See paragraph 12(2) in Unidroit, *Study LXXII - Doc. 5 (1992)* 6.

[24] See paragraph 13 in ibid. This solution can be seen as an indirect acknowledgment of the party choice option (as long as the laws of the forum recognise it) and also as a reflection of the option which, according to Cuming, had not received meaningful support among the respondents: to 'leave all matters of inter partes rights and remedies upon default to the law of the forum': cf question 7(b) and paragraph 18 in Unidroit, *Study LXXII - Doc. 3 (1991)* 11–12.

[25] cf paragraph 8 and paragraph 9 in Unidroit, *Study LXXII - Doc. 5 (1992)* 4–5.

[26] See paragraph 1 in Unidroit, *Study LXXII - Doc. 6 Add. 2 (1993)* 1. See also paragraph 5(a) in Unidroit, *Study LXXII - Doc. 6 Add. 3 (1993)* 2.

[27] See section 2.4.

[28] Unidroit, *Study LXXII - Doc. 8 (1993)* 28.

Despite a number of proposals to provide certain basic enforcement rules in the text of the Convention itself,[29] the first draft set of articles of the CTC contained no such provisions[30] and merely stated:

> In any proceedings for enforcement of an international interest in mobile equipment, the courts of a Contracting State shall recognise the validity and effects of that interest where the issue before the court is a non-domestic issue.[31]

The lack of dedicated rules on enforcement[32] and the lack of clarity as to what kinds of 'effects' of an international interest were to be recognised gave rise to commentator criticism[33] and led to a detailed discussion during the second session of the First Draft Subcommittee in 1995, which adopted a number of conclusions relating to remedies. First, the Convention was to include a list of minimum remedies, which were to be limited to *in rem* remedies.[34] Second, remedies could be set out separately for different (security interest, title reservation, lease) agreements in view of conceptual difficulties.[35] Third, the Convention was not supposed to preclude the use of other remedies chosen by the parties.[36] Fourth, possible Convention remedies could include self-help repossession, judicial sale and judicially supervised sale.[37] Fifth, the Convention enforcement provisions could not apply in the absence of 'a genuinely foreign element'.[38] Later the same year most of these conclusions[39] were reflected in the subsequent draft of the CTC, which for the first time included a dedicated Chapter IV on remedies entitled 'Effects of an International Interest as Between the Parties'.[40]

This new chapter essentially formed the early prototype of the present-day enforcement provisions in the Convention. It included separate remedies for the secured party under a security agreement (taking possession and sale or lease of the object on reasonable terms) (Article 6(1))[41] and for the lessor or seller under a

[29] See, eg, ibid 45; paragraph 5 in Unidroit, *Security Interests Study Group Sub-committee 1st Session Misc. 3 Add. (1994)* 2.

[30] A possible explanation for this decision is that the Drafting Group viewed the preceding discussions of the First Draft Subcommittee as inconclusive and lacking sufficient guidance. For example, the discussions on remedies concluded with a warning to 'avoid reference to recovery of possession', which was not allowed in civil law jurisdictions: see paragraph 6(xviii) in Unidroit, *Study LXXII – Doc. 12 (1994)* 6. On the other hand, the same subcommittee did end up formulating a solution 'in terms of the secured party's right to look to the equipment for satisfaction of the debt and … to have the equipment realised and the proceeds applied towards satisfaction of the debt' – see ibid. It is thus plausible for the Drafting Group to postpone formulating the remedy provisions until a later draft.

[31] See Article 5 in Unidroit, *Study LXXII – Doc. 13 (1994)* 4.

[32] The plans for the introduction of such rules were clearly contemplated by the earlier session of the First Draft Subcommittee – see paragraph 6(xvi) in Unidroit, *Study LXXII – Doc. 12 (1994).*

[33] See, eg, Unidroit, *Study LXXII – Doc. 14 Add 1 (1994)* 1; Unidroit, *Study LXXII – Doc. 14 (1994)* 3.

[34] See paragraph 10(xii) in Unidroit, *Study LXXII – Doc. 15 (1995)* 6.

[35] ibid.

[36] See paragraphs 10(xiii) and 10(xviii) in ibid 6–7.

[37] See paragraph 10(xiv) in ibid 6.

[38] See paragraph 10(xvi) in ibid.

[39] The idea of internationality was left out.

[40] Unidroit, *Study LXXII – Doc. 18 (1995)* 7.

[41] cf Article 8 of the CTC.

title reservation agreement (Article 7(1)),[42] an option for the transfer of ownership over the collateral to the secured party in satisfaction of its claims (Article 6(2))[43] and for the voluntary redemption of the collateral by the debtor (Article 6(3)),[44] as well as provisions permitting the parties to agree on any additional remedies (Articles 6(4) and 7(2)).[45] No rules on advance relief (currently found in Article 13 of the CTC) were envisaged at that stage – the development of these rules is analysed separately in section 5.3.3.

At the same time, the draft had one distinct feature that warrants a deeper look. The entire Chapter IV applied on a party 'opt-in' basis, meaning that each of the basic Convention remedies required a corresponding agreement of the parties and was not available to the financier by default.[46] This issue is examined in section 5.3.2.

5.3.2. Convention Remedies: Party Opt-in or Opt-out?[47]

By mid-1995 it was already clear that the future Convention would include substantive rules governing enforcement, listing certain minimum remedies available to financiers.[48] The mode of application of these rules, however, was subject to interesting debate. The decision of the Drafting Group to make all remedy provisions exercisable only following an agreement of the parties[49] was approved during the subsequent meeting of the First Draft Subcommittee, which confirmed that 'parties would have to opt into, as opposed to being required to opt out of' the relevant rules.[50] The subcommittee's intention was relatively straightforward: to leave parties 'free to choose whatever rules they wished to govern their relations *inter se*'.[51]

It did not take long, however, before the Drafting Group changed its view on the same provision it had originally proposed: what had previously been drafted as an 'opt-in' provision was reformulated as two alternatives. Alternative I essentially reflected the previous version of Article 4, whereas Alternative II turned the

[42] cf Article 10 of the CTC.

[43] cf Articles 9(1)–(2) of the CTC.

[44] cf Article 9(4) of the CTC.

[45] cf Article 12 of the CTC.

[46] See Article 4 in Unidroit, *Study LXXII – Doc. 18 (1995)* 7.

[47] *Party* opt-in and opt-out should not be confused with *state* opt-in and opt-out, ie ability of contracting states to apply or disapply a certain optional provision. The Convention and its protocols tackle these by means of a system of declarations: see n 150 in section 7.3 and the corresponding discussion. In the context of remedies, the key declarations are listed in Articles 54 and 55 and, on the one hand, give contracting states the freedom not to apply certain remedies (Articles 54(1) and 55), while, on the other hand, requiring clarity from participating countries as to whether self-help remedies are excercisable without leave of court (Article 54(2)).

[48] See paragraph 10(xii) in Unidroit, *Study LXXII – Doc. 15 (1995)* 6.

[49] See Article 4 in Unidroit, *Study LXXII – Doc. 18 (1995)* 7.

[50] See paragraph 12 in Unidroit, *Study LXXII – Doc. 21 (1995)* 7.

[51] See paragraph 16 in ibid 8 (emphasis in the original).

provision on its head by giving Convention remedies direct application, subject only to an agreement of the parties to the contrary (ie 'opt-out'): 'The parties may agree in writing to exclude, wholly or in part, any right or remedy conferred on the chargee, seller or lessor by this Chapter'.[52]

While there was no unanimity among commentators in favour of either option,[53] the subsequent session of the Study Group approved the 'opt-out' version of the article, citing the importance of avoiding a 'legal vacuum' in situations when parties have for some reason failed to reach an agreement on specific remedies.[54] There is little doubt that this decision was influenced by the position of the aviation industry reflected in Article 6(1) of the Draft Aviation Text proposed by the AWG, which followed the 'opt-out' route:

> The parties may agree in writing to exclude, wholly or in part, any rights conferred on the chargee, seller or lessor, security assignment assignee, assignee, transferee, engine rights grantee [*sic*] by this Chapter.[55]

The following draft of the Convention essentially reproduced, almost word for word, Alternative II cited above, subject only to minor technical changes.[56] On its face, nothing changed in terms of the ability of the financier to pressure the debtor into a creditor-friendly agreement. A deeper look, however, shows that this is not quite true. The reason for this lies in a fundamental change of approach envisaged during the second session of the Study Group in 1996, which agreed that the draft Convention 'should … incorporate a general rule providing that the remedies exercisable by the chargee … were to be exercised in a *commercially reasonable manner*'.[57] Despite the opposition from the AWG suggesting the removal of restrictions on the exercise of remedies,[58] the Study Group reasoned that the absence of such general protections for the debtor could 'constitute an impediment to the willingness of States to agree that self-help remedies should replace remedies exercised through judicial proceedings'.[59] The issue was particularly relevant for civil law jurisdictions, where self-help was less common and which generally relied on courts to protect the interests of other stakeholders and – in cases when self-help was not available – did not provide the corresponding protections known to many common law countries, such as a duty to obtain the best price and respect the interests of other parties in the collateral. To allow unqualified use of self-help

[52] See Article 7 in Unidroit, *Study LXXII – Doc. 22 (1996)*. See also paragraph in ibid ii.
[53] cf the views of the Banking Federation of the European Union in Unidroit, *Study LXXII – Doc. 26 (1996)* 4 and the preference for the 'opt-in' version by Peter Nesgos and Shiva Falsafi in Unidroit, *Study LXXII – Doc. 26 Add. 3 (1996)* 2.
[54] See paragraph 46 in Unidroit, *Study LXXII – Doc. 27 (1996)* 23.
[55] See Article 6(1) of Annex 1 in Unidroit, *Study LXXII – Doc. 23 (1996)*.
[56] See Article 13 in Unidroit, *Study LXXII – Doc. 30 (1996)* 13.
[57] See paragraph 53 in Unidroit, *Study LXXII – Doc. 27 (1996)* 26 (emphasis added).
[58] The AWG proposed to delete the words 'on reasonable terms', which qualified the remedy of sale or granting a lease of an object: see ibid.
[59] ibid.

remedies in such jurisdictions would effectively mean leaving the debtor at the mercy of the financier.

In the context of the 'opt-out' rule, this change had an important effect (in addition to the obvious extension of scope of debtor protection), which can be demonstrated by comparing the self-help remedies in the different drafts of the Convention prepared in late 1995 and in late 1996. In the earlier draft, the requirement to act reasonably was not treated as a separate duty of the financier but was 'built into' the remedy. In other words, the Convention's remedy was not the right to 'sell or grant a lease of an object' – it was the right to 'sell or grant a lease of any such object *on reasonable terms*'.[60] Since parties were free to exclude 'any right or remedy'[61] (but not a duty), all that was necessary to exclude the debtor protection mechanism was to remove the remedy, as drafted, replacing it with a right to sell or grant a lease of an object (a non-Convention remedy). This would not work in the later draft,[62] which detached the reasonable enforcement test from the actual remedy (now formulated simply as a right to 'sell or grant a lease of any … object'),[63] turned it into a duty and applied to self-help remedies of the secured party generally.[64]

Formulation of the general restriction on the exercise of remedies had another important effect: it indirectly restricted the scope of party autonomy, which even in the revised version allowed the exclusion of *rights* or remedies only.[65] Since Article 8(2) was formulated as an obligation ('any remedy … *shall* be exercised in a commercially reasonable manner'),[66] it can be treated as the first substantive restriction on the exercise of party autonomy in respect of remedies (in addition to the straightforward obligation not to exercise other remedies in contravention of the Convention). This restriction was formalised in 1997, when the Drafting Group finally came up with the modern version of the 'opt-out' provision, which, instead of permitting parties to exclude rights and remedies only, allowed to 'derogate from or vary the effect of any of the provisions of the Convention',[67] subject to certain mandatory, non-derogable, provisions.[68]

The first (tentative) list of such mandatory provisions was proposed by the Drafting Group in July 1997 and was surprisingly close to the final text of Article 15 of the CTC.[69] In fact, the only notable changes involve (i) Article 13(2) of the CTC protecting 'interested persons' in cases of issuing advance relief (which protection was not envisaged back in 1997), and (ii) the general requirement that additional

[60] See Article 9(1)(c) in Unidroit, *Study LXXII – Doc. 22 (1996) (emphasis added).*
[61] See Article 7(1) of Alternative II in ibid.
[62] Unidroit, *Study LXXII – Doc. 30 (1996).*
[63] See Article 8(1)(b) in ibid.
[64] See Article 8(2) in ibid.
[65] See Article 13(1) in ibid.
[66] See Article 8(2) in ibid (emphasis added).
[67] See Article 5 in Unidroit, *Study LXXII – Drafting Group Fourth Session (1997).*
[68] cf Article 15 of the CTC.
[69] See paragraph 21 in Unidroit, *Study LXXII – Doc. 35 (1997)* 5.

remedies should not be inconsistent with the provisions of the Convention.[70] While the first of these two changes is relatively straightforward (it emerged only during the governmental expert stage),[71] the documentary history of the CTC does not give a definitive answer as to why the second restriction on party autonomy was removed from the final text. In fact, this limitation on the exercise of additional remedies consistently maintained its mandatory status throughout all the subsequent drafts[72] preceding the Third Joint Session in 2000, without any major review or documented discussion.[73]

The report of the Third Joint Session contains absolutely no mention of any discussion of Article 5 (which listed the non-derogable provisions) and virtually no opposition to Article 13 (which stipulated the restriction on the exercise of additional remedies) either.[74] Nevertheless, the resulting draft prepared at its conclusion, which changed the order of some provisions (including Article 5, which became Article 14, and Article 13, which became Article 11), no longer treated the restriction on the exercise of additional remedies as non-derogable.[75] A thorough review of all the working papers relating to the Third Joint Session provides an explanation: the *ad hoc* Drafting Group, which had been established after the conclusion of the Second Joint Session to complete the work left unfinished by the Drafting Committee of that session,[76] deleted from Article 5 the reference to Article 13,[77] without any documented explanation and disregarding the fact that both provisions had been previously approved by the delegates without discussion. As a result, the delegates and the Drafting Group at the Third Joint Session were considering the amended version of Article 5 – yet no record of any discussion of this text exists.[78] The result of these developments can now be found in the final text of the CTC, which – similarly – does not treat Article 12 as non-derogable and, by virtue of Article 15, allows parties to deviate from it by agreement in their relations with each other. Whether or not this change is

[70] See Article 13 in ibid. Cf Articles 12 and 15 of the final text of the CTC.

[71] See Article 14(2) in Appendix I to Attachment D in Unidroit, *Unidroit CGE/Int.Int./Report ICAO Ref. LSC/ME-Report (1999).*

[72] See Articles 6 and 14 in Unidroit, *Study LXXII – Doc. 37 (1997)*; Articles 6 and 14 in Unidroit, *Study LXXII – Doc. 39 (1998)*; Articles 6 and 14 in Unidroit, *Study LXXII – Doc. 42 (1998)*; Articles 5 and 13 in Appendix I of Attachment D in Unidroit, *Unidroit CGE/Int.Int./Report ICAO Ref. LSC/ME-Report (1999)*; Articles 5 and 13 in Appendix I of Attachment F in Unidroit, *ICAO Ref. LSC/ME/2-Report Unidroit CGE/Int.Int./2-Report (1999).*

[73] See paragraphs 37 and 49 in Unidroit, *Unidroit CGE/Int.Int./Report ICAO Ref. LSC/ME-Report (1999)* 8; paragraphs 5:8 and 5:19 in Unidroit, *ICAO Ref. LSC/ME/2-Report Unidroit CGE/Int.Int./2-Report (1999)* 5–2.

[74] See paragraphs 104–105 in Unidroit, *Unidroit CGE/Int.Int./3-Report ICAO Ref. LSC/ME/3-Report (2000)* 13.

[75] cf Articles 14 and 11 in Appendix I of Attachment C in ibid.

[76] See paragraph 1 in Unidroit, *Unidroit CGE/Int.Int./3-WP/2 ICAO Ref. LSC/ME/3-WP/2 (2000)* 1.

[77] See Article 5 in Appendix III to ibid.

[78] The report of the Drafting Group of the Third Joint Session shows that Article 5 was relocated to Article 14 without any substantive changes, except renumbering: see Article 5 in Unidroit, *Unidroit CGE/Int.Int./3-WP/40 ICAO Ref. LSC/ME/3-WP/40 30/03/00 (2000).*

appropriate is ultimately a matter of policy that could be examined in case of any future revision of the Convention.[79]

In addition to the formulation of mandatory provisions, the general transition to an 'opt-out' regime in the application of remedies was affected by another important development: certain remedies were given non-automatic effect, requiring the consent of the financier's counterparty. This change affected two categories of Convention remedies[80] – self-help remedies and advance relief[81] – and occurred only at the governmental expert stage, when the results of the work of the Study Group, the APG and the SRC were formally discussed at a governmental level.

The corresponding amendments to the relevant provisions[82] were introduced during the First Joint Session, but, surprisingly, had little in common with the discussions held during the plenary and reflected in the actual report of the session. Following one delegation's mention of difficulties expected to accompany the transposition of Convention remedies into national law,[83] the governmental experts instructed the Drafting Committee to 'review the question of self-help remedies' and consider whether it would be advisable to introduce the concepts of 'good faith' and 'public order'.[84] In respect of advance relief, there is no record of a plenary discussion concerning advisability of turning the relevant article (Article 15) into an 'opt-in' provision.[85]

Despite this, the reports of the Drafting Committee show rather different developments. First, the US delegation came up with a proposal to add the requirement of chargor's consent ('if the chargor has so agreed') to the self-help remedy provisions[86] and later, in a separate submission, to the rules on advance relief ('to the extent the obligor has so agreed').[87] The intermediate reports of the Drafting Committee of the First Joint Session do not reflect the underlying discussion, but the final report shows that both US proposals were accepted by the Drafting Committee, with minor technical adjustments.[88]

[79] See Article 61(2)(d) of the CTC.

[80] There is, of course, the separate remedy exercisable only upon agreement of both the chargee and the debtor (as well as all interested parties), namely the vesting of the ownership over the relevant object in satisfaction of the secured obligations found in Article 9(1) of the CTC. However, the very concept of this remedy is based on the idea that after default (and not earlier than that) parties agree to transfer the ownership over the asset to extinguish the debt. In other words, for this remedy, agreement of the parties is an inherent element. For this reason, the drafting history of Article 9(1) was relatively straightforward: this type of remedy appeared in the first draft that included remedy provisions and similarly referred to the agreement of the parties (together with its alternative, ie court-ordered vesting of the object, which is now found in Article 9(2) of the CTC): see Article 6(2) in Unidroit, *Study LXXII – Doc. 18 (1995)* 7.

[81] The development of advance relief provisions is analysed separately in section 5.3.3.

[82] See Articles 9 and 15 in Unidroit, *Study LXXII – Doc. 42 (1998)* 5, 7.

[83] See paragraph 42 in Unidroit, *Unidroit CGE/Int.Int./Report ICAO Ref. LSC/ME-Report (1999)* 8.

[84] See paragraph 44 in ibid. Although the words 'public order' are used in the report, they should probably be read as references to the concept of *ordre public*, ie public policy.

[85] See paragraphs 51–53 in ibid 9.

[86] See Article 9(1) in Unidroit, *Unidroit CGE/Int.Int. ICAO Ref. LSC/ME DC-WP/7 5/02/99 (1999)* 2.

[87] See Article 15 in Unidroit, *Unidroit CGE/Int.Int. ICAO Ref. LSC/ME DC-WP/10 8/02/99 (1999)* 2.

[88] See Articles 8(1) and 14(1) in Appendix I to Attachment D in Unidroit, *Unidroit CGE/Int.Int./Report ICAO Ref. LSC/ME-Report (1999)*.

The proposal of governmental representatives to consider the introduction of the concepts of 'good faith' and 'public order'[89] is a clear indication of the need to address state sensitivities, such as debtor protection and preservation of public interests. The introduction of the 'opt-in' element in the application of self-help remedies and advance relief certainly goes some way towards achieving the former (although not as strongly as the mandatory restrictions on the exercise of creditor's authority),[90] but does little (if anything) to address the latter (ie broader public policy concerns). Nevertheless, this change was not challenged in the subsequent meetings of governmental experts and was retained in the final text of the CTC.[91]

As a result, the Convention's remedy rules underwent significant transformation during the development of the CTC: from being entirely optional provisions (party 'opt-in'), to becoming available generally absent party agreement to the contrary (party 'opt-out'), with some instruments (self-help and advance relief) available only with the consent of the debtor (partial party 'opt-in').[92]

5.3.3. Advance Relief

One of the biggest transformations in the history of the Convention's remedy provisions relates to its rules on advance relief, which can now be found in Article 13 of the CTC. Their origins go back to 1995, when the AWG proposed setting up strict time frames for national courts to issue 'non-appealable, final decisions' in respect of remedies: five days for the 'grounding' of aircraft and 30 days for repossession by the financier or judicially supervised sale of the same.[93] The need for prompt access to the asset in case of default was considered so important by the AWG, that this proposal was part of the so-called 'core' provisions, which were expected to apply on a mandatory basis by each contracting state:[94] without such rules the future Convention, it was believed, would provide 'a theoretical right which lacks utility'.[95] Shortly afterwards, having received comments on its original memorandum, the AWG acknowledged the overly ambitious character of its initial proposal and agreed to make the rules on time limits for the Convention's remedies optional, ie applicable only after separate enactment by the state which has decided to opt into this regime.[96]

In its second memorandum, the AWG extended its proposal on mandatory time frames to cover: (i) judicial proceedings relating to the ability of the financier

[89] See paragraph 44 in ibid 8.
[90] cf Article 8(3) of the CTC.
[91] See Articles 8(1) and 13(1) of the CTC.
[92] Note that all the remedies found in the protocols to the CTC, except remedies on insolvency, also follow the party 'opt-in' route: see Articles IX(1) and X(3) of the Aircraft Protocol, Articles VII(1) and VIII(3) of the Rail Protocol, Article XX(2) of the Space Protocol, Article VIII(1) of the MAC Protocol.
[93] See paragraph 5.1 in Unidroit, *Study LXXII – Doc. 16 (1995)* 16–17.
[94] ibid 6.
[95] ibid 17.
[96] Unidroit, *Study LXXII – Doc. 19 Add. 4 (1995)* 1.

to take possession of collateral (5 working days); (ii) judicial proceedings relating to any other claim under the Convention (30 days),[97] (iii) repossession in the context of insolvency proceedings (30 days);[98] and (iv) deregistration of aircraft by the aviation authorities, as well as export and removal of the object from the jurisdiction upon default (7 days).[99] The first three scenarios were scrutinised by the Study Group during its second session in 1996, which immediately noted the difficulties[100] with the practical implementation of strict time limits by national courts and sought an alternative method to address the AWG concerns that would be 'perceived as somewhat lighter from the point of view of their potential interference with the sensitivities of States'.[101] In seeking such method, the Study Group reasoned that, instead of having to adjudicate on the merits of the case (outside insolvency proceedings), courts could be relied on to provide 'interim relief or similar protective measures' reflecting two fundamental elements: (i) the ability to have the asset held in one place under judicial supervision, and (ii) the power of the court to appoint a receiver to realise the value of the asset.[102]

In response to this new solution, which immediately gained broad support of the Study Group (but not of the AWG, which initially reserved its position on this matter), the Drafting Group made the first attempt to craft an appropriate solution by introducing a new article giving the financier a new remedy in the form of 'speedy provisional or interim judicial relief'.[103] At the time, the draft Convention was still conceived as a single instrument, incorporating certain aircraft-specific provisions.[104] This changed very quickly, when the AWG and IATA proposed the umbrella structure for the treaty,[105] which created an excellent opportunity for the AWG to reassert its requirement of strict time frames for various proceedings: it accepted the Drafting Group's solution as part of the base Convention, but insisted on having a maximum period of 30 days for the relevant proceedings relating to the equipment in the aircraft-specific protocol.[106] Most importantly, however, the

[97] See Articles 13(1)–(2) and 31(2)(a)(iii) of the Draft Aviation Text in Annex 1 to Unidroit, *Study LXXII – Doc. 23 (1996)*. Note that these provisions were drafted by the AWG as 'state opt-out', rather than 'state opt-in' rules: contracting states could disapply the relevant rules by virtue of corresponding 'reservations'.

[98] See Articles 14(a)(i) and 31(2)(a)(iv) in ibid. This provision was clearly modelled after Section 1110 of the US Bankruptcy Code: this was subsequently acknowledged in Unidroit, *Study LXXII – Doc. 27 (1996)* 40.

[99] See Article 23(2)(b) in Unidroit, *Study LXXII – Doc. 23 (1996)*.

[100] In addition to the obvious state sensitivities, some commentators noted that mandatory time frames for courts were not practicable generally, given the 'general absence of any enforcement system to deal with judges and court officers who ignore the legally-specified timetable': see paragraph 73 in Unidroit, *Study LXXII – Doc. 26 Add. 2 (1996)* 20–21.

[101] See paragraph 95 in Unidroit, *Study LXXII – Doc. 27 (1996)* 41.

[102] See paragraph 96 in ibid.

[103] See Article 15 in Unidroit, *Study LXXII – Doc. 30 (1996)* 14.

[104] See draft Chapter X 'Special Provisions for Aircraft Property' in ibid 22.

[105] See section 4.3. The Drafting Group convened on 23–24 October 1996, while the AWG/IATA proposal was received by UNIDROIT on 16 December 1996. Cf paragraph 1 in ibid 1 and Introduction in Unidroit, *Study LXXII – Doc. 32 (1996)* 1.

[106] Unidroit, *Study LXXII – Doc. 32 Add. 2 (1997)* 3.

AWG and IATA accepted the distinction between 'judicial proceedings *relating to the asset* on the one hand, and judicial proceedings *relating to the ultimate liability*, on the other':[107] the thirty-day limit proposed for the future protocol was directed at the former and did not purport to represent the time required to determine the final liability of the parties. The AWG and IATA were also the first to stress the *sui generis* nature of the interim measures envisaged in the draft, distinct from 'traditional notions of injunction relief and the particular national standards associated therewith'.[108]

The scope of advance relief found in Article 13 of the CTC took years to crystallise in its current form. The first draft included four measures: (i) preservation of the object; (ii) possession, custody or management of the object; (iii) sale of the object; and (iv) immobilisation of the object.[109] The AWG and IATA soon added the fifth option: application of proceeds or retention of income resulting from the sale or lease of the object.[110] With technical amendments and revisions (including the addition of lease to the 'sale' option), these five measures remained in all the subsequent drafts of the Convention preceding the governmental expert stage.[111]

Despite this continuity, this combination was the subject of significant criticism from various commentators for treating sale and lease of collateral in the same way as other, essentially 'conservatory' measures aiming to preserve the status quo pending the final determination of the claim.[112] The same criticism was raised by the governments,[113] but it was not until the Third Joint Session in 2000 that the opposition raised a major discussion warranting amendment of the underlying provision. To address this issue, the governmental experts convened a dedicated working group (consisting of representatives of Canada, France, Japan, Singapore and Sweden and attended by the AWG), which reached a consensus in recommending the removal of sale and the application of proceeds from the baseline Convention rules on advance relief and placing them into the draft Aircraft Protocol as an optional provision to which contracting states could 'opt in'.[114] These rebalancing changes explain the interplay between Article 13(1) of the CTC and Articles X(1), (3) of the Aircraft Protocol: the most intrusive measures became

[107] ibid (emphasis in the original).

[108] ibid 12. The *sui generis* nature of advance relief was later confirmed in the Official Commentaries: see, eg, paragraph 2.132 in Goode, *Convention on International Interests in Mobile Equipment and Protocol thereto on Matters Specific to Aircraft Equipment: Official Commentary* (4th edn, International Institute for the Unification of Private Law (UNIDROIT) 2019) 84–85.

[109] See Article 15 in Unidroit, *Study LXXII - Doc. 30 (1996)* 14.

[110] See Article 15(3)(d) in Appendix to Unidroit, *Study LXXII - Doc. 32 Add. 2 (1997).*

[111] See Article 14(2) in Unidroit, *Study LXXII - Drafting Group Fourth Session (1997)*; Article 14(2) in Unidroit, *Study LXXII - Doc. 35 (1997)*; Article 13(1) in Unidroit, *International Interests Study Group 4th Session Misc. 5 (1997)*; Article 15(1) in Unidroit, *Study LXXII - Doc. 37 (1997)*; Article 16(1) in Unidroit, *Study LXXII - Doc. 39 (1998)*; Article 15(1) in Unidroit, *Study LXXII - Doc. 42 (1998).*

[112] See paragraphs 130, 131, 133 in Unidroit, *Study LXXII - Doc. 36 (1997)* 32; see also Unidroit, *Study LXXII - Doc. 44 (1998)* 3.

[113] See, eg, paragraph 5:21 in Unidroit, *ICAO Ref. LSC/ME/2-Report Unidroit CGE/Int.Int./2-Report (1999)* 5-4.

[114] See Unidroit, *Unidroit CGE/Int.Int./3-WP/24 ICAO Ref. LSC/ME/3-WP/24 (2000).*

subject to non-automatic application requiring express state approval in the first place (as opposed to passive non-objection in the case of 'basic' forms of advance relief).[115]

As history sometimes tends to repeat itself, so was this the case with the time limits for court-sanctioned remedies in the Convention, when in the course of the Third Joint Session the US delegation came up with a proposal for a new provision in the draft Aircraft Protocol, which stated in its first paragraph:

> A Contracting State shall ensure that judicial proceedings relating to the remedies under the Convention will be completed within the period set forth in a declaration to this Protocol.[116]

This provision, which effectively put to the test the discussions within the Study Group back in 1996 that gave birth to the rules on advance relief in the first place, was summarily dismissed by the governmental representatives as 'highly controversial'.[117] It will be recalled that the AWG and IATA previously supported the idea of limiting the time during which the protective measures could be issued.[118] Indeed, the early drafts of the Aircraft Protocol incorporated such a provision,[119] but the more the negotiations progressed, the more watered-down version of the corresponding article emerged as a result. At the conclusion of the First Joint Session, the fixed time frame of 30 days was replaced with an empty placeholder reference ('not exceeding [...] calendar days'), and the whole provision was put into square brackets.[120] By the start of the Third Joint Session, even the placeholder provision was removed and replaced with reference to the number of days specified in a declaration made by a contracting state, thus eliminating any attempt for the draft Aircraft Protocol to impose the time limits on domestic proceedings affecting advance relief (while still leaving the whole provision in square brackets).[121]

Bearing in mind these developments and the fact that neither of the earlier drafts of the Aircraft Protocol ever attempted to establish time limits outside advance relief proceedings, it is no wonder that the US proposal to reintroduce a hard cap on the timing of *all* domestic judicial proceedings was met with such a strong opposition during the Third Joint Session. Even though this proposal was

[115] cf Article X ('Declarations regarding relief pending final determination') in Appendix I to Attachment C in Unidroit, *Unidroit CGE/Int.Int./3-Report ICAO Ref. LSC/ME/3-Report (2000)* and Article X(1) in Appendix II to Attachment C in ibid.

[116] See Unidroit, *Unidroit CGE/Int.Int./3-WP/25 ICAO Ref. LSC/ME/3-WP/25 (2000)*.

[117] See paragraph 118 in Unidroit, *Unidroit CGE/Int.Int./3-Report ICAO Ref. LSC/ME/3-Report (2000)* 14.

[118] See n 106.

[119] See, eg, Article XVIII(1) in Unidroit, *Study LXXIID – Doc. 1 (1998)* and Article X(1) in Unidroit, *Study LXXIID – Doc. 3 (1998)*.

[120] See Article X(1) of Appendix II to Attachment D in Unidroit, *Unidroit CGE/Int.Int./Report ICAO Ref. LSC/ME-Report (1999)*.

[121] See Article X in Appendix IV to Unidroit, *Unidroit CGE/Int.Int./3-WP/2 ICAO Ref. LSC/ME/3-WP/2 (2000)*.

firmly rejected, it was instrumental in testing the limits of state sensitivities: while disagreeing with the overly ambitious scope of the US proposal, several delegations nevertheless expressed their preparedness to accept the time limits, on the understanding that the provision would apply only subject to express consent by the states.[122] It is conceivable that the final decision to open the square brackets around the article[123] dedicated to the time limits for advance relief proceedings was influenced a great deal by the US initiative to go above and beyond the (then) existing draft.

5.3.4. Achieving a Balance of Interests in Remedy Provisions

The challenges in drafting the remedy provisions of the CTC were not limited to finding the most appropriate enforcement provisions and determining the limits of party autonomy: of no less importance was the need to carefully consider the needs of all the stakeholders, stressing how vital it was 'as a matter of general policy for the rules of the future Convention to be perceived as reflecting a balance between the interests of *all* the parties concerned'.[124] The instruments used to achieve this balance in the final text of the Convention are many and include mechanisms protecting not only the debtor (eg the obligation to exercise remedies in a commercially reasonable manner in Article 8(3) or the definition of 'default' in Article 11), but other creditors as well (eg the rules on redistribution of surplus among holders of subsequently ranking interests in Article 8(6) or the concept of 'interested persons' in Article 1(m) protecting the providers of credit insurance and other holders of rights in the collateral). This section focuses on two such instruments that took longest to crystallise in their final form.

i. Duty to Exercise Remedies in a Commercially Reasonable Manner

From a historical perspective, the test of 'reasonableness' was the first restriction on the exercise of remedies to appear in the draft Convention. Its initial purpose was very limited: to restrict the ability of the secured party to sell and lease the collateral under a security agreement.[125] As noted in section 5.3.2,[126] the test was subsequently transformed into a standalone restriction on the exercise of *all* non-judicial remedies of the chargee generally.[127] This decision, however, was

[122] See paragraph 119 in Unidroit, *Unidroit CGE/Int.Int./3-Report ICAO Ref. LSC/ME/3-Report (2000)* 14.

[123] See paragraph 121 in ibid.

[124] See paragraph 94 in Unidroit, *Study LXXII – Doc. 27 (1996)* 40 (emphasis added).

[125] See Article 6(1)(b) in Unidroit, *Study LXXII – Doc. 18 (1995)* 7.

[126] See n 66 and the corresponding discussion.

[127] See Article 8(2) in Unidroit, *Study LXXII – Doc. 30 (1996)* 11.

preceded by a proposal by the AWG to delete the words 'on reasonable terms',[128] on the basis that they 'were unclear and could lead to litigation.[129] A better solution, according to the AWG, was to include a general reference to the terms of the underlying security agreement ('to the extent and on the terms set forth in the security agreement').[130] Despite this, the Study Group reasoned that the absence of a relevant restriction on the exercise of remedies would be a serious impediment to the willingness of states to agree to self-help remedies, particularly from the point of view of civil law jurisdictions, which relied on courts to balance the interests of various parties concerned.[131] Interestingly, while the test of 'reasonableness' was considered appropriate for this role, another possible solution – the duty of the chargee to act in good faith – was not.[132] As a compromise, the proposal of the AWG to refer to the terms of the underlying agreement was also incorporated in the revised draft, this time not as alternative to the test of reasonableness, but as its part.[133]

The compromise suggested by the Study Group, nonetheless, did not satisfy the AWG, which soon returned, in tandem with IATA, with a strong critique of such an approach, adding two new arguments against the test of 'reasonableness': (i) its interpretation would vary widely between jurisdictions, and (ii) it could be used to justify preferential court treatment of nationals in cross-border litigation.[134] Essentially, the AWG reasserted its earlier position, but the tone of its argument shifted slightly: this time, it acknowledged the possibility of including general restrictions on the exercise of remedies. The suggested restrictions would take two forms: (i) a mandatory notice period for the exercise of non-judicial sale, and (ii) any other limitations on the ability of the parties to agree on the method for the exercise of remedies.[135]

The uncertainties underlying the concept of 'reasonableness' were soon emphasised by various commentators, who characterised it as introducing 'an element of subjectivity'[136] and even as having 'no meaning either for lawyers from civil law countries or for lawyers engaged in international commercial law'.[137] Mooney and Whalen came up with an alternative solution to strengthen the reference to the agreement of the parties, which would be conclusive 'unless manifestly unreasonable'.[138] This peculiar transformation of one reasonableness test into

[128] See Article 8(1) of the Draft Aviation Text in Annex 1 to Unidroit, *Study LXXII – Doc. 23 (1996)*.

[129] See paragraph 53 in Unidroit, *Study LXXII – Doc. 27 (1996)* 26.

[130] See Article 8(1) of the Draft Aviation Text in Annex 1 to Unidroit, *Study LXXII – Doc. 23 (1996)*.

[131] See n 59.

[132] See paragraph 53 in Unidroit, *Study LXXII – Doc. 27 (1996)* 26. In the view of the Study Group, a 'good faith' requirement 'would lead to uncertainty'. However, this argument is hardly convincing, since the same critique, as will be shown later, can be directed at the test of 'reasonableness' with equal force.

[133] See Article 8(2) in Unidroit, *Study LXXII – Doc. 30 (1996)*. The relevance of the party agreement was fairly weak, as courts were merely expected to 'have regard' to the terms of the agreement.

[134] Unidroit, *Study LXXII – Doc. 32 Add. 2 (1997)* 9.

[135] ibid 10.

[136] See paragraph 83 in Unidroit, *Study LXXII – Doc. 36 (1997)* 24.

[137] See paragraph 82 in ibid.

[138] See paragraph 81 in ibid.

another implied more deference to party autonomy, effectively allowing court interference only in the more extreme cases, but did not solve the problem at its core: in one form or another, the test of 'reasonableness' remained. Nonetheless, the draft produced following the fourth session of the Study Group in 1997 reflected this approach.[139]

An interesting change occurred after the transition to the umbrella structure of the Convention: the APG, which was initially responsible for the preparation of the draft Aircraft Protocol, concluded that the test of reasonableness should apply not only in the case of remedies exercised under security agreements, but also in respect of conditional sale and leasing agreements – at least in relation to aircraft objects.[140] This idea was supported by the chairman of the SRC, Roy Goode, who removed the corresponding provision from the article addressing remedies of chargee under the security agreement and included it in the draft as a standalone restriction applicable to *all* Convention remedies.[141] The change was, however, quickly reversed by the SRC, which felt that its mandate did not permit interference with the substance of provisions established previously by the Study Group and left the matter for consideration of the governmental experts, recalling that the approach envisaged by the draft Aircraft Protocol had previously been met with 'fierce opposition' from the leasing circles on the ground that the lessor – as owner of the relevant asset – should be allowed to 'do whatever he liked with that asset' in jurisdictions which did not treat leases as security interests.[142] This decision marked the separation of different approaches taken by the Convention and its protocols in addressing the test of 'reasonableness'. Another difference stemmed from the fact that the early drafts of the Aircraft Protocol got rid even of the residual test of 'manifest unreasonableness' qualifying the ability of the parties to agree on rules of enforcement, as suggested by Mooney and Whalen and reflected in the draft CTC: the protocol treated party agreement as conclusive.[143]

Overall, the draft Convention and the Aircraft Protocol reached the governmental stage in an odd state: in an attempt to restrain the enforcement powers of the financier, they relinquished the challenging concept of good faith by replacing it with the notion of party autonomy, restricted by the test of 'manifest unreasonableness' in one case and the idea of 'public order' in the other. Neither option provided a conclusive solution devoid of uncertainty, making it sometimes difficult to tell which solution made more practical sense. This is best illustrated by the results of deliberations during the First Joint Session, where the governmental experts eventually instructed the Drafting Committee to consider 'whether the

[139] See Article 9(2) in Unidroit, *Study LXXII – Doc. 37 (1997)*.

[140] Unidroit, *Study LXXII – Doc. 40 (1998)* 15.

[141] See Article 15 in Unidroit, *Study LXXII – Doc. 39 (1998)*.

[142] See paragraphs 28, 94 and 117 in Unidroit, *Study LXXII – Doc. 41 (1998)* 13, 25, 29.

[143] See Article IX(3)(b)(2) in Unidroit, *Study LXXIID – Doc. 3 (1998)* 8. To address political sensitivities, the draft Aircraft Protocol limited enforcement by prohibiting the taking of possession or control over collateral in a manner contrary to 'public order': see Article IX(3)(b)(3) in ibid.

concept of "good faith" should be inserted instead of that of "a commercially reasonable manner"'.[144]

The sensitivities involved in balancing the interests of various parties reached their peak during the Third Joint Session, when the ICAO Secretariat presented its paper on 'remedies and interim relief'.[145] The paper was a radical attempt to influence the enforcement regime under the Aircraft Protocol that extended well beyond the safeguards envisaged by the Convention. First, it deleted references to the conclusive nature of party agreement relating to enforcement. Second, it included a duty of the creditor to 'have due regard of all relevant circumstances' when determining commercial reasonableness. Third, it entitled the debtor to claim compensatory damages in court in case of losses resulting from the exercise of remedies provided by the Convention or the Aircraft Protocol.[146] Despite some limited support, the ICAO proposal was not reflected in the subsequent drafts.

Overall, the three sessions of governmental experts produced inconclusive results. On the one hand, the only material change in the draft Convention related to the scope of the 'reasonableness' test, which now applied to advance relief measures, in addition to self-help remedies of the chargee.[147] This change, however, had little practical effect, since the Aircraft Protocol displaced the Convention rules anyway, extending the 'reasonableness' test to the exercise of all remedies.[148] On the other hand, the Aircraft Protocol ultimately strengthened the role of party autonomy by getting rid of any of its restrictions, first, by replacing the duty to observe public order with references to the exercise of remedies by lawful means[149] and, second, by removing references to the latter at the conclusion of the Third Joint Session.[150] Thus, the draft protocol had the potential of reaching both goals at once: (i) extending the scope of the reasonableness test to all remedies, and (ii) ensuring that agreement of the parties as to the scope of this test is not challenged.

This changed during the Cape Town Diplomatic Conference, where a number of delegations (South Africa, Jamaica, Kenya and India) strongly opposed the idea that party agreement should control without any qualification.[151] As a result, the corresponding provision in the draft Aircraft Protocol was referred to the Drafting Committee, which found no better solution than to reproduce the same restriction

[144] See paragraph 45 in Unidroit, *Unidroit CGE/Int.Int./Report ICAO Ref. LSC/ME-Report (1999)* 8.

[145] See Unidroit, *Unidroit CGE/Int.Int./3-WP/12 ICAO Ref. LSC/ME/3-WP/12 (2000).*

[146] ibid 6.

[147] cf Article 9(2) in Unidroit, *Study LXXII – Doc. 42 (1998)* and Article 7(2) in Appendix I of Attachment C in Unidroit, *Unidroit CGE/Int.Int./3-Report ICAO Ref. LSC/ME/3-Report (2000).*

[148] See Article IX(3) in Appendix II of Attachment C in Unidroit, *Unidroit CGE/Int.Int./3-Report ICAO Ref. LSC/ME/3-Report (2000).*

[149] cf Article IX(3)(b)(3) in Unidroit, *Study LXXIID – Doc. 3 (1998)* and Article IX(3)(b)(3) in Appendix II of Attachment F in Unidroit, *ICAO Ref. LSC/ME/2-Report Unidroit CGE/Int.Int./2-Report (1999).*

[150] See Article IX(3)(b) in Appendix II of Attachment C in Unidroit, *Unidroit CGE/Int.Int./3-Report ICAO Ref. LSC/ME/3-Report (2000).*

[151] Unidroit, *Diplomatic Conference to Adopt a Mobile Equipment Convention and an Aircraft Protocol: Acts and Proceedings; [Convention on International Interests in Mobile Equipment and Protocol thereto on Matters Specific to Aircraft Equipment]* (UNIDROIT 2006) 824–29.

that had already existed in the text of the Convention (ie 'manifest unreasonableness'). The test of 'reasonableness' thus went full circle, as the protocol lost its (previously) defining feature: unlimited party autonomy in determining the manner of enforcement. Nevertheless, the Aircraft Protocol still extended the scope of the 'reasonableness' restriction to all the remedies – a decision that was subsequently reproduced in every other adopted protocol.[152]

ii. Meaning of 'Default'

The concept of 'default' appeared in the draft Convention together with the first provisions on remedies as a trigger for their exercise and was closely linked to the idea of party autonomy: even the draft articles in 1995 allowed parties to agree as to what events give rise to the enforcement rules of the treaty.[153] The idea of party agreement regarding the meaning of 'default' was never the subject of any substantial criticism,[154] which cannot be said about the application of the term when the parties have chosen to remain silent.

At its second session held in 1996, the Study Group labelled the default provisions as 'draconian', as the existing draft permitted enforcement following *any* default whatsoever, however small or brief.[155] Two solutions were considered necessary to 'ensure … the fair and balanced character' of the draft Convention: (i) introduction of the element of 'materiality'; and (ii) incorporation of a provision giving the defaulting party a reasonable opportunity to remedy the default before the enforcement rules could apply with full force. The Study Group relied on two existing international treaties for inspiration: the CISG, which permits avoidance of the contract by the buyer or the seller in case of a 'fundamental breach'[156] or following the failure to perform the obligation within a reasonable time period fixed by the counterparty,[157] and the Financial Leasing Convention, which allows termination of the leasing contract in the event of 'substantial default'[158] and requires the lessor to give the lessee 'a reasonable opportunity of remedying the default' before termination.[159] The Drafting Group's response to the guidance from the Study Group was laconic: it borrowed the 'substantial default' concept from the Financial Leasing Convention and introduced a new (undefined) concept of 'persistent default'.[160] The latter does not appear analogous to the grace period

[152] See Article VII(3) of the Rail Protocol, Article XVII(1) of the Space Protocol and Article VIII(3) of the MAC Protocol.

[153] See Article 5 in Unidroit, *Study LXXII – Doc. 18 (1995)* 7.

[154] In fact, the scope of party autonomy was broadened further, by allowing parties to agree that events other than default may give rise to the Convention remedies: see paragraph 56 in Unidroit, *Study LXXII – Doc. 27 (1996)* 27.

[155] See paragraph 56 in ibid.

[156] See Articles 49(1)(a) and 64(1)(a) of the CISG.

[157] See Article 49(1)(b) and 47(1); Articles 64(1)(b) and 63(1) of the CISG.

[158] See Article 13(2) of the Financial Leasing Convention.

[159] See Article 13(5) of the Financial Leasing Convention.

[160] See Article 11(1) in Unidroit, *Study LXXII – Doc. 30 (1996)* 13.

provisions of the above two conventions, as it was not based on the right or duty of the financier to give the defaulting party an opportunity to cure the breach – instead, it signalled a degree of longevity of the violation.

The obvious problem with the new 'twin' elements resulted from the applied drafting technique, which made the default criteria concise, but also abstract. As a result, a very serious breach lasting only a moment could trigger the enforcement provisions, just like a minor technical omission persisting for a long period. Of course, these matters were routinely handled in commercial contracts using various techniques, such as the notion of 'continuing' default, which permits the use of remedies only insofar as the breach has not been remedied by the counterparty. However, as noted earlier, the new default criteria were meant to deal with situations when the parties failed to agree as to what constitutes a default beforehand.

Failure to acknowledge the uncertainty resulting from any attempt to qualify the term 'default' using abstract criteria resulted in a series of unfortunate changes – all with little practical effect. First, following critique by Charles Mooney and Thomas Whalen,[161] the Drafting Group replaced the two alternative characteristics of default ('substantial' and 'persistent') with a single one ('material').[162] This change, in turn, triggered even more criticism from commentators, who stressed the insufficient clarity of the new term[163] and enquired whether 'material default' had the same meaning as 'fundamental breach' under the CISG and 'fundamental non-performance' under UPICC (UNIDROIT Principles of International Commercial Contracts)[164] and PECL (Principles of European Contract Law).[165] As a result, the reference to 'material default' was replaced with 'substantial default' at the conclusion of the fourth session of the Study Group in 1997,[166] clearly with no improvement in terms of clarity.[167]

The only meaningful attempt to resolve the 'default' conundrum during the governmental expert stage took place at the Third Joint Session, when the plenary discussed the ICAO proposal to qualify this term by limiting default, first, to the non-fulfilment of a 'primary obligation' and, second, to instances of breach of payment obligations in the case of leases or sales involving payments by instalment.[168] The proposal was rejected by the delegates, who nonetheless agreed to adjust the definition of 'default': as if in an attempt to pick every possible combination of various abstract terms, it was agreed to bring back the 'materiality'

[161] Unidroit, *Study LXXII – Doc. 32 Add. 3 (1997)* 5.

[162] See Article 11(2) in Unidroit, *Study LXXII – Doc. 35 (1997).*

[163] See paragraph 108 in Unidroit, *Study LXXII – Doc. 36 (1997)* 28.

[164] Article 7.3.1(1) of UPICC 1994 reads: 'A party may terminate the contract where the failure of the other party to perform an obligation under the contract amounts to a fundamental non-performance'.

[165] Article 8.103 (previously Article 3.103) defines 'fundamental' non-performance. See paragraph 107 in Unidroit, *Study LXXII – Doc. 36 (1997)* 28.

[166] See Article 12(2) in Unidroit, *Study LXXII – Doc. 37 (1997).*

[167] Prior to the start of governmental consultations, the Australian government submitted comments requesting more guidance 'on what type of default would be regarded as "substantial"': see Unidroit, *Study LXXII – Doc. 44 (1998)* 3.

[168] Unidroit, *Unidroit CGE/Int.Int./3-WP/12 ICAO Ref. LSC/ME/3-WP/12 (2000)* 5.

criterion, this time not as replacement for the word 'substantial', but as a standalone trigger of the enforcement provisions.[169] As a result, throughout the years the term 'default', which first appeared without any clarification, was qualified by a whole array of various criteria in different combinations: (i) 'substantial or persistent'; (ii) 'material'; (iii) 'substantial'; and (iv) 'substantial or material'.

For reasons that are not evident from the documentary history alone, the Drafting Committee nonetheless did not incorporate the decision of the plenary into the draft submitted to the Cape Town Diplomatic Conference, which simply read: 'In the absence of such an agreement, "default" ... means a substantial default'.[170]

Overall, this omission did not change much, since without a corresponding definition the provision remained abstract and unclear in either case. This situation changed during the Cape Town Diplomatic Conference, when the African States presented a paper suggesting the first definition of 'substantial default':

> Substantial default means a default which deprives materially the non-defaulting party [of] the expected economic benefits it would obtain had performance been carried out by the defaulting party.[171]

This proposal not only defined the relevant term – it incorporated a measure for assessing the magnitude of breach, by reference to perceived economic benefits of the non-defaulting party.[172] In response, the Drafting Committee took a more conservative approach, adding a definition into the text, but essentially reproducing (in part) the already well-known formula of 'fundamental breach' used in the CISG.[173] The more ambitious proposals (default by the creditor or reference to the expected economic benefit) never appeared in the actual text of the Convention.

Interestingly, the final text of the CTC uses the same term to identify the trigger for the enforcement provisions ('default') that was used in the initial draft which included remedy rules.[174] Over the years, the text lost all the abstract qualifying criteria ('substantial', 'material' etc) and instead gained a more concrete definition.[175] The value of this definition is of course questionable (particularly given that the CTC is aimed at sophisticated parties) – yet it is an important step in guiding domestic courts enforcing the rule.

[169] See paragraphs 98 and 102 in Unidroit, *Unidroit CGE/Int.Int./3-Report ICAO Ref. LSC/ME/3-Report (2000)* 12–13.

[170] See Article 10(2) in Appendix I to Attachment C in ibid.

[171] See paragraph 3.4 in Unidroit, *Diplomatic Conference to Adopt a Mobile Equipment Convention and an Aircraft Protocol: Acts and Proceedings; [Convention on International Interests in Mobile Equipment and Protocol thereto on Matters Specific to Aircraft Equipment]* (UNIDROIT 2006) 169. The proposal by the African States went much further in attempting to reach the balance of interests of various parties and proposed a dedicated provision governing the consequences of a default committed by the *creditor*: see paragraph 3.2 in ibid.

[172] See ch 7 and section 7.2.2 specifically for the discussion relating to the role of economic benefit.

[173] cf Article 11(2) of the CTC and Article 25 of the CISG.

[174] cf Article 5 on Unidroit, *Study LXXII – Doc. 18 (1995)* 7.

[175] The word 'substantial' was deleted from the final text of Article 11(2).

6

Addressing Matters Affecting Third Parties: Key Considerations

6.1. Overview

Without substantive priority provisions in the text of the CTC, the creation of the autonomous concept of international interest discussed in section 2.3.2 would have achieved very little, except further complicating the existing national regimes by adding a new type of *in rem* interest on top of the existing types. The Convention priority rules eliminate this uncertainty by putting international interests ahead of their counterparts established by domestic law in terms of priority (with certain exceptions), provided that the perfection requirements (in the form of registration) have been complied with.

However, the priorities in the CTC do not stop at regulating the position of international interests vis-à-vis private property interests existing under national law. The abandonment of the concept of internationality (subject to declarations on internal transactions discussed in section 2.4.3) has effectively 'locked in' the industries affected by the relevant protocols,[1] essentially making registrations in the international registry mandatory even for purely domestic financings: an unregistered interest would lose priority to any registered interest, regardless of the time of its creation (except for pre-existing rights or interests under Article 60 of the CTC).[2]

Further extension of the scope of the priority system has resulted in the expansion of the list of registrable interests and introduction of various exceptions,[3] but the end result was worth the effort: the principal first-to-file rule found in Article 29(1)–(2) of the CTC is exceptionally strong and affects all types of interests, even those which are not registrable under the Convention.

This chapter examines the history of the twin facets of the Convention affecting third parties: the rules on priorities and the international registration system.

[1] The lock-in effect exists only where the relevant protocol is in force, and thus at the time of writing only applies to the aviation industry.

[2] See n 81 and the corresponding discussion.

[3] See paragraphs 2.212–2.224 in Goode, *Convention on International Interests in Mobile Equipment and Protocol thereto on Matters Specific to Aircraft Equipment: Official Commentary* (4th edn, International Institute for the Unification of Private Law (UNIDROIT) 2019) 124–30.

6.2. Development of the System of Priorities

At the early stages of the UNIDROIT project to develop a treaty on international interests in mobile equipment there was very limited international guidance in terms of structuring the system of priorities.

On the one hand, the Financial Leasing Convention, adopted just before the review of the Canadian Proposal by the UNIDROIT Governing Council in June 1988,[4] adopted a very cautious approach to priorities. First, its priority rules were limited to the recognition of the lessor's real rights against the lessee's trustee in bankruptcy.[5] Second, it did not attempt to regulate the priority position of any creditors having (i) liens or security interests in the leased equipment arising outside attachment or execution, or (ii) rights of arrest, detention or disposition over ships or aircraft.[6] Such a restrictive approach did not, however, reflect the original thinking of the study group working on that treaty, which had initially proposed a very simple and broad provision stating that '[the] lessor's title to the equipment shall be enforceable against *all third parties*' (subject to compliance with public notice requirements, if any).[7] This straightforward provision, which essentially incorporated the *nemo dat quod non habet* rule to protect the lessor in all dealings of the lessee with third parties, could not withstand the opposition of civil law jurisdictions (during the intergovernmental discussions), which utilised the principle *en fait de meubles possession vaut titre* protecting the innocent third party rather than dispossessed legal owner.[8]

On the other hand, existing asset-specific conventions included certain limited substantive priority provisions.[9] However, these priority rules mostly addressed the problem of liens ranking ahead of other security interests, and neither convention attempted to create a self-contained regime governing priorities.

Cuming's Questionnaire did not provide any conclusive guidance either. The majority of respondents (36) preferred a dedicated set of priority rules in the future convention on international interests in mobile equipment to deal with disputes involving not only secured parties, but also execution creditors and buyers. At the same time, 23 respondents opted for a hands-off approach, leaving all matters of priority to the applicable law.[10] Despite these mixed signals, the initial preference within the Study Group was to follow the majority view and regulate priority issues by including dedicated substantive provisions in the future Convention.[11]

[4] See n 1 in section 2.2.1.

[5] Article 7(1) of the Financial Leasing Convention.

[6] Article 7(5) of the Financial Leasing Convention.

[7] See Article 5 in Unidroit, *Study LIX – Doc. 16 (1984)* 2 (emphasis added).

[8] See paragraph 89 in Unidroit, *Study LIX – Doc. 48 (1987)* 49.

[9] See, eg, Articles IV(1), V, VII(4), VIII, X(3) of the 1948 Geneva Convention; Articles 3, 5, 6 of the 1926 Brussels Convention; Articles 5, 6 of the 1967 Brussels Convention; Article 6 and Chapter III of Protocol No. 1 Concerning Rights in rem in Inland Navigation Vessels to the 1965 Geneva Convention.

[10] Unidroit, *Study LXXII – Doc. 3 (1991)* 11.

[11] See paragraph 13 in Unidroit, *Study LXXII – Doc. 7 (1993)* 6.

This solution, however, had a limited reach, since it permitted co-existence of parallel systems of priorities.

6.2.1. Multiple Priorities Problem

The multiplicity of priority regimes stemmed from one of the early design choices to avoid the application of the future Convention in 'purely domestic situations'.[12] The difficulties in attempting to differentiate between domestic priorities, on the one hand, and their truly 'international' counterparts, on the other, surfaced very early.

The Study Group at its first session in March 1993 expressed 'significant support' for introducing two joint criteria necessary for the application of the future Convention's priority rules: (i) the relevant mobile equipment subject to a domestic or Convention security interest is taken from one state to another (the second state being a party to the Convention), and (ii) a competing interest in such equipment arises in the second state.[13] This solution gave the financier only limited control over its priority position, as the priority of any competing interests arising under the laws of the first state before the equipment is moved to a Convention state (or after the return of the equipment back to the first state) was determined by the laws of the first state, and not by the future Convention.[14] To test the application of the original solution, Cuming reviewed nine different hypothetical scenarios, where various interests were created (and the relevant equipment was located) in different states. In most cases the suggested priority system yielded satisfactory results, however the possibility of simultaneous application of more than one priority system (ie national and international) gave rise to the problem of circular priorities.

A circular priority could be created, for example, in a situation when the equipment was moved from State A to State B (a Convention state) and three security interests were created in the following order: first, in favour of Creditor 1 (when the equipment was still in State A), second, in favour of Creditor 2 (when the equipment was in State B), third, in favour of Creditor 3 (also when the equipment was in State B). To trigger a circular situation in this scenario, two additional assumptions were necessary: (i) Creditor 1 has failed to perfect its interest in accordance with the Convention (to trigger the application of its priority rules) before Creditor 2, and (ii) Creditor 2 has failed to perfect its interest in accordance with the laws of State B and, as a result, lost its priority to Creditor 3

[12] See paragraph 9 in ibid 5. Note, however, the existence of a minority view 'that even a domestic priority issue should be decided under the Convention once an international security interest had been created'.

[13] Unidroit, *Study LXXII – Doc. 8 (1993)* 20.

[14] In addition, obvious additional risks would arise in the case of moving the equipment to a non-Convention state, followed by the creation of competing interests in that state.

under those laws. In this scenario, Creditor 2 has priority over Creditor 1 (under the Convention), Creditor 1 has priority over Creditor 3 (under the Convention), but at the same time Creditor 3 has priority over Creditor 2 (under the laws of State B).[15]

A major change of thinking occurred in late 1994 during the second session of the First Draft Subcommittee, which considered the key characteristics of the future system of priorities. On the one hand, it confirmed the first-to-file principle based on registration in the international register and giving priority over 'all domestic security interests in the same equipment, whether filed on a national register or not and regardless of whether the national filing was first in time or not'.[16] On the other hand, it abandoned the idea of establishing a special priority regime for purely domestic situations, noting that a corresponding provision 'would complicate life enormously for the secured party'.[17] The subcommittee thus removed one source of multiplicity of priority rules (different priorities for domestic and international situations), but the next draft of the Convention soon added another one in the form of Article 12(4), which stated:

> An international interest is not valid against any third party who acquired an interest in the equipment under an agreement with the debtor, lessee or buyer at a time when the international interest was not registered.[18]

This exception made it possible for a third party to obtain priority over the holder of an international interest, and this priority could not be superseded by subsequent registration of the international interest. The First Draft Subcommittee later explained that to obtain such priority the interest of the third party had to be 'an interest other than an international interest'.[19] In other words, the above provision did not regulate priority conflicts among a registered and an unregistered international interest (for which there was a simple rule in Article 12(3) giving priority to the holder of the registered interest): it aimed to protect the third party (such as the holder of a non-consensual interest) who was not capable of safeguarding its priority position through registration.

The same draft created one more exception from the first-to-file rule: the holder of a first ranking registered international interest was subordinated to the holder of a second ranking interest in respect of advances made after notice of the existence of the second interest (except where such advances were mandatory).[20] This provision aimed to protect the junior creditors against new borrowings from the senior creditor.

[15] See footnote 10 in Unidroit, *Study LXXII - Doc. 8 (1993)* 27. In his circular priorities scenario Cuming assumed that priority disputes between holders of interests created in the same state (in this case – Creditors 2 and 3) were governed by domestic law, and not by the Convention.

[16] See paragraph 10(xxii) in Unidroit, *Study LXXII - Doc. 15 (1995)* 8.

[17] See paragraph 10(xxvi) in ibid 9.

[18] Unidroit, *Study LXXII - Doc. 18 (1995)* 9.

[19] See paragraph 34 in Unidroit, *Study LXXII - Doc. 21 (1995)* 12.

[20] See Article 12(2) in Unidroit, *Study LXXII - Doc. 18 (1995)* 9.

Each of these two exceptions created complications by itself: the former reduced the value of registration, both for the creditor and for any third parties, as it could not guarantee priority, while the latter raised the problem of determining whether or not the advance was made with knowledge of a second interest.[21] Taken together, they could lead to circular priorities in a situation when: (i) Creditor 1 registers its international interest first; (ii) an interest not registrable under the Convention in favour of Creditor 2 arises second; (iii) Creditor 3 registers its international interest third; and (iv) Creditor 1 makes an advance to the debtor with knowledge of subsequent interests and without an obligation to do so. In this situation, in respect of the latter advance, Creditor 1 has priority over Creditor 2 (as first in time under the first exception), Creditor 2 has priority over Creditor 3 (as first in time under the first exception), but Creditor 3 has priority over Creditor 1 (under the second exception).[22]

The complexity resulting from the use of the two exceptions outlined above generated opposition from various commentators, including the AWG,[23] and the priority rules were substantially simplified, first, by giving registered interests priority over any unregistered interests (including those that were not registrable under the Convention) and, second, by making references to actual knowledge or value given with such knowledge irrelevant in the context of priorities.[24] The resulting system of priorities emerged remarkably simple and straightforward, recognising the primacy of registration as the main source of priority. Nevertheless, the Convention could not get rid of all the provisions overriding this default approach. Such remaining provisions are rather limited, relate to preferred national creditors and are examined in section 6.2.2.

The establishment of a self-contained system of priorities excluding multiple overlapping priority regimes was particularly useful for the autonomous concept of international interest,[25] which was created by the Convention itself and coexisted with its national law counterparts (or existed regardless of their invalidity): any exclusions from a single comprehensive set of rules in the form of references to domestic priorities would inevitably require courts to attempt to integrate international interests into their national rules, presumably by way of finding the 'nearest equivalent' or using some other form of approximation. The solid basic priority rule now found in Article 29(1)–(2) mostly eschews the need to do so, although one hypothetical scenario (however unlikely it may seem in the context of sophisticated parties targeted by the CTC) may still prove somewhat puzzling, as it is not fully addressed by the Convention's priority regime: in a situation when

[21] The latter clearly follows from the later draft – see Article 19(1) in Unidroit, *Study LXXII – Doc. 22 (1996)* 7.

[22] See comments by Charles Mooney and Thomas Whalen in Unidroit, *Study LXXII – Doc. 32 Add. 3 (1997)* 7–8.

[23] See, eg, Unidroit, *Study LXXII – Doc. 32 Add. 2 (1997)* 13; Unidroit, *Study LXXII – Doc. 32 Add. 3 (1997)* 7–8; paragraph 164 in Unidroit, *Study LXXII – Doc. 36 (1997)* 39–40.

[24] See Article 25 in Unidroit, *International Interests Study Group 4th Session Misc. 5 (1997)* 9.

[25] See section 2.3.2.

two domestic security interests are validly constituted and compete for priority, but for some reason neither party to the underlying agreements has registered the relevant international interest (assuming that both international interests have arisen), there are, in fact, a total of four competing interests (two of which arise by virtue of applicable national law, while two others arise automatically under the CTC). In this scenario, it is too early for the Convention priorities to apply, since neither international interest has been registered (although the one to register first will automatically get priority over the other three), but too late in the sense that the international interests have already arisen under the Convention and cannot simply be disregarded.[26]

Despite the simplicity of the basic priority rule contained in Article 29(1)–(2) of the CTC, the Convention eventually developed a number of exceptions relating to proceeds (Article 29(6)), contractual subordination (Article 29(5)), prospective international interests (Article 19(4)), pre-existing interests (Article 60(1)), items that are not standalone objects covered by the protocols (Article 29(7)), survival of international interests in bankruptcy (Article 30(1)), non-consensual rights or interests (Articles 39 and 40), outright buyers, conditional buyers and lessees (Article 29(3)–(4)), assignment and subrogation (Articles 35–36 and 38) and even the ability of the debtor to trump its own creditor (which cannot be found in the text of the Convention and stems from the Official Commentary).[27] The following section 6.2.2 focuses on the exceptions from the basic rule which underwent the biggest transformation during the development of the Convention.[28]

6.2.2. Priority Position of Nationally Preferred Creditors

Early discussions about the prospects of regulating the priority position of preferred non-consensual creditors suggested a hands-off approach: at its second session in 1994, the First Draft Subcommittee concluded that the international interest 'would inevitably have to yield priority' to statutory liens in favour of preferential creditors.[29] The loss of priority of the international interest was not, however, the only problem, since it was recognised that state courts, if left to their

[26] Michel Deschamps suggests the existence of an 'implied' principle whereby after the start of a dispute a party may not improve its position by registering under the Convention: see Deschamps, 'The Perfection and Priority Rules of the Cape Town Convention and the Aircraft Protocol: A Comparative Law Analysis' (2013) 2 *Cape Town Convention Journal* 51, 58. This view, however, does not correspond to the straightforward first-to-file rule of Article 29(1)–(2) of the CTC and does not explain the interplay between all the four interests described in the example.

[27] See paragraph 2.221 in Goode, *Convention on International Interests in Mobile Equipment and Protocol thereto on Matters Specific to Aircraft Equipment: Official Commentary* (4th edn, International Institute for the Unification of Private Law (UNIDROIT) 2019) 128.

[28] For a detailed analysis of the priority provisions under the Convention as adopted see Roy Goode, 'The Priority Rules Under the Cape Town Convention and Protocols' (2012) 1 *Cape Town Convention Journal* 95.

[29] See paragraph 10(xxiii) in Unidroit, *Study LXXII – Doc. 15 (1995)* 8.

own devices, would be faced with the task of integrating this Convention-specific interest into their national legal systems in order to determine its priority relative to domestically preferred creditors. This task was further complicated by two problems. First, a number of jurisdictions did not recognise the concept of non-possessory security interests, title reservation and leasing in the first place, making it necessary for the Convention to spell out certain minimum legal characteristics of the international interest. Second, the national legal systems varied substantially in ranking various preferred creditors among themselves and in relation to security interests.[30]

The early involvement of the aviation industry challenged the hands-off approach, suggesting a more active role of the Convention in regulating the priority of preferred national creditors. The Boeing Company went quite far by suggesting that the first-to-file priority rule should cover, among other things, 'non-contractual security involving governmental creditors', such as EUROCONTROL (European Organisation for the Safety of Air Navigation) and tax creditors.[31] The AWG as a whole, however, considered five alternative approaches to the issue of regulating nationally preferred creditors: (i) a 'hard' rule in the Convention overriding domestic priorities; (ii) imposing a duty on states to declare all types of preferred creditors, but without an option to enlarge or modify the list; (iii) imposing an obligation to declare preferred creditors, but with a right to amend the list (amendments to take effect without retrospective effect); (iv) imposing a duty on states to declare the preferred creditors, also with the right to amend the list at any time, but without any consequence; and (v) a hands-off rule deferring the matter to local creditors.[32] The third option was viewed by the AWG as providing the best balance between state interests and the objective of increasing legal certainty for private parties.

Although the AWG proposal was limited to priority rules applicable in the context of aviation financing, the First Draft Subcommittee nevertheless recognised the utility[33] of this approach 'in respect of the generality of equipment to be covered by the proposed Convention', but only provided that it would not permit states to designate other consensual interests as having priority over the international interest.[34]

In its Draft Aviation Text prepared in 1996, the AWG took its original proposal one step forward, by bifurcating all interests held by the (initially) single category of nationally preferred creditors into two: 'preferred national interests' and 'registrable national interests'.[35] The former comprised national interests receiving automatic priority and existed outside the Convention registration system

[30] ibid.

[31] See Appendix to the comments by Scott Scherer in Unidroit, *Study LXXII – Doc. 14 Add 1 (1994).*

[32] Unidroit, *Study LXXII – Doc. 16 (1995)* 21–22.

[33] This was notwithstanding the view of certain commentators that such approach would be 'unworkable and very difficult to oversee and implement': see Unidroit, *Study LXXII – Doc. 17 (1995)* 7.

[34] Unidroit, *Study LXXII – Doc. 21 (1995)* 13.

[35] See paragraphs 26 and 33 in Annexure to Unidroit, *Study LXXII – Doc. 23 (1996).*

(insofar as they were designated as such by the relevant state), while the latter derived their priority from the act of registration, equally with international interests. The second kind of priority, according to the AWG draft, was provided to: (i) attachment or execution creditors; (ii) lien holders; (iii) persons acquiring a national interest by virtue of the application of national accession rules or through the installation of the property in question onto other types of property in which such person had an interest; and (iv) creditors having claims arising from non-payment of taxes, fees or similar governmental charges.[36]

The above separation of two types of interests held by preferred national creditors later formed the basis of Articles 39 and 40 of the CTC, although initially the interests enjoying automatic priority were part of the 'basic' priority rules,[37] while the registrable national interests formed a dedicated chapter.[38] This was soon changed by placing both groups of interests, first, in a separate single article[39] and, shortly afterwards, into two dedicated provisions.[40]

Interestingly, the two articles passed through the governmental expert stage and the Cape Town Diplomatic Conference differently: the proviso on registrable non-consensual rights or interests made it into the final text with minimal changes, whereas its counterpart giving 'super-priority' without registration generated debate. Most of the criticism related to the ability of states to designate national non-consensual interests and resulted in the gradual relaxation of the rule by way of (i) allowing state declarations to be formulated in broad terms,[41] and (ii) permitting state declarations to cover non-consensual interests created in the future.[42] Following an intervention of the UK delegation, states were given the ability to apply the 'super-priority' retrospectively, but only upon ratification (in order to protect the non-consensual rights and interests of states against international interests already entered on the register as a result of another state ratifying the Convention first).[43]

The final challenge to the provision during the Cape Town Diplomatic Conference was presented by EUROCONTROL, which intended to protect its ability to collect route charges on behalf of its member states. The difficulty stemmed from the fact that the charges in question, which were secured by a lien attaching to the aircraft, remained payable to EUROCONTROL itself (rather than

[36] See paragraph 33 in Annexure to ibid.

[37] See Article 26(4) in Unidroit, *Study LXXII - Doc. 30 (1996)* 19.

[38] See draft Chapter IX in ibid 21–22.

[39] See Article 35 in Unidroit, *Study LXXII - Doc. 35 (1997).*

[40] See Articles 39–40 in Unidroit, *Study LXXII - Doc. 42 (1998)* 15–16.

[41] See paragraph 89 in Unidroit, *Unidroit CGE/Int.Int./Report ICAO Ref. LSC/ME-Report (1999)* 13. Note the qualifying words 'generally or specifically' in Article 39(1) of the CTC, which are not present in Article 40.

[42] ibid. Cf Article 39(2) of the CTC.

[43] See proposal by the United Kingdom in Unidroit, *Diplomatic Conference to Adopt a Mobile Equipment Convention and an Aircraft Protocol: Acts and Proceedings; [Convention on International Interests in Mobile Equipment and Protocol thereto on Matters Specific to Aircraft Equipment]* (UNIDROIT 2006) 127. Cf Article 39(4) of the CTC.

its member states) – but EUROCONTROL, incapable of becoming a party to the Convention,[44] enjoyed no dedicated protection under the Convention's system of priorities applicable to non-consensual rights and interests.[45] Possible solutions considered by the delegates varied greatly, from allowing EUROCONTROL to become party to the Convention, to changing the mechanism of collecting route charges. Eventually, a dedicated working group was established to come up with a compromise solution. The resulting proposal was surprisingly short and essentially cosmetic in nature. First, it sought to amend the definition of 'non-consensual right or interest' by making express reference to obligations owed to 'an intergovernmental or private organization'. However, this did not really extend the scope of the definition in any way, since any mention of entities to which obligations may be owed was not more than a clarification, as is clear from the proposed text:

> 'Non-consensual right or interest' means a right or interest conferred under a declaring States's law to secure the performance of an obligation, including an obligation to a State, State entity or an intergovernmental or private organization.[46]

Second, the proposal envisaged a dedicated clarification to be added to the *travaux preparatoires* suggesting that states should include 'reasonable information' on the nature of the non-consensual interest, as well as nature of the obligation it may secure.

Interestingly, the final text of Article 39 goes beyond these very modest recommendations and incorporates one important addition in the form of Article 39(1)(b), which is broad enough to protect EUROCONTROL's enforcement rights (but only insofar as they are permitted under the laws of the relevant state making the declaration). Perhaps as a result of its last-minute nature, this provision has a number of clear drafting omissions.[47]

6.3. Development of the Registration System

The importance of a registration-based public notice system for a secured transactions regime is well articulated in the UNCITRAL Legislative Guide on Secured Transactions:

> The promotion of certainty and transparency of security rights in movable assets is a key objective of a modern secured transactions regime. Nothing is more central

[44] This right was reserved for states and Regional Economic Integration Organisations (see Article 48 of the CTC), and EUROCONTROL did not possess such status.

[45] See proposal by Belgium in Unidroit, *Diplomatic Conference to Adopt a Mobile Equipment Convention and an Aircraft Protocol: Acts and Proceedings; [Convention on International Interests in Mobile Equipment and Protocol thereto on Matters Specific to Aircraft Equipment]* (UNIDROIT 2006) 242–43.

[46] See proposal presented by South Africa in ibid 293.

[47] See paragraph 4.285 in Goode, *Convention on International Interests in Mobile Equipment and Protocol thereto on Matters Specific to Aircraft Equipment: Official Commentary* (4th edn, International Institute for the Unification of Private Law (UNIDROIT) 2019) 428.

to the realization of this goal than the establishment of a general, notice-based, registry system.[48]

The creation of an international asset-based system of registration has provided the key to the proper functioning of the priority rules established by the CTC and attracted significant attention among the commentators. One of the members of the UNIDROIT Governing Council characterised the creation of the international registration system as 'the single most important innovation of the … Convention'.[49] In a recent comparative study of the registry provisions of the first three protocols, the authors similarly identified the concept of international registry as the 'key creation' of the CTC.[50] Others have used the success of the Convention's registration system as a source of inspiration for an ambitious idea of an international registry of general application to record domestic security interests in respect of all movables – both tangible and intangible.[51]

This section tracks the key challenges underpinning the development of the registration provisions of the CTC.

6.3.1. Origins of the Registration System

The philosophy underpinning the registration system established by the CTC goes back to UNIDROIT's preceding project – the Financial Leasing Convention. The study group working on that treaty 'recognised the ultimate desirability of a system of registration as the most effective means of giving notice … to third parties', but considered the idea unrealistic at the time, noting, however, that in many countries registration was only considered feasible 'for large unit goods that were easily identifiable'.[52] The Canadian Proposal to adopt an international treaty on international interests in mobile equipment[53] soon provided an excellent opportunity to revisit the idea of setting up an international registration system.

The early vision of the future registration system was inspired by an outline of main features of the Canadian personal property registries prepared by Ronald Cuming in early 1993 for the attention of the Study Group at its first session. The experience in Canada included the establishment of fully computerised registries, searchable on a 24-hour basis without human involvement and allowing registration of short 'financing statements' (rather than entire agreements).[54] This practice

[48] United Nations, *UNCITRAL Legislative Guide on Secured Transactions (2010)* 149.

[49] Unidroit, *Study LXXII – Doc. 40 (1998)* 22.

[50] Rory McPhillips and others, 'Comparative Analysis of Aircraft, Rail and Space International Registries and Their Regulatory Provisions' (2016) 5 *Cape Town Convention Journal* 29.

[51] Charles W Mooney, 'Cape Town Convention's Improbable-but-Possible Progeny Part One: An International Secured Transactions Registry of General Application, The Essay' (2014) 55 *Va J Int'l L* 163, 174–75.

[52] See paragraph 87 in Unidroit, *Study LIX – Doc. 48 (1987)* 48.

[53] See n 1 in section 2.2.1.

[54] Unidroit, *Security Interests Study Group 1st Session Misc. 5 (1993)* 7.

was used by Cuming to prepare the first outline of the future registry system to be established under the Convention.[55]

Despite the evidence and the proposal submitted by Ronald Cuming, sessions of the First Draft Subcommittee produced more questions than answers. First, the registration system was initially envisaged as 'being primarily against the debtor', while registration against the asset was considered merely a possibility.[56] However, soon the position was reversed: an asset-based register became the preferred option, but a separate register of interests registrable against the debtor was considered a valid addition, particularly for those assets which did not lend themselves to identification.[57] Second, there was no agreement on the consequences of failure to register.[58] Third, no clear consensus existed on the effects of registration and the possibility of triggering the Convention provisions if no interest was registered in the registry.[59] In addition, the relationship between registration and constitution of an international interest changed from draft to draft: the initial logic that an international interest is *created* by registration[60] was replaced by a new approach whereby registration merely perfects an already existing international interest.[61]

Overall, the discussion did not move beyond the basic features of the future registration system due to insufficient expert knowledge on the matter, and the decision was made to convene a corresponding group of technical experts to consider both the legal and technical aspects of the registry.[62] This marked the first primary challenge in the whole process of development of the registration provisions: the very technical nature of the problem and reliance on expert submissions. Registration working groups were later formed at various stages of the development of the Convention: during the work of the Study Group[63] and during the governmental expert stage.[64] Following the adoption of the CTC and the relevant protocols, the work on the establishment of asset-specific registries continued in dedicated preparatory commissions.[65]

[55] See section V in Unidroit, *Study LXXII - Doc. 8 (1993)*.

[56] See paragraph 6(xi) in Unidroit, *Study LXXII - Doc. 12 (1994)* 5.

[57] See paragraph 10(ii) in Unidroit, *Study LXXII - Doc. 15 (1995)* 3–4; see also Article 5(3) in Unidroit, *Study LXXII - Doc. 22 (1996)* 3.

[58] See paragraph 6(xix) in Unidroit, *Study LXXII - Doc. 12 (1994)* 6.

[59] See paragraph 10(i) in Unidroit, *Study LXXII - Doc. 15 (1995)* 3.

[60] See Article 2(c) in Unidroit, *Study LXXII - Doc. 13 (1994)* 2; paragraph 10(xxii) in Unidroit, *Study LXXII - Doc. 15 (1995)* 8.

[61] See paragraph 10 in Unidroit, *Study LXXII - Doc. 18 (1995)* 3.

[62] See paragraph 39 in Unidroit, *Study LXXII - Doc. 21 (1995)* 13.

[63] The sessions were held in April 1996 and May 1997: see Unidroit, *Study LXXIIC - Doc. 2 (1997)*; Unidroit, *Study LXXIIC - Doc. 3 (1997)*.

[64] See paragraph 14 in Unidroit, *Unidroit CGE/Int.Int./Report ICAO Ref. LSC/ME-Report (1999)*; Attachment D in Unidroit, *ICAO Ref. LSC/ME/2-Report Unidroit CGE/Int.Int./2-Report (1999)*.

[65] The work of the preparatory commission established by Resolution No 2 of the Cape Town Diplomatic Conference resulted in the establishment of the Aircraft Registry, which commenced its operation on 1 March 2006. The work of the rail preparatory commission established by Resolution No 1 of the Luxembourg Diplomatic Conference in 2007 led to the appointment of the Registrar – Regulis SA in November 2014 (although the rail registry itself is not yet in operation). The space preparatory commission established by Resolution No 1 of the Berlin Diplomatic Conference is still in the early stages of its work and has so far obtained a preliminary agreement from the ITU to become

The second challenge revolved around choosing between asset and debtor-based mechanisms. The transition to the present, purely asset-based, system, happened quite late. In April 1996, the Study Group at its second session still considered the possibility of registration against the name of the debtor 'for the limited purpose of preserving the validity of the international interest against the trustee in bankruptcy and judgment creditors of the chargor, buyer and lessee'.[66] The final decision was left until a later time, pending feedback from the special registration working group. The latter expressed overall preference towards eliminating the debtor-based element due to a technical reason: such registration was likely to cause difficulties with recording all names in different alphabets (a problem that is non-existent in the case of serial numbers).[67] In response, the Drafting Group deleted all references to the registration against the debtor from the draft Convention.[68]

The third challenge of the process of development of the registration system stemmed from the need to correspond to the system of priorities, which was gradually expanding its scope, eventually turning into a single self-contained regime.[69] As a result, the registration system, initially established solely for the registration of national interests[70] (and later – international interests),[71] subsequently accommodated registrations of assignments and subordinations,[72] prospective international interests, prospective assignments and registrable non-consensual interests[73] and acquisitions of international interests by subrogation.[74] Following extensive debate at the Third Joint Session relating to the feasibility of extending the scope of the Convention to 'purely internal transactions',[75] the registration system was used to protect the priority position of those financiers who could not register an international interest as a result of a declaration on internal transactions adopted by their home state (by allowing such financiers to register notices of national interests and treating them as 'registered interests' giving priority).[76]

the Supervisory Authority, but more work is required before the Registrar can be appointed and the space registry begins its operation: see Unidroit, *Unidroit 2015 Prep. Comm. Space/4/Doc. 7 rev. (2015)* 8. The adoption of the MAC Protocol was also followed by the establishment of a dedicated preparatory commission (pursuant to Resolution No 1 of the Pretoria Diplomatic Conference in 2019) – although at the time of writing the work of the commission (which only had its first session on 21–22 May 2020) was still in the early stages.

[66] See paragraph 39 in Unidroit, *Study LXXII – Doc. 27 (1996)* 20.

[67] Unidroit, *Study LXXIIC – Doc. 2 (1997)* 8.

[68] See Article 17(2) in Unidroit, *Study LXXII – Doc. 30 (1996)* 15.

[69] See section 6.2.1.

[70] See Articles 2(1), 1(2)(b)–(c) in Unidroit, *Study LXXII – Doc. 13 (1994)* 1–2.

[71] See Article 2(1) in Unidroit, *Study LXXII – Doc. 18 (1995)* 6; Article 5(1) in Unidroit, *Study LXXII – Doc. 22 (1996)* 3.

[72] See Articles 16(1) and 17(4) in Unidroit, *Study LXXII – Doc. 30 (1996)* 14–15.

[73] See Article 15(1)(a) in Unidroit, *Study LXXII – Doc. 35 (1997)*.

[74] See Article 15(1)(c) in Appendix I to Attachment C in Unidroit, *Unidroit CGE/Int.Int./3-Report ICAO Ref. LSC/ME/3-Report (2000)*.

[75] See section 2.4.3.

[76] See Article 1(cc) of the CTC. This provision was further strengthened by Article 1(n) of the CTC, which requires the establishment of national machinery for the transmission of notices to the international registry.

The Aircraft Protocol and the Space Protocol further enhanced the scope of the registration system by making it possible to register sales.[77] Contrary to this example, the Rail Protocol[78] and the MAC Protocol[79] do not permit registration of sales as such, but nevertheless make it possible to register notices of sale. This turns the international registry into a conduit through which parties may attempt to secure priority under national law, although the effects of such registrations will eventually depend on the applicable law rules on giving notice.[80]

The history of development of Article 60 of the CTC provides another example of the broad scope of the registration mechanics established by the Convention. This provision regulates the application of the treaty to 'pre-existing rights or interests', ie rights or interests that emerged before the effective date of the CTC,[81] and seeks to prevent the loss of priority by creditors who obtained their rights in the collateral prior to the entry into force of the Convention. In pursuit of this objective, the delegates of the Cape Town Diplomatic Conference were choosing between two alternatives, the first of which was very simple:

> This Convention does not apply to a pre-existing right or interest, which shall retain the priority it enjoyed before this Convention entered into force.[82]

This straightforward provision quickly gained the support of most delegations, including the United Kingdom, Switzerland, the United States, Sweden, Australia and Argentina.[83] The overwhelming support of this option was, however, countered by the South African delegation speaking on behalf of African States in favour of the second alternative, which envisaged an important change.[84] In contrast to the above simple provision, which provided for essentially infinite protection of pre-existing rights or interests, the second option gave financiers only a limited amount of time (provisionally ten years) to register their existing rights or interests in the international registry. Upon such registration, the priority position of such rights and interests would be the same as prior to the entry into force of the Convention, but failure to register in time would subject the financiers to the standard priority rules of the treaty, with the inevitable result of being subordinated (as unregistered interests) to any registered interests.[85]

[77] See Article III of the Aircraft Protocol; Article IV of the Space Protocol.

[78] See Article XVII of the Rail Protocol.

[79] See Article XX of the MAC Protocol.

[80] See paragraph 5.70 in Goode, *Convention on International Interests in Mobile Equipment and Luxembourg Protocol thereto on Matters Specific to Railway Rolling Stock: Official Commentary* (2nd edn, International Institute for the Unification of Private Law (UNIDROIT) 2014) 437.

[81] See Article 1(v) of the CTC.

[82] See Article 55 (Alternative A) in Unidroit, *Diplomatic Conference to Adopt a Mobile Equipment Convention and an Aircraft Protocol: Acts and Proceedings; [Convention on International Interests in Mobile Equipment and Protocol thereto on Matters Specific to Aircraft Equipment]* (UNIDROIT 2006) 25.

[83] ibid 794.

[84] ibid 794–95.

[85] See Article 55 (Alternative B) in ibid 55.

The South African approach, supported by Ghana and Pakistan,[86] attempted to significantly strengthen the role of the international registration system by ensuring that following a set number of years the records of the registry would become conclusive and not subject to any 'hidden' unrecorded priorities of pre-existing transactions. In his recollection of this debate, Charles Mooney notes that the primary reasoning of the dissenting states 'was based on perceived inadequacies of their existing domestic registries' and their resulting interest in allowing pre-existing transactions to 'migrate' to the international registry. On Mooney's account, it was not the modern regime of secured transactions – but rather the international *registration system* itself – that made the CTC so attractive to such developing states.[87] As a result, the final text of Article 60(3) (or, rather, its history) is a fine illustration of the perceived benefits of the registration system going beyond the simple recordation of competing interests.

6.3.2. Structure of the Registration System

The CTC created the first ever international system of registration of security interests. In the absence of existing international precedent,[88] the development of the most appropriate registration machinery was a particularly difficult task.

The early design choices relating to the structure of the international registration system established by the CTC go back to the work of the First Draft Subcommittee, which reflected a rather simplistic view that such a system would operate under the general oversight of the UNIDROIT Governing Council – the latter to have the authority to appoint and replace the relevant body administering the register. The administering body was to be given powers to adopt additional regulations supplementing the rules of the Convention.[89]

This approach was reflected in one of the earlier drafts[90] and further revised by the AWG, which proposed to add an intermediate level between the Governing Council and the operator, labelled the 'supervisory body' and possessing expert knowledge in the relevant area of asset finance practice and technical matters. The role of the supervisory body was to promulgate initial and ongoing rules and regulations implementing the future Convention. Registration would only be possible through 'satellite registrars' designated by each contracting state upon ratification to transmit the registration details to the central registrar.[91] The latter proposal was

[86] ibid 795.

[87] Charles W Mooney, 'Cape Town Convention's Improbable-but-Possible Progeny Part One: An International Secured Transactions Registry of General Application, The Essay' (2014) 55 *Va J Int'l L* 163, 169.

[88] Other existing registration systems relating to security interests (whether general, as in the case of the Canadian personal property registries, or asset specific, such as registries for the registration of rights in aircraft) operated on a domestic level.

[89] See paragraph 10(vii) in Unidroit, *Study LXXII – Doc. 15 (1995)* 5.

[90] See Article 5(2) in Unidroit, *Study LXXII – Doc. 22 (1996).*

[91] Unidroit, *Study LXXII – Doc. 23 (1996)* 15.

subsequently relaxed by the AWG and IATA, which agreed to make registration through satellite registries optional, rather than mandatory.[92] On the one hand, this decision would permit all states to take advantage of the registration system, regardless of existing technical infrastructure. On the other hand, direct filings would require an international registry operating on a 24-hour basis to accommodate time zone differences. In the context of aviation industry, the transition to direct registrations circumventing the national aircraft registries would essentially result in a bifurcation of registration functions, with the domestic registries handling matters of safety and operation and the central registry recording private property rights.[93]

1997 saw a fundamental change in the approach to the design of the future Convention and, with it, the establishment of the APG to prepare the draft aviation protocol.[94] Both the special registration working group and the APG were considering the question of the most appropriate structure of the future registration system and came up with different results.

In May 1997, the special registration working group completed its work at its second session and prepared its recommendations on the structure of the registration system. It favoured a binary system whereby each protocol would establish an intergovernmental organisation to act as the 'Intergovernmental Regulator' overseeing the operation of the international registry. The registry itself was to be operated by a separate entity, the 'Registrar', which was independent from the Intergovernmental Regulator. An international organisation in the role of the Intergovernmental Regulator was deemed essential (though potentially problematic for certain categories of equipment) to 'establish the international credibility' of the registry and gain the confidence of the relevant industry.[95]

In October 1997, the APG presented its own version of the registration provisions specific to the draft Aircraft Protocol. The principal changes from the registration working group proposal related not just to the level of specificity of the protocol provisions (reflected, for example, in the provisional designation of an affiliate of IATA as the operator of the registry), but to the overall approach to the registration structure. In addition to the binary scheme, it proposed an alternative, whereby the international registry was operated by the 'International Registry Authority'.[96] In the latter scenario, the APG explained, an intergovernmental entity would both operate and regulate the registry at the same time.[97]

As a result of the added flexibility provided by the APG text, the draft Convention and the draft Aircraft Protocol reached the governmental stage reflecting different approaches: the former followed the logic of the registration

[92] Unidroit, *Study LXXII – Doc. 32 Add. 2 (1997)* 6.
[93] ibid 7.
[94] See section 4.3 and n 45 specifically.
[95] See paragraph 16(v) in Unidroit, *Study LXXIIC – Doc. 3 (1997)* 8.
[96] See draft Article XVIII (Alternative A) in Unidroit, *Study LXXII – Doc. 36 Add. 3 (1997).*
[97] See paragraph 29 in ibid vii.

working group, and the latter reflected the vision of the APG. The two instruments were ultimately reconciled in the report of the Registration Working Group of the Second Joint Session, which agreed to separate the roles of the Registrar and the Intergovernmental Regulator (this time renamed to 'Supervisory Authority').[98] At the same time, as regards the procedure for appointment of the Supervisory Authority, the working group proposed three different alternatives: (i) to specify in the protocol the international organisation appointing or constituting it; (ii) to designate in the protocol the international organisation responsible for the appointment and substitution of its members; or (iii) to provide for the appointment of the Supervisory Authority by the contracting states after the entry into force of the Convention.[99] In the absence of definitive guidance from the governmental experts, the Drafting Committee opted for the first alternative ('The Supervisory Authority shall be …')[100] and the matter was eventually left for the Cape Town Diplomatic Conference, which ultimately invited ICAO to act as the Supervisory Authority under the Aircraft Protocol.[101]

The choice of ICAO was a simple one, given its authority in international aviation practice and the fact that most countries of the world are ICAO members. The nomination of the Supervisory Authority under the Space Protocol followed the same pattern, as the ITU (also practically a universal international organisation) was invited to perform the function right at the conclusion of the Berlin Diplomatic Conference.[102] The situation with the Rail Protocol was quite different due to the limited membership of OTIF (essentially European, with several member states in North Africa and Near East), the only candidate intergovernmental organisation considered for the role. Reliance on OTIF as Supervisory Authority was considered problematic from the point of view of states outside its membership, and an entirely different mechanism for the appointment of the Supervisory Authority was established to make it possible for all the contracting states to have confidence in this body.[103] As a result, the Supervisory Authority under the Rail Protocol is a collegial body consisting of representatives of state parties, states designated by UNIDROIT and states designated by OTIF.[104]

The most recent challenge in terms of selecting the Supervisory Authority surfaced in March 2017, during the first session of the MAC Protocol Committee of Governmental Experts. In contrast to the other protocols, the MAC Protocol covers a diverse group of assets,[105] which makes it particularly difficult to

[98] See paragraph 13 in Attachment D to Unidroit, *ICAO Ref. LSC/ME/2-Report Unidroit CGE/Int. Int./2-Report (1999).*

[99] See Article C in Appendix II of Attachment D to ibid.

[100] See paragraph 207 and Article XVI(1) in Appendix II of Attachment C to Unidroit, *Unidroit CGE/Int.Int./3-Report ICAO Ref. LSC/ME/3-Report (2000).*

[101] See Resolution No 2 of the Cape Town Diplomatic Conference.

[102] See Resolution No 2 of the Berlin Diplomatic Conference.

[103] Unidroit, *Study LXXIIH – Doc. 13 (2003)* 15–16.

[104] See Article XII of the Rail Protocol.

[105] See section 3.5.

identify a single existing international organisation for the role of the Supervisory Authority. Nevertheless at the conclusion of the Pretoria Diplomatic Conference the International Finance Corporation (IFC) of the World Bank Group was invited to accept the functions of the Supervisory Authority.[106] The IFC was initially given six months to make a decision, however this term was subsequently extended due to the state of emergency declared due to the COVID-19 pandemic in the United States, the seat of the IFC. At the time of writing, the role of the Supervisory Authority under the MAC Protocol remained vacant, although the urgency of this matter prompted the preparatory commission to go back to considering the alternative candidates discussed during the 2019 Diplomatic Conference, such as the OECD and UNIDROIT itself.[107]

[106] Resolution No 2 of the Pretoria Diplomatic Conference.
[107] Unidroit, *Unidroit 2020 MACPC/1/Doc. 9 rev. (2020)* 7–8.

7

Measuring the Feasibility of the Convention: Commercial Concerns and State Sensitivities

7.1. Overview

This is the first out of two chapters (alongside chapter eight) that do not focus on the genesis of certain key provisions of the Cape Town Convention but analyse the challenges associated with the entire process of development of the CTC. It examines how the feasibility of the Cape Town Convention was assessed during the development process by looking at two groups of factors: commercial concerns and various state sensitivities.

First, it argues that commercial factors were dominant in assessing the viability of the CTC but shows that the first attempt to quantify the economic benefits of the CTC appeared almost ten years after the start of the project. Before that, any attempts to provide some kind of commercial justification to the draft treaty remained abstract and based on qualitative, rather than quantitative, criteria.

Second, this chapter demonstrates that, despite being a commercial law treaty, the Cape Town Convention was greatly influenced by state sensitivities that reduced its overall reach and impact. It shows that one of the key obstacles to the promotion of commercial objectives in the CTC was the notion of sovereignty: the perception of governments as to what can or cannot be realistically regulated in an international treaty significantly changed the scope of many provisions of the Convention and its protocols (such as the decision to abandon a functional approach to security interests, the last-minute overhaul of the whole system of assignment under the CTC during the Diplomatic Conference in 2001, or the sophisticated system of declarations). Other relevant challenges included the need to achieve an adequate balance of interests between parties and the public service exemption (both of which restrict the authority of the creditor during enforcement), as well as more elaborate factors, such as 'treaty fashion' (ie reliance on the current trends in international treaty-making to determine whether a proposed change constitutes an unacceptable departure from the status quo).

7.2. The Role of Commercial Factors in the Development of the CTC

How does one assess ex ante whether a proposed international convention is actually worth the effort? Without some form of economic analysis showing how the new instrument could enhance the position of various stakeholders or otherwise improve the existing regime, a draft treaty may lack the support of states, international organisations and domestic end users. In a commercial law context, the role of such analysis increases significantly: in the words of Herbert Kronke, former Secretary-General of UNIDROIT, the only working criterion to determine the success of a treaty is whether it 'reduces costs and enhances benefits in a given area of transnational commercial transactions'.[1] Once this is accepted, the opening question in this paragraph can be superseded by a different one: how does one measure the economic benefit of a proposed treaty?

The first attempt to quantify the economic benefits of the CTC appeared only in 1998, ie almost ten years after the start of the project. Before that, any attempts to provide some kind of commercial justification to the Convention remained abstract and based on qualitative, rather than quantitative, criteria. At the core of these attempts lay the 'twin' factors of certainty and predictability.[2]

7.2.1. Certainty/Predictability and its Role in the Development of the CTC

Two distinct characteristics of certainty and predictability are relevant for the purposes of this section in the context of transnational commercial law. On the one hand, greater certainty does not automatically translate into economic benefit. By way of example, an international convention might result in the adoption of a uniform, but wholly inappropriate connecting factor to a particular type of transaction: the resulting harmonisation would enhance certainty and may somewhat reduce the need for ex ante legal research – but is unlikely to lead to any meaningful cost savings. On the other hand, predictability carries with it *ipso facto* a subjective element: the need to take into account the particular actors for whom the new instrument is intended. In a sense, it implies a certain bond with the recipients of the new rules, a factor of paramount importance in commercial law. In the field of mobile equipment financing the principal recipients are, essentially, creditors

[1] Herbert Kronke, 'International Uniform Commercial Law Conventions: Advantages, Disadvantages, Criteria for Choice' (2000) 5 *Uniform Law Review* 13, 16.

[2] In this book, these two concepts are used interchangeably, in the same manner as they are treated (and labelled 'twin factors') in the 1998 UNIDROIT Report of the SRC: see paragraph 44 in Unidroit, *Study LXXII – Doc. 41 (1998)* 16.

who provide financing protected by security interests created over mobile assets. These creditors operate within a system that monetises risks: whenever the timely return of a loan and payment of respective interest cannot be guaranteed, the potential risk factors are analysed to assess the likelihood of being repaid and, depending on the severity of the risks involved, the cost of financing grows proportionately. This system is pragmatic at its core and is indifferent to achievements of harmonisation insofar as they do not make the return of the creditors' investment more likely, or rather, more commercially predictable.

As was noted in chapter two, at the very early stages of development of the Convention the key challenge was to solve the problem of different connecting factors used by states to determine the law applicable to security interests created over mobile assets.[3] Unification of conflict of laws rules could no doubt provide some increased predictability for commercial parties, but its scope would remain limited to ensuring that various courts apply the *same rules* in order to identify the national legal system governing a particular relationship, translating into equally limited cost reduction for end users.

Later developments showed that the degree of legal certainty generated by conflict of laws unification depended not only on the adoption of a uniform connecting factor, but also on the degree of deference to applicable law. In 1995, the AWG proposed to the Study Group to include in the draft Convention an optional provision requiring those states which elect to apply it to respect the choice of applicable law made by the parties to a transaction without any condition or qualification whatsoever.[4] This approach, in the view of the AWG, would 'give international financiers and lessors the benefit of the certainty and predictability … through the application of well-developed and commercially recognized laws'.[5] On top of that, 'the need for commercial certainty and predictability … [were] sufficient reasons in and of themselves for selecting law which is otherwise wholly unrelated to the parties and the transaction'.[6]

This proposal by the AWG was later criticised by Giuseppe Guerreri of the International Law Association as making possible the creation of a parallel system of rules which may conflict with the uniform rules envisaged in the draft Convention.[7] In his comments, Guerreri stressed that a wholly permissive approach to the choice of law 'would … impair the general applicability of the Convention and its importance as uniform international law'.[8] This observation is particularly important for the purposes of this section, since it demonstrates

[3] See section 2.2.1.
[4] Unidroit, *Study LXXII – Doc. 16 (1995)* 24.
[5] ibid 25.
[6] ibid 26. See also footnote 52 in ibid for a list of other concerns and objections to an unqualified recognition of the law chosen by the parties to a transaction.
[7] The criticism was expressed in Mr Guerreri's personal capacity.
[8] Unidroit, *Study LXXII – Doc. 17 Add. 3 (1995).*

how the aims of commercial certainty and unification of law may differ and even contradict each other.

The position of the aviation industry, represented by the AWG, reflected a most pragmatic approach: while unification of laws in the area of secured transactions would be helpful, the desired level of legal certainty could be achieved more realistically through the ability to choose the laws of a creditor-friendly jurisdiction, provided that this choice of law was not qualified by any conditions other than the agreement of the parties. The pragmatism of this approach is easier to appreciate assuming that a wholesale unification of the law of secured transactions laws is not realistic: in this scenario, the unqualified recognition of the law of a well-known and respected chosen jurisdiction is indeed an acceptable compromise that provides essentially the same amount of legal certainty. From a financier's standpoint, such alternative might even seem *more* attractive compared to actual unification, since it promotes regulatory competition among states.

The demand for certainty on a deeper, substantive level, surfaced very early: in 1989 Ronald Cuming acknowledged the need to ensure recognition of security interests created under the laws of other jurisdictions[9] and later the Study Group opted for the creation of the new concept of 'international interest'[10] and an international system of priorities overriding the domestic regime.[11] These developments aimed to achieve predictability of applicable rules themselves, rather than the ways to identify them. In the terms of legal risk assessment, the benefits of this approach are clear: as long as the respective substantive law provisions are not harmonised on a universal level, a proper risk assessment may involve the analysis of dozens of legal systems – a scenario so improbable that it hardly justifies further consideration. The cost of obtaining legal advice (both in terms of money, time spent and logistics) with respect to multiple legal systems is generally high enough to justify taking a shorter and easier route: the risks involved are translated into additional cost of financing and transferred to the debtor. The result is generally a lose-lose situation, in which the creditor has no efficient means of ascertaining the contents of the rules to be applied by a court in case of a potential dispute, and the debtor is often charged disproportionate interest to compensate for such lack of assurance. Accordingly, the amount of resources required to achieve this level of commercial predictability is inversely proportional to the level of substantive law harmonisation in the field of security interests in mobile equipment. Conflict of laws unification is incapable of achieving this degree of predictability simply because it cannot exclude the need to analyse the laws of different states.

[9] See section 2.2.2.
[10] See section 2.3.
[11] See section 6.2.

A key to understanding the specific nature of substantive level predictability in the Convention lies in the mechanics underlying the notion of 'international interest'. When this concept became autonomous, ie detached from the national legal systems, the CTC effectively started building a parallel system of regulation coexisting with domestic laws and the property interests created under such laws.[12] In effect, despite the increased predictability, there was minimal actual unification of the national legal regimes: the Convention is built around the functional approach to security, but applies it to the concept of international interests rather than their domestic law counterparts. As a result, states are able to maintain any national distinctions between the different types of agreements covered by the Convention (the domestic characterisation is acknowledged in Article 2(4) of the CTC) and are free to regulate them independently: there is no pressure to unify. If international interests are not registered, the national regimes will continue to apply: the relevant parties will still be able to utilise the Convention remedies (as these do not depend on registration), but the CTC priorities will be rendered ineffective until a registration occurs. As a result, the international regime established by the Convention achieves greater predictability not by harmonising the domestic security regimes as such (except setting a number of minimum remedies), but by creating very strong incentives to make use of the international regime (via the system of priorities).

It is true, at the same time, that the concept of international interest itself generated a degree of confusion even within the UNIDROIT Study Group,[13] which acknowledged 'the need to minimise the degree of uncertainty that would inevitably flow from the creation of the new autonomous interest'[14] and decided against the inclusion in the text of the draft Convention of a list of factors which cannot invalidate an international interest. Such a list was initially proposed by the AWG in Article 5(2)(a)–(d) of the Draft Aviation Text essentially for illustrative purposes and contained a number of criteria that could not affect the existence or validity of the international interest: (i) recognition of the form of the interest in a contracting state; (ii) additional actions or formalities required by domestic laws; (iii) application of otherwise applicable conflict of laws rules of a contracting state to determine the validity of the interest; and (iv) other grounds existing under national law (except in relation to the capacity to enter into a corresponding agreement) that might result in invalidation or non-recognition of such interest.[15]

[12] The level of detachment of this parallel system from domestic laws is not absolute, however, as a number of matters are left to be decided by the applicable law: see paragraphs 2.72–2.74 in Goode, *Convention on International Interests in Mobile Equipment and Protocol thereto on Matters Specific to Aircraft Equipment: Official Commentary* (4th edn, International Institute for the Unification of Private Law (UNIDROIT) 2019) 55–58.

[13] See, eg, n 120 in section 2.3.2 and the corresponding discussion relating to the misconception in the commentary of some members of the Study Group in Unidroit, *Study LXXII – Doc. 26 Add. 1 (1996)*.

[14] Unidroit, *Study LXXII – Doc. 27 (1996)* 21–22.

[15] See Article 5 of the Draft Aviation Text in Annex 1 to Unidroit, *Study LXXII – Doc. 23 (1996)*.

Despite the general preference towards achieving greater predictability by including these 'potentially invalidating factors', the Study Group expressed concern that the list could be missing other similar factors and thus be *non-exhaustive* – and, as a result, any court interpreting the relevant provision might reason 'that, such other potentially invalidating factors not having been specifically referred to, they were not intended to be covered'.[16] Eventually, the Study Group agreed that corresponding clarifications relating to the various 'potentially invalidating factors' could be included in the explanatory report or commentary to the future Convention.[17]

The involvement of business circles in the project highlighted another important dimension of the twin concepts of certainty and predictability: they can be effectively increased in a commercial treaty even regardless of *any* change of the rules governing a particular legal relationship, whether on a domestic or an international level. It will be recalled from section 6.2.2 that, in its memorandum submitted to the Study Group in 1995, the AWG came up with five alternative options of regulating the priority position of nationally preferred creditors (ie categories of creditors who, as a result of their importance for the national legal system, should be allowed to retain priority regardless of the time of registration of the international interest), ranging from the most intrusive into the area of national laws (namely a complete override of domestic priority rules) to the least intrusive one (in the form of deference to the priority position under the domestic law).[18] In its commentary, the AWG explained that, in its view, the draft Convention 'should embody a system in which maximum information is provided to financiers and lessors in order for them to calculate legal risks and appropriately price such risks in transactions'.[19]

In other words, greater certainty could be achieved not only via changes to the rules applicable to a particular category of secured transactions, but also through transparency-enhancing mechanisms, such as an obligation on contracting states to disclose the list of national creditors having priority over the holders of an international interest. Although the AWG clearly favoured a more intrusive option where any subsequent change to the list of such preferred creditors would have no retrospective effect (thus protecting the priority position of financiers against changes in the law), it also envisaged an alternative whereby countries would only be required to record nationally preferred creditors, but 'their ability to do so would be without consequence'.[20] The latter option, it was noted, would not affect priorities in any way, but 'it might reduce uncertainty and transaction/litigation costs'.[21] Concerns about the freedom of states to determine the priority position of their preferred national lien creditors, on the one hand, and reservations about the

[16] Unidroit, *Study LXXII – Doc. 27 (1996)* 21.
[17] ibid 22.
[18] See n 32 in section 6.2.2.
[19] Unidroit, *Study LXXII – Doc. 16 (1995)* 22.
[20] ibid.
[21] ibid.

feasibility of requesting states to give public notice of domestic creditors granted preferential status,[22] on the other, later resulted in the introduction of two separate categories of non-consensual preferred creditors in the CTC,[23] now found in Articles 39 and 40 of the Convention.

Other examples of enhanced certainty in the CTC on a substantive level cover various criteria for determining the applicability of the Convention. First, one should note the abandonment of idea of 'internationality':[24] in the view of the AWG, 'aircraft are simply too mobile, aircraft financings are too complex, and the need for commercial certainty and predictability is too great, to condition the applicability of the proposed convention on factual predicates of this kind'.[25] Second, the Study Group opted for a closed list of asset types covered by the CTC to make it clear for third parties when the Convention applies: the alternative approach, it was felt, would 'sacrifice an essential element of legal certainty'.[26] Third, during discussions concerning the feasibility of treating 'true leases' separately for the purposes of the draft Convention,[27] the AWG expressed a strong view that all leases should be covered by the new treaty, noting the need to 'avoid complex characterisation issues that could only end up creating more uncertainty regarding the Convention's applicability'.[28]

Overall, it was the need for greater certainty – not unification as such – that formed the main driving force behind the development of the CTC.[29] Many other considerations were affected by this overarching objective, directly or indirectly. By way of example, the need for greater certainty was only one of the objectives pursued by the aviation industry through the work of the AWG, which summarised its position by stating in its second memorandum to the Study Group in 1996 that the rules of the future Convention 'must, *in addition to providing certainty*, ensure that the basic commercially oriented, and contractually agreed, rights of asset-based financiers and lessor are protected'.[30] To address the latter concern, the AWG proposed a number of 'asset-finance-facilitating "optional" provisions':[31] (i) unqualified recognition of choice of law selected by the parties;[32] (ii) protection

[22] Unidroit, *Study LXXII – Doc. 27 (1996)* 37.

[23] See section 6.2.2.

[24] See section 2.4 for a more detailed discussion of the development of the concept of internationality.

[25] See footnote 14 in Unidroit, *Study LXXII – Doc. 16 (1995)* 7. Later, in 1999, an attempt to define the term 'purely domestic transaction' was met with similar criticism that 'the very essence of the Convention was to offer the holders of international interests clear predictability of their rights' – see paragraph 5.37 in Unidroit, *ICAO Ref. LSC/ME/2-Report Unidroit CGE/Int.Int./2-Report (1999)*.

[26] See paragraph 26 in Unidroit, *Study LXXII – Doc. 27 (1996)* 16.

[27] For a more detailed discussion of the legal issues concerning various types of leases see section 2.2.4.i generally.

[28] See paragraph 35 in Unidroit, *Study LXXII – Doc. 27 (1996)* 19.

[29] By way of example, comments prepared jointly by IATA and the AWG for the Committee of Governmental Experts in 1998 expressly state: 'Vague standards, inconsistent with the basic objective of providing commercial predictability, should be avoided': see Unidroit, *Study LXXII – Doc. 45 / Study LXXIID – Doc. 6 (1998)*.

[30] See footnote 10 in Unidroit, *Study LXXII – Doc. 23 (1996)* 3 (emphasis added).

[31] ibid.

[32] Unidroit, *Study LXXII – Doc. 16 (1995)* 24.

of the financier upon the initiation of insolvency-related proceedings against the debtor/lessee by way of mandatory return of the equipment (or, alternatively, requirement to cure all defaults and perform contractual obligations);[33] and (iii) mandatory time frames for issuing final non-appealable court decisions in respect of remedies under the Convention.[34] It is not hard to notice, however, that each of these additional measures also aims to achieve greater certainty, respectively, in the application of substantive laws, on initiation of bankruptcy proceedings (and other bankruptcy-related events) and in the course of enforcement of remedies.[35] The separation of these three groups of measures into a separate category by the AWG may thus seem somewhat misleading.

The Draft Aviation Text prepared by the AWG in 1996 – or rather its level of detail – suggests another certainty-enhancing feature generated by the aviation industry, which later translated into the final text of the CTC. The AWG text comprised 32 articles and Annexure with 51 definitions (25 pages overall) and more than tripled the size of the previous draft of the Convention, which had only 19 articles and 15 definitions across 8 pages.[36] While the increase in size can partly be explained by the introduction of aircraft-specific provisions (which had not existed in the earlier draft) and the new 'optional' provisions discussed in the previous paragraph, the drastic change of the overall volume cannot be attributed to these two factors alone. Indeed, the aircraft-specific provisions were reduced to a single article,[37] while the 'optional' provisions were also quite limited.[38]

The main reasons behind the dramatic increase of the size of the document lay in the different drafting technique utilised in the Draft Aviation Text: the latter added (i) numerous technical provisions, as well as (ii) extra clarificatory language to achieve greater certainty of the treaty rules. The new technical provisions included a number of definitions, such as 'contractual rights and obligations', 'courts', 'judicial proceedings', 'party', 'ratification instrument', 'relevant Contracting State', 'selected law', 'take possession' and others.[39] The extra clarificatory language was either integrated into the existing provisions of the draft Convention, or added as part of the new articles proposed by the AWG. Examples of such language included: (i) adding

[33] ibid 26.

[34] See paragraph 2 in Unidroit, *Study LXXII – Doc. 19 Add. 4 (1995)*. It should be noted that this proposal was initially considered by the AWG as mandatory, rather than optional: see paragraph 5.1 in Unidroit, *Study LXXII – Doc. 16 (1995)* 16–17. However, later the position was reversed.

[35] During the second session of the Study Group in 1996, the AWG acknowledged that 'an important element in the creation of that degree of legal certainty … was the ability for prospective financiers to know that, in the event of default and/or insolvency, their right to repossess and sell a charged asset would be enforced on a reasonable time scale': see Unidroit, *Study LXXII – Doc. 27 (1996)* 40.

[36] See Unidroit, *Study LXXII – Doc. 22 (1996)*.

[37] See Article 23 of the Draft Aviation Text in Unidroit, *Study LXXII – Doc. 23 (1996)*.

[38] See Article 13, Article 24(3) and Article 31(2)(a)(iii) (for time limits of court proceedings), Articles 14–15 and Articles 31(2)(a)(iv)–(v) (for insolvency-related protections), Article 7(a), Article 25 and Article 31(2)(a)(i) (for recognition of contractual choice of law) of the Draft Aviation Text in ibid.

[39] See Annexure to ibid.

detail to an otherwise self-sufficient provision;[40] (ii) suggesting criteria or situations which did not affect the application of existing provisions;[41] and (iii) incorporating provisions essentially confirming the status quo which would have existed anyway in the absence of such provisions.[42]

The inclusion of these technical provisions and extra clarificatory language was a deliberate and informed act by the AWG – in his summary of the key concepts underlying the AWG submission to the Study Group in 1996 Jeffrey Wool explained that the future Convention was expected to 'provide a sufficient level of detail as to its meaning and application so as materially to enhance the certainty of risk assessment in asset-based financing'.[43] The Study Group subsequently recognised the need for a 'sufficient measure of predictability' for aviation financiers, but at the same time noted the amount of detail that 'was uncommon and … probably … undesirable in an international Convention'.[44] To balance these 'twin' considerations, the Study Group considered the idea of treating various detailed provisions as matters of interpretation that could be addressed in a separate report or commentary.[45]

Interestingly, the earlier conclusion about the primacy of certainty and predictability in the development of the CTC finds support even in the context of ships, which have been excluded from the scope of the Convention despite the very good reasons for their inclusion.[46] The aviation industry, represented by the AWG

[40] See Article 5(1)(a) of the Draft Aviation Text in ibid, which supplemented 'in writing' with extra language: 'signed by or on behalf of the parties'. See also Article 8(1) of the same, which stressed that the various remedies could apply to 'all or part of' of the relevant property (cf Article 9 in Unidroit, *Study LXXII – Doc. 22 (1996)*). See also Article 9 of the Draft Aviation Text in Unidroit, *Study LXXII – Doc. 23 (1996)*, which clarified that the remedy of taking possession could be exercised not only in respect of 'all or any' of the property, but also 'to the extent and on the terms set forth in the agreement' (cf Article 10 in Unidroit, *Study LXXII – Doc. 22 (1996)*).

[41] See Article 5(2) of the Draft Aviation Text in Unidroit, *Study LXXII – Doc. 23 (1996)*, which listed four groups of factors that could not affect the creation of a valid international interest.

[42] See Article 27 of the Draft Aviation Text in ibid, which provided that 'all legal matters not expressly addressed in [the] Convention shall be governed by otherwise applicable law'.

[43] Unidroit, *Study LXXII – Doc. 25 (1996)* 1.

[44] See paragraph 9 in Unidroit, *Study LXXII – Doc. 27 (1996)* 9. In their subsequent comments the AWG, joined by IATA, further stressed the need for greater detail in the text of the treaty: 'While we appreciate the advantages of keeping the proposed convention light and simple, this objective is in tension with the parallel objective of obtaining a high degree of commercial certainty': see paragraph 2.2 in Unidroit, *Study LXXII – Doc. 32 Add. 2 (1997)*.

[45] This gave rise to the compromise solution, whereby the more technical and detailed provisions were removed from the CTC, on the assumption that the relevant matters would be addressed in the corresponding explanatory materials. See also paragraphs 47, 56, 91 in Unidroit, *Study LXXII – Doc. 27 (1996)* 23, 27, 39. The AWG and IATA subsequently proposed a combination of (i) an 'explanatory report' (providing a general background, discussion and illustration) and (ii) 'official comments' (addressing specific points required to achieve greater certainty), suggesting that the latter should be obligatory in nature: see paragraph 2.2 in Unidroit, *Study LXXII – Doc. 32 Add. 2 (1997)* 4. See also the summary of comments made by Jeffrey Wool in Unidroit, *Study LXXII – Doc. 41 (1998)* 6, 10. Finally, see paragraph 25 in ibid 13 and paragraph 2 in Unidroit, *Study LXXII – Doc. 45 / Study LXXIID – Doc. 6 (1998)* 2.

[46] See section 3.4.

(and later joined by IATA and ICAO), and the shipping circles, supported by the CMI, IMO and UNCTAD, took diametrically opposed views in relation to the future Convention while citing essentially the same reasons: the need to promote certainty and predictability. The only substantive argument[47] of the shipping industry against the inclusion of ships into the UNIDROIT treaty concerned the new International Convention on Maritime Liens and Mortgages adopted in 1993. According to UNCTAD, in the light of this new instrument the extension of scope of the draft Convention to ships 'could only cause confusion and uncertainty'.[48]

While the absence of any meaningful documented analysis of the provisions of the two instruments for potential conflicts or overlaps during the development process clearly signals the lack of interest from the shipping circles in the first place, it is not material for the purposes of this chapter. The UNCTAD's speculation about uncertainty resulting from the co-existence of the two treaties could be real even in the absence of contradiction between them: in the end, having more than one instrument affecting security interests over ships could indeed cause some confusion.[49] What is relevant, however, is the fact that the shipping industry highlighted the importance of the need to adjust to the new rules and the uncertainty resulting from their adoption.

A different course of action taken by each of the two (aviation and shipping) industries demonstrates a different overall perception of the impact of this factor, but does little in terms of measuring its relevance. Without a quantitative analysis in the form of an economic benefit assessment, involving calculations of both the positive and negative impacts of the new treaty, both sides essentially relied on the abstract notion of certainty and chose different ways. One can only presume that a separate study showing that the legal certainty resulting from the elimination of legal risks for the shipping industry would outweigh any adjustment costs could go a long way towards swaying the shipping circles in favour of the draft Convention. However, since UNIDROIT, IMO, the CMI and UNCTAD left things as they were, one should not be surprised by the lack of progress and eventual exclusion of ships from the scope of the CTC.

Despite the above examples, the relevance of the twin notions of certainty and predictability is probably best illustrated by the history of development of Article 5(1) of the CTC, which establishes the basic rules of interpretation of the

[47] The other argument was essentially the urge to avoid the interference by UNIDROIT with the development of rules impacting ships and shipping operations, which, according to Rubens Ricupero, the (then) Secretary-General of UNCTAD, '[had] always been elaborated within the *competent* international/intergovernmental organizations with full participation of the shipping community': see Appendix I in Unidroit, *Study LXXII – Doc. 29 (1996)* (emphasis added).

[48] ibid.

[49] This does not explain, however, the negative reaction of the international organisations representing the shipping industry: after all, sophisticated parties involved in ship financing transactions could be expected to have the ability and resources to navigate the complex legal framework of maritime law, let alone two standalone conventions governing security over ships.

Convention. The first draft of this provision can be found in Article 30 of the Draft Aviation Text proposed by the AWG in 1996, which read:

> In the interpretation and application of the terms of this Convention and the regulations regard shall be had to their international character and of the desirability of achieving uniformity in their interpretation and application.[50]

This article was clearly modelled after Article 7(1) of the CISG, except that reference to the 'observance of good faith in international trade' was omitted. The omitted reference was, however, reinstated by the Drafting Group later the same year in the revised draft of the Convention: the newly added Article 6 reproduced Article 7 of the CISG word for word in its entirety.[51]

Following the third session of the Study Group held in Rome in January 1997, the Drafting Group prepared a revised draft of the Convention, which added for the first time a new overarching objective in interpretation of the treaty: the need to promote 'predictability' in its application.[52] This new objective did not replace any of the existing objectives (which included promotion of uniformity in the interpretation and the observance of good faith in international trade), but expressly recognised the relevance of commercial certainty for the proper understanding of the instrument. Despite the intense subsequent debate about the appropriateness of including a reference to 'good faith' as part of the interpretation process, the reference to 'predictability' was never omitted from subsequent drafts, even in cases when alternative wordings of the same text were proposed by the Drafting Group[53] or when the general formula of this provision was revised by adding reference to the Convention's object and purpose.[54]

Of crucial importance here is the fact that 'predictability' as another primary objective (i) was added prior to the removal of the reference to the 'good faith' principle, and (ii) was included in each of the Alternative A and Alternative B proposed by the Drafting Group in 1997 at the conclusion of its fourth session.[55] Accordingly, it never came in direct conflict with the 'good faith' principle and thus the statement in the Official Commentary that in Article 5(1) 'predictability has been *substituted* for good faith'[56] is not entirely accurate. While there is no denying that predictability is one of the main principles on which the CTC as a whole is based, a deeper look at the drafting history of Article 5(1) clearly shows that 'predictability' did not replace 'good faith' (as would seem to be the case upon a simple comparison of Article 5(1) of the CTC with Article 7(1) of the CISG):

[50] See Annex I in Unidroit, *Study LXXII – Doc. 23 (1996).*

[51] See Article 6 in Unidroit, *Study LXXII – Doc. 30 (1996).*

[52] See Article 6(1) in Unidroit, *Study LXXII – Drafting Group Fourth Session (1997).*

[53] See Alternative A and Alternative B of Article 6 in Unidroit, *Study LXXII – Doc. 35 (1997).*

[54] See Article 5(1) in Unidroit, *International Interests Study Group 4th Session Misc. 5 (1997).*

[55] See Article 6 in Unidroit, *Study LXXII – Doc. 35 (1997).*

[56] See paragraph 4.67 in Goode, *Convention on International Interests in Mobile Equipment and Protocol thereto on Matters Specific to Aircraft Equipment: Official Commentary* (4th edn, International Institute for the Unification of Private Law (UNIDROIT) 2019) 323 (emphasis added).

the former earned its own place among the primary interpretation objectives and would have existed regardless of the outcome of the dispute concerning 'good faith'.

The history of the CTC shows that predictability was the principal commercial factor that determined the outcome of many drafting conflicts and shaped the CTC in its present form. This important factor, however, essentially remained abstract and did not lend itself to quantification, which significantly limited its usefulness, especially when different commercial factors counteracted each other (as was the case with the shipping industry involvement and the perceived uncertainty generated by the draft Convention). Nevertheless, limited attempts to quantify the economic benefits generated by the CTC were made several times and at various stages of development of the Convention and its protocols. These are addressed in greater detail in the following section.

7.2.2. Economic Benefit Studies in the History of the CTC

The first attempts to explain the relevance of the economic benefit generated by the CTC can be tracked back to the second memorandum prepared by the AWG in 1996. The utterly pragmatic approach of the aviation industry is illustrated by the basic premise that 'the value of the proposed convention is directly related to the extent to which its terms … result in an increase in the availability of credit, and/or a reduction in the cost of such credit, to owners/operators of aircraft equipment'.[57] This premise was based on the high amount of credit required to finance future aircraft deliveries, which, according to the estimates by the major airframe manufacturers, could be in the range of USD 900–1,000 billion over the next 20 years.[58]

A conceptual and qualitative, rather than quantitative, analysis of economic advantages of a new treaty governing security interests in movable assets was later provided jointly by the three members of the Center for Economic Analysis of Law (CEAL): Nuria de la Pena, Lance Girton and Heywood Fleisig.[59] Instead of attempting to quantify the prospective benefits of the future treaty, which at the time consisted of only 19 draft articles,[60] the authors suggested several economic conclusions resulting from their analysis of the draft text, some of which appeared rather basic. First, they simply concluded that 'the more narrow the application of the convention to a list of specific equipment, the more limited its economic impact'.[61] Second, on the basis of abstract figures and hypothetical scenarios, the paper stressed the importance of priority rules, particularly in relation to future advances.[62] Third, it observed the relevance of balancing costs and benefits when

[57] Unidroit, *Study LXXII – Doc. 23 (1996)* 3.
[58] See footnote 9 in ibid.
[59] See Unidroit, *Study LXXII – Doc. 26 Add. 2 (1996).*
[60] See Unidroit, *Study LXXII – Doc. 24 (1996).*
[61] Unidroit, *Study LXXII – Doc. 26 Add. 2 (1996)* 11.
[62] ibid 12–14.

designing rules governing purchase money security interests.[63] Fourth, the authors outlined a number of issues relating to the prospects of establishing an international registry: (i) choosing between domestic registries and a wholly international registry; (ii) the need for greater access to registration records; (iii) the greater efficiency of a notice filing system; and (iv) the relevance of pre-filing as a mechanism protecting the lender in cases when the debtor uses the loan to purchase the equipment used as collateral.[64] Fifth, the document focused on the economic relevance of the ability of the secured creditor to enforce its security and concluded that 'the greatest diminution in the economic value of collateral arises from problems in enforcing security interests'.[65] The authors identified two primary economic factors in assessing enforcement-related provisions: (i) the size of collection costs, and (ii) correlation between the economic life of collateral and the time period required to seize and sell such collateral.[66] They also highlighted the importance of creditor protection in case of debtor's insolvency, but at the same time expressed reservations as to the viability of the time limits for court judgments proposed by the AWG resulting from the lack of any enforcement system to deal with judges and court officers who ignore the legally-specified timetable.[67]

While the CEAL paper did not include any empirical economic benefit analysis, its role should not be underestimated: it identified those elements of the draft Convention which were capable of generating quantifiable economic benefit. In other words, it helped bridge the gap between the abstract notion of 'certainty' and the concrete reduction of costs to the end users of the future treaty. The second session of the Study Group held shortly afterwards, in April 1996, brought the draft Convention one step closer to an actual economic benefit analysis: it was suggested that the pricing of secured financing transactions was 'directly related to perceptions of the probable timetable for repossession and sale in the event of default and/or insolvency'.[68] These considerations formed the basis of some of the future economic benefit studies.

The first quantitative economic benefit analysis was commissioned by the Aircraft Protocol Group and prepared in 1998 by Anthony Saunders and Ingo Walter under the Auspices of INSEAD and the New York University Salomon Center[69] (the 'INSEAD Study'). The study was limited to the aviation sector and estimated the savings in the region of USD 5 billion per annum based on 20-year projected aircraft deliveries.[70] In select cases, the cost savings generated by the

[63] ibid 16.
[64] ibid 16–19.
[65] ibid 19.
[66] ibid.
[67] ibid 20–21.
[68] See paragraph 93 in Unidroit, *Study LXXII – Doc. 27 (1996)* 40.
[69] Anthony Saunders and Ingo Walter, *Proposed Unidroit Convention on International Interests in Mobile Equipment as Applicable to Aircraft Equipment through the Aircraft Equipment Protocol: Economic Impact Assessment* (A Study Prepared Under the Auspices of INSEAD and the New York University Salomon Center, 1998).
[70] ibid iii.

future Convention were deemed infinite, since in certain circumstances credit would be extended where it was simply unavailable before.[71]

These savings were expected to be further supplemented by a variety of micro- and macroeconomic benefits. The former included: (i) benefits for commercial air carriers in the form of enhanced fleet planning, operational flexibility and resulting profit maximisation; (ii) reduction of transaction costs through simplification and standardisation; (iii) assumed pass-through of interest cost savings to reduce fares; (iv) reductions in litigation costs and delays; and (v) reduced pressure for sale of used aircraft under conditions of financial distress. The latter amounted to a 2–3 per cent reduction in external country debt for certain emerging market countries.[72]

On its face, the INSEAD Study took into account three asset finance enhancing principles embodied in the draft Convention. The first (the 'transparent priority principle') stated that a financier or lessor must be able to determine and ensure its first-ranking priority. The second (the 'prompt enforcement principle') implied the ability of the financier or lessor, upon default of the debtor, to promptly realise the value of collateral or redeploy the asset to generate proceeds that could be applied against the amount of unpaid debt. The third (the 'bankruptcy law enforcement principle') required that the rights of a financier or lessor under the first two principles remained unaffected by the bankruptcy of the party providing the relevant security.[73]

Despite the very broad and far-reaching expected gains from the draft Convention, the methodology utilised by the authors of the INSEAD Study was based on very generous assumptions[74] and lacked sufficient data for a truly global research: it involved very limited country-specific data.[75] The study involved two main stages: (i) a calculation of costs savings by US airlines resulting from the adoption of the Bankruptcy Reform Act of 1994 (and Section 1110 of the US Bankruptcy Code[76]), and (ii) generating broad estimates of possible cost savings by the global airline industry resulting from the draft Convention as applied to aircraft.[77] In essence, the study was built on a 'what if' basis: the analysis used

[71] ibid.
[72] ibid iv.
[73] ibid 11.
[74] The estimated savings assumed 'a 100-basis-point reduction in the overall cost per annum of 12-year fixed-rate aircraft loans, and comparable savings in the case of asset-backed bond rating upgrades': see ibid iii.
[75] See Table 2 'Hypothetical savings in $ million for 1992–1997' and Table 3 'Projected savings in $ million for 1997–2016'. In each case, country-specific data was based on the airline spending: actual in the first case and projected in the second case.
[76] Title 11 of the United States Code.
[77] Anthony Saunders and Ingo Walter, *Proposed Unidroit Convention on International Interests in Mobile Equipment as Applicable to Aircraft Equipment through the Aircraft Equipment Protocol: Economic Impact Assessment* (A Study Prepared Under the Auspices of INSEAD and the New York University Salomon Center, 1998) 15.

hypothetical pricing to form the basis of some of the key calculations[78] and did not take into account the implementation costs of the new treaty.

Despite its limited scope and methodology, the INSEAD Study remained the only ex ante quantitative economic benefit study prepared prior to the adoption of the Convention in 2001.[79] Although this study was referred to multiple times as evidence of possible practical gains resulting from the CTC,[80] such references primarily focused on the (quite lucrative) conclusions that the draft Convention '[would] achieve significant economic gains' and that 'the economic gains [would] be substantial and complementary',[81] or on the three 'principles underlying asset-based financing'.[82]

Interestingly, there appears to be no record of a substantive review or critique of the INSEAD Study, despite its very real limitations. There is limited evidence suggesting that an element of peer feedback was involved in the development of the document and that the research 'was coupled with contributing "economic fora" where a range of experts – airlines, financial institutions, international credit rating agencies, export credit agencies, and manufacturers – discussed the subject with the authors'.[83] It should be noted, however, that most, if not all, of the above participants were also the key stakeholders and prospective beneficiaries of the proposed reform generated by the Convention.

The above concerns should not, however, underestimate the crucial role the INSEAD Study played in the development of the CTC. It was prepared in the run-up to the governmental consultations relating to the draft Convention and the Aircraft Protocol and provided 'an invaluable pointer to the practical benefits that [Governments] could expect to derive from the proposed new international regimen'.[84] Perhaps even more importantly, it connected quantitative analysis with the three asset finance enhancing principles (transparent

[78] The projected cost savings were based on hypothetical interest rate spread savings between hypothetical secured and unsecured financing transactions assigned to hypothetical secured transactions. Such spread savings amounted to 100 basis points (in case of reduction from LIBOR plus 140 basis points to LIBOR plus 40 basis points) or 50 basis points (in case of reduction from LIBOR plus 90 basis points to LIBOR plus 40 basis points): see paragraphs 4.10 and 4.11 in ibid 22–23. The authors explained that some figures were provided 'as reasonable indicators both of hypothetical secured and unsecured rates, as well as differentials between them', and acknowledged that 'actual rates and/or differentials may be higher or lower depending on a wide variety of factors': see footnote 47 in ibid 20.

[79] For completeness, note a reference to a 'Draft Economic Impact Assessment Study' in the report of the 77th session of the UNIDROIT Governing Council: see Unidroit, *Study LXXII – Doc. 40 (1998)* 30. It is impossible to confirm or deny whether this reference relates to the INSEAD Study.

[80] See, eg, paragraph 4(a) in Unidroit, *Study LXXII – Doc. 43 / Study LXXIID – Doc. 4 (1998)* 3; paragraph 153 in Unidroit, *Study LXXII – Doc. 41 (1998)* 36–37.

[81] See footnote 7 in Jeffrey Wool, 'The Case for a Commercial Orientation of the Proposed UNIDROIT Convention as Applied to Aircraft Equipment' (1999) 4 *Uniform Law Review* 289, 290.

[82] Jeffrey Wool, 'Treaty Design, Implementation, and Compliance Benchmarking Economic Benefit – a Framework as Applied to the Cape Town Convention' (2012) 17 *Uniform Law Review* 633, 644.

[83] Jeffrey Wool, 'Economic Analysis and Harmonised Modernisation of Private Law' (2003) 8 *Uniform Law Review* 389, 391.

[84] Unidroit, *Study LXXII – Doc. 40 (1998)* 30.

priority, prompt enforcement and bankruptcy enforcement),[85] essentially turning them into assumptions underlying the projected economic benefit. These assumptions, as was succinctly noted by Jeffrey Wool, had 'in terrorem' effect during the subsequent negotiations: any dilution of these principles in the final text would be perceived as diminishing the expected impact of the Convention. In addition, the INSEAD Study had an interesting connection to some of the following impact studies relating to the CTC: Appendix 4 briefly discussed the feasibility of analysing repossession delays as an alternative method of economic assessment.[86]

The delay between a debtor's default and repossession of the collateral by the financier formed the basis of two economic benefit studies prepared by Vadim Linetsky in 2009 and 2010. The first measured the risk and financing cost reduction to the lender resulting from the shortening of existing repossession delays to the 60-day maximum. The 60-day limit originated from Section 2(a) of Annex 1: Qualifying Declarations to the Sector Understanding on Export Credits for Civil Aircraft ('ASU 2007') adopted by the OECD on 27 July 2007[87] and formed one of the mandatory criteria established by the ASU 2007 that had to be fulfilled before a state could qualify for a special Cape Town Convention discount.[88] The data on existing repossession delays was calculated on the basis of the World Bank statistics on contract enforcement delays, which were not specific to aircraft financing contracts, but were subsequently adjusted by applying certain commercial data on aircraft repossessions submitted by financial institutions.[89] The study concluded that the worldwide reduction of aircraft repossession delay from the median 10 months to 60 days could generate total savings on the order of USD 161 billion between 2009 and 2030. The following 2010 study assessed the economic benefits of reducing aircraft repossession delays in the context of a single jurisdiction – the United Kingdom – and projected savings of between

[85] While these principles were applied in the text of the INSEAD Study, they were not developed by its authors. This follows from the acknowledgement in footnote 1 in Anthony Saunders and Ingo Walter, *Proposed Unidroit Convention on International Interests in Mobile Equipment as Applicable to Aircraft Equipment through the Aircraft Equipment Protocol: Economic Impact Assessment* 1 (A Study Prepared Under the Auspices of INSEAD and the New York University Salomon Center, 1998).

[86] Appendix 4 is not present in the article form of the INSEAD research, co-authored by Jeffrey Wool and Anand Srinivasan: see Anthony Saunders and others, 'The Economic Implications of International Secured Transactions Law Reform: A Case Study' (1999) 20 *U Pa J Int'lL* 309.

[87] OECD, *Sector Understanding on Export Credits for Civil Aircraft* (2007).

[88] The ASU 2007 established certain rules governing the financing that export credit agencies could provide for the purchase of aircraft. Its principal objective was to 'foster a level playing field for such export credits, in order to encourage competition among exporters based on quality and price of goods and services exported rather than on the most favourable officially supported financial terms and conditions': see section 1(a) in ibid. According to the ASU 2007, its participants providing official support were required to charge, for the credit amount officially supported, no less than the minimum premium rate set out in the document (section 12(a)). The Cape Town Convention discount effectively reduced that minimum premium rate. Subsequently, the ASU 2007 was superseded by a new version adopted in 2011 (ASU 2011).

[89] Vadim Linetsky, *Economic Benefits of the Cape Town Treaty* 4 (2009).

GBP 538 and 2,705 billion in funding costs of financing aircraft deliveries over the next 20 years.[90]

The two economic benefit studies by Vadim Linetsky focused on microeconomic benefits and employed a more robust methodology to calculate the impact generated by the CTC. This was possible for two principal reasons. First, both the Convention and the Aircraft Protocol had been finalised, allowing researchers to focus more on the actual provisions of these documents rather than their general principles. Second, the ASU 2007, which set the 60-day threshold for qualifying declarations, provided a much-needed actual, rather than hypothetical, starting point for measuring the delta of economic benefit.[91] In addition, as was noted by Jeffrey Wool, the published methodology of major credit rating agencies had shown that 'the presence of the CTC (with the qualifying declarations and implementation) could result in up to a two notch upgrade in the rating of the relevant securities'.[92]

Although most economic benefit studies relating to the CTC focused on the aviation sector and the Aircraft Protocol, certain limited attempts have been made to cover other protocols. These studies, however, either remained essentially qualitative in nature,[93] or were based on very generous assumptions and broad hypotheticals.[94]

Overall, the practice of preparing economic benefit studies to measure the impact of the CTC is difficult to assess. On the one hand, the studies played an important role in the development of new protocols and the assessment of existing ones by signalling the level of change resulting from the adoption and implementation of the new instruments. On the other hand, the methods used to prepare such studies have been extremely diverse, and the results are hard to verify. How could the situation be improved? First, greater emphasis should be made on quantitative,

[90] Vadim Linetsky, *Accession to the Cape Town Convention by the UK: An Economic Impact Assessment Study* 2 (2010).

[91] cf Anthony Saunders, Anand Srinivasan and Ingo Walter, 'Innovation in International Law and Global Finance: Estimating the Financial Impact of the Cape Town Convention' (2006) http://ssrn.com/abstract=894027. This study, prepared shortly before the adoption of the ASU 2007, had to rely on broad assumptions and general comparisons. On the one hand, the authors assumed that the ratification of the CTC would result in the improvement in the debt ratings of the airlines and prepared a study on a 'what if' basis, asking what savings may accrue to an airline if its rating were improved. On the other hand, the study used a single-country 'event study' of the reaction of the stock market to the US signature and ratification process in 2003 and 2004 to estimate the stock market valuation of publicly-traded airlines generally.

[92] Jeffrey Wool, 'Treaty Design, Implementation, and Compliance Benchmarking Economic Benefit – a Framework as Applied to the Cape Town Convention' (2012) 17 *Uniform Law Review* 633, 648–49.

[93] See Souichirou Kozuka and Fuki Taniguchi, 'An Economic Assessment of the Space Assets Protocol to the Cape Town Convention' (2011) 16 *Uniform Law Review* 927; Unidroit, *Study 72K – CGE 1 – Doc. 10 (2017).*

[94] See the paper 'Extending UNIDROIT's Cape Town Convention to Mining, Agricultural, and Construction Equipment: Economic Issues' by Heywood Fleisig in Unidroit, *Unidroit 2013 C.D. (92) 5(b) (2013).* This study broadly projected that the MAC Protocol would increase sales of mining, agricultural and construction equipment by about USD 600 billion over a period of five to seven years and facilitate using USD 2 trillion in such equipment as collateral for loans.

as opposed to qualitative economic research. The latter often ends up repeating the basic asset financing principles on which the CTC is based, adding little in terms of actual impact analysis. Second, economic benefit studies should become more sophisticated and include multiple micro and macroeconomic indicators. Third, impact assessments should address not only the expected benefits of adopting the new instruments, but also the corresponding costs of implementation and other countervailing factors.

7.3. State Sensitivities

It is clear from the previous section that the development of the CTC, as a whole, was driven by commercial objectives. These objectives are reflected in the preamble of the Convention and include, among other things, the desire 'to provide broad mutual economic benefits for all interested parties'. At the same time, a whole range of factors (for simplicity referred to as 'state sensitivities') limited the reach of purely commercial objectives in the text of the CTC, resulting in a set of provisions pursuing other, non-economic, aims.[95] This dualism can be best illustrated by the words of members of the Study Group at its second session in 1996, who stressed 'how vital it would be as a matter of general policy for the rules of the future Convention to be perceived as reflecting a balance between the interests of all the parties concerned, as well as responding to the underlying objectives of the Convention, and as being consistent with the requirements of other branches of the law'.[96]

One of the key obstacles to the promotion of commercial objectives in the CTC was the notion of sovereignty: the perception of governments as to what can or cannot be regulated in an international treaty significantly changed the scope of many provisions of the Convention and its protocols.

An obvious example of such sovereignty-driven non-commercial factors can be found in Article 2(2) of the CTC, which retains the distinction between security, leasing and title reservation agreements. As was explained in greater detail in section 2.2.4, the perceived conceptual differences between various legal traditions precluded the universal consensus to adopt a functional approach to security.[97] Although in the end all three types of agreements ended up being covered in the Convention, the explicit reference to each of them is a clear reminder of the very real distinction in approach adopted by the national legal systems.

[95] An acknowledgment of the existence of other, non-commercial aims of the CTC based on state sensitivities can be found in an early article by Jeffrey Wool, who recognised the so-called 'diplomatic objective' (in addition to the 'commercial objective'), namely the need to 'generate a high level of international consensus': see Jeffrey Wool, 'The Case for a Commercial Orientation of the Proposed UNIDROIT Convention as applied to aircraft equipment' (1999) 4 *Uniform Law Review* 289, 291.

[96] See paragraph 94 in Unidroit, *Study LXXII – Doc. 27 (1996)* 40.

[97] See n 41 in section 2.2.4.

Another conceptual problem can be found in the records of the governmental expert stage in the run-up to the Cape Town Diplomatic Conference, where a last-minute intervention during the Third Joint Session eventually demolished the system of assignment that had been created by the draft Convention. At the time, the assignment provisions were following a simple logic that 'an assignment of an international interest in an object … transfers to the assignee … (a) all the interests and priorities of the assignor … and (b) all associated rights'[98] (ie rights to payment or other performance under the agreement secured by the relevant object). The underlying rationale was clear: since the draft CTC regulated international interests (rather than receivables generally), it only seemed intuitive to follow that approach and provide for the mechanism of assignment of such interests. This view, however, was challenged by the French delegation, which submitted that the existing draft completely overturned French 'ideas regarding the assignment of debts': the latter followed the reverse logic that assignment of debt carries with it the accessory transfer of security (Articles 1690, 1692 of the French Civil Code).[99] The dramatic departure of the draft Convention from the French domestic notions of assignment prompted that delegation to request a mechanism permitting states not to apply the relevant chapter.[100] To address this matter, the delegations of Canada, France and the United States came together to propose two alternative versions of the assignment provisions.[101] Despite this effort, the matter was referred to the Cape Town Diplomatic Conference, which approved the current text that follows the French approach.[102]

Bankruptcy law was another area which proved to be largely impenetrable by the CTC. The difficulties associated with unification of matters of bankruptcy law can perhaps be best illustrated by the fact that this problem was brought up during the very first discussion of the Canadian Proposal[103] by the UNIDROIT Governing Council in 1989, when Roy Goode expressed the view that 'bankruptcy rules should … be totally excluded although rights created outside bankruptcy law would in many cases be given effect within bankruptcy law'.[104] This succinct comment, in essence, summarises quite well the future development of the bankruptcy-related provisions of the CTC. In the summary of responses to his 1990

[98] See Article 30(1) in Appendix III to Unidroit, *Unidroit CGE/Int.Int./3-WP/2 ICAO Ref. LSC/ME/3-WP/2 (2000)*.

[99] Unidroit, *Unidroit CGE/Int.Int./3-WP/4 ICAO Ref. LSC/ME/3-WP/4 (2000)* 3.

[100] ibid 4.

[101] See paragraphs 223, 232–37 in Unidroit, *Unidroit CGE/Int.Int./3-Report ICAO Ref. LSC/ME/3-Report (2000)*. See the actual text of proposal in Unidroit, *Unidroit CGE/Int.Int./3-WP/31 ICAO Ref. LSC/ME/3-WP/31 Rev. 29/03/00 (2000)*.

[102] See Chapter IX of the CTC. Note that the change of approach significantly complicated the priority rules applicable to assignment (see Article 36 of the CTC) to protect general receivables financiers: see paragraphs 4.263–4.272 in Goode, *Convention on International Interests in Mobile Equipment and Protocol thereto on Matters Specific to Aircraft Equipment: Official Commentary* (4th edn, International Institute for the Unification of Private Law (UNIDROIT) 2019) 415–21.

[103] See n 1 in section 2.2.1.

[104] Unidroit, *Governing Council C.D. 68 – Doc. 26 (1989)* 34.

Questionnaire, Ronald Cuming concluded that there was 'considerable support for a minimalist, but not a hands-off, approach': while an attempt to influence national bankruptcy laws in any significant way was considered 'completely unrealistic', most respondents favoured the need to ensure that transactions creating security interests governed by the future Convention were treated in bankruptcy as security agreements.[105] This outcome later translated into a unanimous decision by the Study Group that 'the Convention should in no way seek to displace national bankruptcy rules but should rather simply seek to ensure the survival of the international security interest in bankruptcy proceedings'.[106] In the words of Charles Mooney and Thomas Whalen, preservation of the international interest in bankruptcy '[was], perhaps, the single most fundamental role for the Convention'.[107]

The insolvency-related articles of the different protocols establishing various alternatives went beyond the original modest limits outlined above:[108] the relevant provisions in each protocol impose obligations on domestic insolvency administrators[109] and even domestic courts[110] in the course of insolvency proceedings. Nonetheless, neither of these provisions applies by default, as each requires a corresponding declaration – a clear indication of the special character of bankruptcy provisions. Following the adoption of the CTC and the Aircraft Protocol, the aviation industry was instrumental in designing economic incentives for the adoption of certain declarations in the form of the ASU 2007 and, later, the ASU 2011, but the more intrusive bankruptcy-related provisions remain optional in nature.

A very similar position applies to procedural matters under the Convention: the latter does not stipulate specific time limits for courts or other authorities, while the protocols allow corresponding declarations.[111] The complexity of the issue of establishing hard cut-off time frames is further strengthened by the due process concerns of fair hearing.[112]

Another taboo area untouched by the CTC concerns the enforcement of Convention provisions by the contracting states. Despite several attempts to establish some form of supranational body for the resolution of disputes arising under the Convention, the CTC incorporates no international control mechanism over its compliance. In 1997, Vladislav Kouvshinov came up with an idea – inspired by

[105] Unidroit, *Study LXXII – Doc. 4 (1992)* 9–10.

[106] Unidroit, *Study LXXII – Doc. 7 (1993)* 6.

[107] Unidroit, *Study LXXII – Doc. 36 (1997)* 43.

[108] See n 84 in section 8.3 for a brief account of the history of the relevant provisions.

[109] See, eg, Article XI(2) (Alternatives A and B) of the Aircraft Protocol, Article IX(3) (Alternatives A, B and C) of the Rail Protocol, Article XXI(2) (Alternatives A and B) of the Space Protocol and Article X(3) of the MAC Protocol.

[110] See, eg, Article XII(2) of the Aircraft Protocol, Article X(2) of the Rail Protocol, Article XXII(2) of the Space Protocol and Article XI(2) of the MAC Protocol.

[111] See, eg, Article X(2), Article XI(3) (Alternative A) and Article XI(2) (Alternative B) of the Aircraft Protocol; Article VIII(2), Article IX(4) (Alternative A), Article IX(3) (Alternative B) and Article IX(15) (Alternative C) of the Rail Protocol; Article XX(2), Article XXI(4) (Alternative A) and Article XXI(2) (Alternative B) of the Space Protocol; Article IX(2) and Article X(4) of the MAC Protocol.

[112] See Unidroit, *Study LXXII – Doc. 19 Add. (1995)* 9.

the arbitration procedure established under the 1965 ICSID Convention[113] – to set up an 'International Centre for Settlement of Disputes Arising out of or in Connection with the Implementation of the Convention on International Interests in Mobile Equipment, Protocols to this Convention and the Regulations of the Intergovernmental Regulator' (the 'Centre'). According to this proposal, the jurisdiction of the Centre would cover: (i) disputes between holders of international interests (and, potentially, holders of registered registrable national interests); (ii) disputes between such holders and the Registrar regarding acts and omissions of the latter; and (iii) claims for the granting of speedy relief. The Centre's Secretariat was expected to maintain a Panel of Arbitrators and a Panel of Conciliators consisting of duly qualified persons.[114] A different, more modest, suggestion was made by Ioannis Voulgaris, who proposed the institution of 'Boards of Appeal' to hear appeals brought against the actions of the international registrar, modelled after the Board of Appeal set up under the European Regulations on the Community trade mark.[115]

Eventually, neither proposal was successful. Interestingly, the same is true in respect of recognition by contracting states of court judgments and rulings issued by other contracting states under the Convention. In 1997, the Space Working Group came up with the following proposal, which, however, was subsequently rejected:

> Subject to the public policy of each Contracting State, a Contracting State shall recognise the orders, rulings and judgments issued by courts of competent jurisdiction of other Contracting States that arise out of this Convention and are consistent with this Convention.[116]

Another area of state sensitivity relates to the special rules governing 'internal transactions'.[117] Given the importance of the twin notions of certainty and predictability for the development of the CTC,[118] it might seem puzzling why the Convention treats the internal transactions separately.[119] Nevertheless, the difficult history of the concept of internationality explained in section 2.4 and the number of declarations[120] made under Article 50(1) of the CTC demonstrate how difficult it has been for states to relinquish full control over transactions firmly associated with their national jurisdiction.

One of the most recent sovereignty-driven challenges concerns the MAC Protocol and relates to mobile equipment associated with immovable property.

[113] Convention on the Settlement of Investment Disputes between States and Nationals of Other States (adopted 18 March 1965, entered into force 14 October 1966) 575 UNTS 159.

[114] See paragraph 198 in Unidroit, *Study LXXII – Doc. 36 (1997)* 52–54.

[115] Unidroit, *Study LXXII – Doc. 40 (1998)* 19–20.

[116] See paragraph 129 in Unidroit, *Study LXXII – Doc. 36 (1997)* 32.

[117] See section 2.4.3.

[118] See section 7.2.1.

[119] See Articles 1(n) and 50 of the CTC, Article IV(2) of the Aircraft Protocol, Article XXIX(2) of the Rail Protocol and Article I(3) of the Space Protocol.

[120] See n 195 in section 2.4.3.

This problem is new in the context of the CTC, since it had no relevance for any of the existing protocols, and originates from the fact that under certain legal systems mining, agricultural or construction equipment can become so associated with immovable property that the interests in the latter can extend to such equipment under domestic law. This created the possibility for serious objections from states to the transition to an international regime governing security interests in mining, agricultural and construction equipment, since immovable property interests are generally considered a matter of national sovereignty. Naturally, this factor was a radical departure from the autonomous concept of mobility in the Convention, which does not depend on the domestic classification or characterisation of the relevant objects: for example, for the purposes of the CTC it is irrelevant that under Russian law an aircraft that is subject to state registration is considered immovable property (section 130 of the Civil Code of the Russian Federation).[121]

At first, this factor was not considered a major obstacle, as it was understood that the degree of 'association' with the immovable property necessary to trigger the application of the relevant domestic rules involved some kind of *physical connection* with the land (eg in the case of cranes). A comparative law analysis performed by the UNIDROIT Secretariat, however, revealed that in certain jurisdictions such rules could apply regardless of physical attachment: what mattered was whether or not the equipment was 'utilised for the economic exploitation of the immovable property'.[122] To address this issue, the UNIDROIT study group came up with three alternatives from which contracting states must choose (the relevant declarations are mandatory), ranging from a hands-off approach leaving the consequences of association with immovable property to domestic law (Alternative C), to a provision preserving both the existence and priority position of the international interest in the equipment which has been so associated (Alternative A).[123] Alternative A (as initially drafted) was particularly problematic for equipment so connected with the immovable property that it would lose its individual legal identity or that it cannot be removed without material damage to the immovable property or the equipment itself.[124] As a result, the final text adopted in 2019 was revised to only cover 'severable' immovable-associated equipment, ie equipment whose 'estimated value after physical disconnection … from the immovable property would be greater than the estimated cost of the disconnection and of any restoration of the immovable property'.[125]

As noted in section 5.3.4, the desire to achieve a balance of interests is one of the important features of the system of remedies established by the CTC and its protocols. The Convention has set up a number of safeguards restricting the freedom of creditor in case of enforcement. These include the requirement to exercise

[121] See further paragraphs 2 and 11(2) in Unidroit, *Study 72k - CGE1 - Doc. 9 (2017)* 1, 3.
[122] See paragraph 77 in Unidroit, *Study 72k - CGE1 - Doc. 4 (2017)* 16.
[123] See Article VII in Unidroit, *Study 72k - CGE1 - Doc. 2 corr. (2017)*.
[124] See paragraph 11(3) in Unidroit, *Study 72k - CGE1 - Doc. 9 (2017)* 3.
[125] Article VII(4) (Alternative A) of the MAC Protocol.

remedies in a commercially reasonable manner,[126] the obligation of the chargee to give reasonable prior notice to 'interested persons' (which category includes the debtor),[127] the need to compare the amount of secured obligation with the value of the relevant object prior to the vesting of ownership to it in satisfaction under Article 9[128] or the right of the court to impose terms protecting interested persons in issuing advance relief under Article 13.[129] The importance of the above protections is further reinforced by the fact that their application cannot be avoided by agreement of the parties.

Another example of non-commercial factors in development of the CTC restricting the exercise of treaty remedies relates to the so-called public service exemption envisaged by the Rail[130] and Space[131] Protocols. At the core of the public service exemptions lies an acknowledgment that rolling stock and space assets (primarily satellites) are objects of special importance that can be utilised in delivery of public services and that 'the denial of public access to such assets will create a disproportionate and greater loss for the greater economy compared to the loss for the individual creditor if there is no removal'.[132] The exemption itself aims to safeguard the ability of contracting states to prevent interruptions to public services upon default of the debtor – even if this causes inconvenience to the creditor – but the two protocols approach this matter differently.

The Space Protocol merely restricts the full exercise of remedies by the creditor during a certain period (but does not deny the relevant remedy),[133] while the Rail Protocol goes further than that and lays down a mechanism of compensation to the creditor in situations when the contracting state blocks repossession, use or control of the collateral.[134] The solution envisaged in the Rail Protocol essentially maintains a balance of interests of both the state and the creditor in respect of rolling stock used for public service: the former is interested in exercising control over the relevant assets, while the latter wants to be repaid.

Two additional factors override commercial concerns in relation to public service exemptions in these two protocols. First, Article XXV(4) of the Rail Protocol contains what can be labelled as one of the most 'anti-commercial' provisions in any of the protocols, allowing contracting states, by virtue of a special declaration, not only to preclude enforcement of the relevant remedies, but also to deprive the creditor of any compensation (although with no retroactive effect).[135]

[126] Article 8(3) of the CTC.
[127] Article 8(4) and Article 1(m)(i) of the CTC.
[128] Article 9(3) of the CTC.
[129] Article 13(2) of the CTC.
[130] Article XXV of the Rail Protocol.
[131] Article XXVII of the Space Protocol.
[132] Howard Rosen, 'Public Service and the Cape Town Convention' (2013) 2 *Cape Town Convention Journal* 131, 133.
[133] Article XXVII(3) of the Space Protocol.
[134] Article XXV(3) of the Rail Protocol.
[135] Article XXV(5) of the Rail Protocol.

This provision effectively nullifies the protections of the CTC in relation to the corresponding rolling stock. Second, Article XXVII(9) of the Space Protocol not only provides that the limitation on the exercise of remedies established by paragraph 3 does not apply to a creditor whose international interest was created prior to the conclusion of the contract with the public services provider, but makes this provision conditional on the lack of *actual* knowledge of the existence of a public services contract by such creditor. The need to ascertain the factual matter of existence or absence of actual knowledge appears only once across all four protocols and the Convention itself and this unusual provision looks very odd in a treaty built around the concept of legal certainty and numerous provisions expressly envisaging that the state of one's mind has no bearing on its application.[136]

Interestingly, a public service exemption is not known to the Aircraft Protocol: in its first memorandum prepared for the UNIDROIT Study Group in 1995, the AWG expressly addressed the potential negative effect of the Rome Convention on the exercise of remedies under the draft Convention and requested an 'express rejection of the rights and remedies accruing to an aircraft operator' under the Rome Convention.[137] This rejection was reflected in the final text of Article XXIV of the CTC. While different possible explanations of this fact exist,[138] it is clear that in the case of aircraft the need to promote financing interests trumped the relevant non-commercial concerns.

Two additional important factors were counteracting the need for greater certainty (and the corresponding high amount of detail) in the CTC: the need to keep the text light and simple[139] and the need to leave room for flexibility and future development of the Convention. The first conflict later resulted in the adoption of explanatory materials, whereas the latter led to the implementation of a mechanism for periodic review of the CTC (Article 61), initially proposed by the AWG in 1997.[140]

A curious example of non-commercial state sensitivities relates to what could be labelled as 'trends' in international treaty-making or 'treaty fashion'. In the history of development of the CTC these matters were raised during the discussions focusing on jurisdiction and interpretation. In 1998, the SRC considered the question whether the three grounds of jurisdiction to grant 'speedy judicial relief'[141] (which included the location of the object within the territory of the relevant state, the location of the relevant parties in the relevant state and the agreement of the parties to confer jurisdiction on a court of their choice) were exclusive, or whether

[136] See Article 29(2)(a)–(b), Article 29(3)(b), Article 29(4)(b) of the CTC, Article XIV(1) of the Aircraft Protocol, Article XXIII(1) of the Space Protocol.

[137] See footnote 40 in Unidroit, *Study LXXII - Doc. 16 (1995)* 17.

[138] See, eg, Howard Rosen, 'Public Service and the Cape Town Convention' (2013) 2 *Cape Town Convention Journal* 131, 133.

[139] See, eg, paragraphs 9 and 11 in Unidroit, *Study LXXII - Doc. 27 (1996)* 10; paragraph 11 in Unidroit, *Study LXXII - Doc. 36 (1997)* 5; Unidroit, *Study LXXII - Doc. 40 (1998)* 7.

[140] See paragraph 2.3 in Unidroit, *Study LXXII - Doc. 32 Add. 2 (1997)* 5.

[141] See Article 16(3) in Unidroit, *Study LXXII - Doc. 39 (1998)* 7.

it was possible to add other grounds. The key issue was whether concurrent jurisdiction could be attributed to the court having *general* jurisdiction over the merits of the case 'in view of the growing trend to give extraterritorial effect to orders *in rem* in cases where the court making such orders was the court having jurisdiction over the merits of the case, where previously such effect would not have been given'.[142]

Adding extraterritorial effect to interim *in rem* orders, it was felt, would 'better fulfil the Convention's vocation to reflect the conditions likely to prevail in the 21st Century'.[143] For essentially the same reasons, the reverse provision, which purported to give general jurisdiction over the merits to the court authorised to grant speedy judicial relief,[144] was subject to additional scrutiny by the SRC: it 'would go against the current international trend by providing for a *forum arresti*, a jurisdiction known only to a very small number of States and one which had been widely criticised as exorbitant'.[145] In a similar fashion, the French delegation later cautioned the other participants of the Third Joint Session that the 'Convention cannot, without incurring the risk of grave dysfunction, derogate in such a flagrant manner from the rules *normally used* by States for the founding of jurisdiction in respect of the granting of interim relief'.[146] During the same Third Joint Session, one delegation similarly observed that the article on interpretation of the CTC was modelled after the corresponding provision of the CISG, noting that 'all commercial law Conventions adopted since 1980 had used [same] formulation and, if it were modified in this instrument, it might cast doubt on those other commercial law Conventions'.[147]

Overall, the many state sensitivities obviously played a secondary role in the development of the CTC – a *commercial* convention at its core. These factors are difficult to compare against their commercial counterparts, as the former are impossible to quantify. At the same time, the history of development of the CTC has shown that many of these factors (including insolvency rules, procedural laws and even matters affecting rights to immovable property) – despite their sensitive nature – can be effectively tackled in a commercial treaty through the use of alternatives,[148] optional provisions and declarations.

[142] See paragraph 121 in Unidroit, *Study LXXII – Doc. 41 (1998)* 30 (emphasis in the original). The report specifically refers to the Helsinki Principles on Provisional and Protective Measures in International Litigation adopted in 1996 (the 'Principles'). These Principles expressly recognise in paragraph 16 that 'where the court is properly exercising jurisdiction over the substance of the matter, it should have the power to issue provisional and protective orders addressed to the defendant personally to freeze his assets, irrespective of their location'.

[143] ibid.

[144] See Article 17(1) in Unidroit, *Study LXXII – Doc. 39 (1998)* 7.

[145] See paragraph 124 in Unidroit, *Study LXXII – Doc. 41 (1998)* 30 (emphasis in the original).

[146] Unidroit, *Unidroit CGE/Int.Int./3-WP/4 ICAO Ref. LSC/ME/3-WP/4 (2000)* 5 (emphasis added).

[147] See paragraph 90 in Unidroit, *Unidroit CGE/Int.Int./3-Report ICAO Ref. LSC/ME/3-Report (2000)* 11.

[148] See section 8.3.

The use of declarations to address state sensitivities deserves a separate mention: throughout the years of development the Convention and its protocols developed an elaborate system of declarations allowing (and in some cases requiring) contracting states to decide on a number of matters for which wholesale unification was not feasible. This system of declarations, coupled with express prohibition on reservations,[149] prevents uncontrolled dilution of the scope and reach of these instruments, while at the same time allowing states to make choices in respect of the most sensitive matters. Available declarations come in five groups: opt-in declarations, opt-out declarations, declarations relating to a contracting state's own laws, mandatory declarations and 'other' declarations.[150]

[149] See Article 56(1) of the CTC, Article XXXII(1) of the Aircraft Protocol, Article XXVIII(1) of the Rail Protocol, Article XLIII(1) of the Space Protocol and Article XXX(1) of the MAC Protocol.

[150] See paragraph 2.327 in Goode, *Convention on International Interests in Mobile Equipment and Protocol thereto on Matters Specific to Aircraft Equipment: Official Commentary* (4th edn, International Institute for the Unification of Private Law (UNIDROIT) 2019) 190.

8

Process-Management Challenges

8.1. Overview

The process of development of the CTC was long and complex: the Convention and its first protocol were adopted more than 10 years after the start of the project by UNIDROIT. Such a marathon is not feasible without careful planning and forward-looking strategic thinking. This chapter examines various solutions utilised during the development of the Convention to make the overall process manageable and realistic.

First, it assesses the key role played by the various working groups in the development of the treaty. Second, it posits that alternatives were the crucial element of crystallising negotiations and identifying the most appropriate solution (which is further stressed by the fact that alternatives were eventually retained in the final text of the document, eg in the form of alternative bankruptcy provisions in the protocols). Third, the chapter examines the complicated interplay of various stakeholders in the process of development of the treaty, with a focus on the need to obtain industry support and, to illustrate this point, the very different outcomes generated by the CTC for different industries.

8.2. The Role of Working Groups in the Development of the Convention

The development of the CTC was a multi-stage process, in which governments were not directly involved until the later stages: the UNIDROIT Governing Council formally included the matter of preparing a treaty on security interests in mobile equipment in its Work Programme in April 1989,[1] whereas the first session of governmental experts took place almost 10 years later, in February 1999.[2] Prior to formally submitting the texts to the review by states, UNIDROIT spent a significant amount of time to produce coherent and balanced draft instruments. This work was carried out by internal working groups and supervised by the

[1] Unidroit, *Governing Council C.D. 68 – Doc. 26 (1989)* 36.
[2] See Unidroit, *Unidroit CGE/Int.Int./Report ICAO Ref. LSC/ME-Report (1999)*.

UNIDROIT Governing Council, which acted as an important check on the overall process and the quality of the emerging solutions.

In the run-up to the governmental expert stage, UNIDROIT established two key working groups with a more general mandate: first, the Restricted Exploratory Working Group (REWG)[3] (meeting once in March 1992)[4] convened to carry out an early feasibility study (and submitting the results of such study to the Governing Council) and, second, the Study Group[5] (meeting four times: in March 1993,[6] April 1996,[7] January 1997[8] and November 1997[9]) established after the REWG to follow up with more substantial work, which culminated in the development of the draft Convention. Most of the fundamental decisions that steered the development of the CTC and its protocols followed from the work of these two working groups, but a large portion of the success of the Convention is attributable to the work of other, more specialised working groups and committees, which are examined in sections 8.2.1 and 8.2.3 below.

8.2.1. Steering and Revisions Committee (SRC)

The SRC was convened in June 1998, following the review by the UNIDROIT Governing Council of the draft Convention and the draft Aircraft Protocol, which revealed the need for the latter to be 'generally aligned, as to both style and terminology, with the preliminary draft Convention'.[10] The differences resulted from the fact that both documents came essentially from different working groups: the draft Convention was prepared by the Study Group, while the draft Aircraft Protocol was created by the APG. The resulting misalignment and complexity of the draft protocol, which was 'drafted in the style of very detailed legislation',[11] was so apparent that some members of the UNIDROIT Governing Council queried 'whether a clearer result might not be obtained by drawing up several *different Conventions* rather than one framework Convention and several different Protocols'.[12] This posed a real challenge to the umbrella structure[13] of the CTC – one of style, rather

[3] The REWG was established in 1991 pursuant to a decision of the UNIDROIT Governing Council – see Unidroit, *Governing Council C.D. (70) 22 (1991)* 62.

[4] See Unidroit, *Study LXXII – Doc. 5 (1992).*

[5] The Study Group was established in 1992 pursuant to a decision of the UNIDROIT Governing Council – see Unidroit, *Governing Council C.D. (71) 18 (1992)* 33.

[6] Unidroit, *Study LXXII – Doc. 7 (1993).*

[7] Unidroit, *Study LXXII – Doc. 27 (1996).*

[8] There is no report for this meeting, but the dates are confirmed in paragraph 3 in Unidroit, *Study LXXII – Doc. 35 (1997)* 1.

[9] There is no report for this meeting, but the dates are confirmed in Unidroit, *Study LXXII – Doc. 37 (1997).*

[10] Unidroit, *Study LXXII – Doc. 40 (1998)* 37.

[11] ibid 7.

[12] ibid 19 (emphasis added).

[13] See section 4.3.

than scope. Without proper alignment, presentation of the two texts to the governments was considered 'wholly inappropriate'.[14]

The role of the SRC was essentially technical: where policy matters were raised, the corresponding provisions were put in square brackets for the attention of state representatives during the governmental expert stage.[15] The committee was careful not to exceed its terms of reference, even where an alternative solution seemed more intuitive.[16] Nonetheless, the proper alignment of the two texts showed that the umbrella structure was indeed possible and realistic.

8.2.2. Drafting Groups and Committees

The collegial nature of deliberations at various stages of development of the CTC required a dedicated body to translate the relevant decisions into the language that was appropriate for an international convention. In the context of development of the Convention itself, this role was performed by: (i) the chairman of the Study Group;[17] (ii) the Drafting Group of the First Draft Subcommittee of the Study Group, which held four sessions in July 1994,[18] June 1995,[19] December 1995[20] and March 1996;[21] (iii) the Drafting Group of the Study Group as a whole, with sessions in April 1996;[22] October 1996,[23] January 1997;[24] (iv) the Drafting Committee of each of the three sessions of governmental experts in 1999 and 2000;[25] and (v) the Drafting Committee of the Cape Town Diplomatic Conference.[26] Special drafting committees were also established for the purposes of development and adoption of other protocols.

Interestingly, the various drafting groups and committees went much further than rubber-stamping the decisions adopted by other working groups in multiple

[14] Unidroit, *Study LXXII – Doc. 40 (1998)* 34.

[15] Unidroit, *Study LXXII – Doc. 41 (1998)* 27.

[16] Despite the proposal of the chairman of the Study Group to amend the draft agreed by the Study Group previously, the SRC left it for the governments to decide whether the chargee's duty to exercise remedies in a commercially reasonable manner should apply to conditional sellers and lessors: see paragraphs 28, 38 and 117 in ibid 29. It will be recalled from section 5.3.4.i that subsequently every protocol extended the scope of the 'reasonableness' test to the exercise of *all* remedies.

[17] See Unidroit, *Study LXXII – Doc. 39 (1998).*

[18] See Unidroit, *Study LXXII – Doc. 13 (1994).*

[19] See Unidroit, *Study LXXII – Doc. 18 (1995).*

[20] See Unidroit, *Study LXXII – Doc. 22 (1996).*

[21] See Unidroit, *Study LXXII – Doc. 24 (1996).*

[22] See Appendix IV to Unidroit, *Study LXXII – Doc. 27 (1996).*

[23] See Unidroit, *Study LXXII – Doc. 30 (1996).*

[24] See Unidroit, *Study LXXII – Drafting Group Fourth Session (1997).*

[25] See Attachment D in Unidroit, *Unidroit CGE/Int.Int./Report ICAO Ref. LSC/ME-Report (1999)*; Attachment F in Unidroit, *ICAO Ref. LSC/ME/2-Report Unidroit CGE/Int.Int./2-Report (1999)*; Attachment C in Unidroit, *Unidroit CGE/Int.Int./3-Report ICAO Ref. LSC/ME/3-Report (2000).*

[26] See Unidroit, *Diplomatic Conference to Adopt a Mobile Equipment Convention and an Aircraft Protocol: Acts and Proceedings; [Convention on International Interests in Mobile Equipment and Protocol thereto on Matters Specific to Aircraft Equipment]* (UNIDROIT 2006) 295.

ways: by suggesting new approaches, formulating new concepts and even breaking deadlocks in negotiations. In doing so, they performed a steering role and significantly affected the course of development of multiple provisions.

Initially, the need for a more active role of the Drafting Group was dictated by practical considerations of drafting efficiency. The second session of the First Draft Subcommittee of the Study Group concluded with a decision to revise the early draft of the Convention[27] in the light of two sets of comments: (i) the conclusions reached during that meeting, and (ii) a memorandum to be prepared by an 'external group representing the interests of the aviation industry' (later known as the AWG).[28] The latter document was not yet ready at the time and was to be produced in due course, yet the First Draft Subcommittee was keen to have the revised draft ready before the next session. Mindful that the future memorandum of the aviation industry might raise new and unexpected issues, the subcommittee empowered the Drafting Group to 'be free, in proposing a revised text, to depart from what had been provisionally agreed to the extent necessary'.[29]

Following the above decision, the Drafting Group continued performing its steering function. One of the prime examples of this role is the decision to follow the model of Article 2 of the Convention for the European Patent for the Common Market and introduce the concept of 'autonomous' nature of the international interest, which served as a turning point in determining the characteristics of the latter.[30] In a similar fashion, the Drafting Group deemed inappropriate the earlier decision of the First Draft Subcommittee to treat an international interest effective if it had been perfected in accordance with domestic law.[31] On a different occasion, the Drafting Group, dissatisfied with the earlier agreement of the First Draft Subcommittee to apply all the remedy provisions on an 'opt-in' basis,[32] proposed two alternative wordings to the same article to draw the attention of the Study Group to the effects of the initial approach in situations when the parties have failed to come to an agreement.[33] While incorporating the early provisions relating to the international registry, the Drafting Group introduced, on its own initiative, the idea of an 'independent adjudicator' authorised to hear complaints in respect of acts or omissions of the Registrar and operators of national registration facilities, citing the 'principles of natural justice'.[34] In the same document, the Drafting Group 'expressed itself to be against the idea of introducing the obligor's written consent as a requirement for a valid assignment', taking the view that this 'would create as many problems as those it sought to solve'.[35] Later, during the First

[27] Unidroit, *Study LXXII – Doc. 13 (1994).*
[28] See paragraph 11 in Unidroit, *Study LXXII – Doc. 15 (1995)* 9.
[29] ibid.
[30] See n 112 and the corresponding discussion in section 2.3.2.
[31] See paragraph 12 in Unidroit, *Study LXXII – Doc. 22 (1996)* ii.
[32] See paragraph 12 in Unidroit, *Study LXXII – Doc. 21 (1995)* 7.
[33] See paragraph 8 in Unidroit, *Study LXXII – Doc. 22 (1996)* ii. See also section 5.3.2.
[34] See paragraph 42 in Unidroit, *Study LXXII – Doc. 35 (1997)* 8.
[35] See paragraph 50 in ibid 9.

Joint Session, the Drafting Committee considered the instruction of the plenary to examine the feasibility of introducing the concepts of 'good faith' and 'public order' in the context of self-help remedies, and proceeded in a totally different direction, by adding the requirement of the chargor's consent instead.[36]

In addition to playing a proactive role by suggesting new alternative solutions and casting a critical eye on the changes agreed by the negotiators, the various drafting groups and committees were often called to decide on matters of policy when the relevant collegial bodies could not come to agreement. In these cases, a referral of a difficult matter to the draftsmen was essentially a shorthand for requesting a *solution* from the drafting experts, often to produce a basis for future discussions. This was the case during the second session of the Study Group, which ended its long and inconclusive discussions with a request to the Drafting Group to 'do its best to capture the various ideas put forward in the course of the Study Group's consideration', even authorising it to enlist the assistance of an expert representing the aviation industry.[37]

Reliance on the Drafting Committee as an instrument for breaking deadlocks in negotiations was even stronger during the governmental expert stage, with delegates often referring to the drafting team matters of higher complexity without adequate guidance due to the absence of an agreement. Examples include a general instruction to revise the bankruptcy provisions in the light of other international conventions and soft law instruments,[38] or an abstract decision that 'the Drafting Committee should look at the entire Chapter VIII'.[39] This led the Drafting Committee to admit in the course of the First Joint Session that in respect of certain issues it 'did not feel that its instructions from the Joint Session permitted it to provide a solution'[40] and to refer the same matters back to the delegates, effectively creating a 'ping-pong' situation.[41] This mutual referral of certain matters sometimes led to absurd results: delegates of the Second Joint Session gave the Drafting Committee the task of considering whether or not the additional language qualifying the right of the creditor to exercise certain remedies should be deleted,[42] without noticing that the additional language in question was in fact proposed by the Drafting Committee itself during the First Joint Session.[43] As a result, the Drafting Committee was essentially authorised to determine the fate of its own proposal.

[36] See n 84 in section 5.3.2 and the corresponding discussion.

[37] See paragraph 105 in Unidroit, *Study LXXII – Doc. 27 (1996)* 46.

[38] See paragraph 73 in Unidroit, *Unidroit CGE/Int.Int./Report ICAO Ref. LSC/ME-Report (1999).*

[39] See paragraph 87 in ibid 13.

[40] See paragraph 6 in Attachment D to ibid 11–12.

[41] See, eg, footnote 10 in Appendix I to Attachment D in ibid.

[42] See paragraph 5:14 in Unidroit, *ICAO Ref. LSC/ME/2-Report Unidroit CGE/Int.Int./2-Report (1999)* 5–3.

[43] See Article 8(2) (noting the words 'and by lawful means' in square brackets) in Appendix I to Attachment D in Unidroit, *Unidroit CGE/Int.Int./Report ICAO Ref. LSC/ME-Report (1999).*

It should be noted that, with some exceptions,[44] the initiatives taken by the drafting groups or drafting committees were appreciated by the competent working groups and governmental representatives, as a sign of the important role played by drafts in crystallising the difficult points in negotiations. Nonetheless, the unfortunate tendency to offload onto the Drafting Committee matters of policy resulted in inefficient use of its time and was no doubt among those factors that prevented the Drafting Committee from finishing its work by the end of the Second Joint Session and led to the establishment of an intersessional ad hoc drafting group to cope with the heavy workload.[45]

8.2.3. Specialist Working Groups and Consultations

Different approaches were used during the development of the CTC and its protocols to tackle complex issues requiring expert knowledge or empirical research unavailable within the relevant negotiating body. These included the commissioning of individual experts or organisations to conduct research,[46] as well as internal research conducted by the UNIDROIT Secretariat.[47] The most sophisticated problems, however, could not be resolved by a single expert or the Secretariat alone to a satisfactory standard and required the pooling of expert knowledge in dedicated specialist working groups.

An example of such approach is the establishment of a 'group of technical experts … to look at both the legal regimen … desirable for the proposed registration system … and the computer technology aspects of this system' at the conclusion of the third session of the First Draft Subcommittee.[48] The relevant working group met twice (in April 1996[49] and May 1997[50]) and produced not only comments regarding the structure and operation of the international registration system envisaged by the draft Convention, but also a set of revised provisions to be included in the draft treaty.[51]

In the run-up to the Cape Town Diplomatic Conference, the practice of setting up specialist working groups continued during the governmental expert stage, where the delegates established, among other things: (i) the Registration Working Group to deal with institutional, legal, operational and other relevant issues regarding the establishment of the international registry;[52] (ii) an informal

[44] See n 140 in section 5.3.4 and the corresponding discussion for an example when the suggested change was reverted as exceeding the scope of prior agreement within the Study Group.

[45] See paragraph 1 in Unidroit, *Unidroit CGE/Int.Int./3-WP/2 ICAO Ref. LSC/ME/3-WP/2 (2000).*

[46] See, eg, Unidroit, *Study LXXII – Doc. 1 (1989)*; Unidroit, *Study LXXII – Doc. 2 (1989).*

[47] See, eg, paragraph 1 in Unidroit, *Governing Council C.D. (86) 8 (d) (2007)* 1.

[48] See paragraph 39 in Unidroit, *Study LXXII – Doc. 21 (1995)* 13.

[49] Unidroit, *Study LXXIIC – Doc. 2 (1997).*

[50] Unidroit, *Study LXXIIC – Doc. 3 (1997).*

[51] See Appendix II in ibid.

[52] See paragraphs 14, 54 and Attachment C in Unidroit, *Unidroit CGE/Int.Int./Report ICAO Ref. LSC/ME-Report (1999)* 5.

working group to consider possible overlap of the draft Convention with the draft UNCITRAL Convention on Assignment in Receivables Financing;[53] (iii) an informal working group to analyse the insolvency-related provisions of the draft Convention and the draft Aircraft Protocol in the context of other existing international insolvency-related rules and instruments[54] (later given a formal status);[55] (iv) the Jurisdiction Working Group to discuss the most appropriate grounds for establishing the jurisdiction of courts under the Convention, the limits of party autonomy to determine such jurisdiction and other pertaining issues;[56] and (v) the Public International Law Working Group to review the relationship between the draft Convention and its protocols, the number of ratifications required for their entry into force and other relevant matters.[57]

While many of the above working groups continued their operation throughout multiple sessions of governmental experts, with the passing of time another important function of specialist working groups became apparent: in the run-up to the Cape Town Diplomatic Conference matters on which delegations struggled to agree were referred to ad hoc working groups to break the deadlock. The Third Joint Session gives two excellent examples. First, the plenary established a small working group to consider the concept of internationality[58] 'in consideration of the division of opinion among delegations'.[59] Second, the delegates convened another small working group to examine the advance relief provisions[60] 'in view of the opposing views that were expressed by a number of delegations'.[61] In each case, the small membership of the working groups helped crystallise the key points of contention and propose a single solution or a number of alternatives.

Composition of working groups created for the purpose of breaking deadlocks deserves a separate mention, as expert knowledge in a specific area was not the only or the primary factor in the selection of participants. Such groups were often intended to achieve a compromise rather than produce new knowledge, acting as think-tanks rather than miniature research bodies. This practice became even more evident during the Cape Town Diplomatic Conference,[62] where the chairman, Antti Leinonen, established a number of working groups, often referred to

[53] See paragraph 74 in ibid 12.

[54] See paragraph 143 in ibid 21.

[55] See paragraph 3:1 in Unidroit, *ICAO Ref. LSC/ME/2-Report Unidroit CGE/Int.Int./2-Report (1999)* 3–1.

[56] See paragraphs 3:1, 3:3, 5:74–5:81 in ibid.

[57] See paragraphs 3:1, 3:4, 5:36 in ibid.

[58] See n 187 in section 2.4.3 and the corresponding discussion.

[59] See paragraph 71 in Unidroit, *Unidroit CGE/Int.Int./3-Report ICAO Ref. LSC/ME/3-Report (2000)* 10.

[60] See n 114 in section 5.3.3 and the corresponding discussion.

[61] See paragraph 110 in Unidroit, *Unidroit CGE/Int.Int./3-Report ICAO Ref. LSC/ME/3-Report (2000)* 13.

[62] I am most grateful to the UNIDROIT Secretariat for providing a transcript of all sessions of the Cape Town Diplomatic Conference between 29 October and 16 November 2001, which helped greatly in preparing this book.

as 'informal consultations', to seek a common solution on a variety of issues, such as: (i) immunity of the Supervisory Authority;[63] (ii) choosing the most appropriate mechanism of assignment;[64] (iii) application of the Convention to pre-existing rights or interests;[65] (iv) treatment of non-consensual rights and interests in the case of insolvency;[66] (v) providing support to states lacking the capacity to establish the connection between national entry points and the international registry;[67] (vi) requirements for the entry into force and the establishment of the international registry;[68] (vii) rules on jurisdiction in light of the European Community legislation;[69] (viii) protection of aircraft liens as security for EUROCONTROL charges;[70] and (ix) procedure for amendments to the Convention and its protocols.[71]

The consensus-building purpose of these informal 'think-tanks' stems not only from their objectives, but also from their composition, which was non-exclusive and open to any interested delegations.[72] Attempts to firmly distinguish between such informal consultations and working groups do not yield a satisfactory result, as the different labels, which were not always uniformly used, essentially reflect the same collaborative engagement of various delegations. What does matter, however, is that the referral of complex negotiation issues to delegates – rather than the Drafting Committee – left the policy matters in the hands of the actual decision makers,[73] reducing the workload of the drafting team.[74]

Overall, the practice of active engagement of delegations in small-group consultations and working groups was a highly effective way of reaching a satisfactory outcome of deliberations during the Cape Town Diplomatic Conference, with some delegations noting that 'the Chairman's role in facilitating sub-groups and

[63] Unidroit, *Diplomatic Conference to Adopt a Mobile Equipment Convention and an Aircraft Protocol: Acts and Proceedings; [Convention on International Interests in Mobile Equipment and Protocol thereto on Matters Specific to Aircraft Equipment]* (UNIDROIT 2006) 779–80.

[64] ibid 784.

[65] ibid 797.

[66] ibid 816. The published summary mentions only referral of the matter to the Drafting Committee, however the transcript reflects the invitation of the chairman to the delegations of Singapore and Canada to hold informal negotiations.

[67] Unidroit, *Diplomatic Conference to Adopt a Mobile Equipment Convention and an Aircraft Protocol: Acts and Proceedings; [Convention on International Interests in Mobile Equipment and Protocol thereto on Matters Specific to Aircraft Equipment]* (UNIDROIT 2006) 836.

[68] ibid 841.

[69] ibid 847.

[70] ibid 845.

[71] ibid 905.

[72] See, eg, the summary of the chairman's response to an intervention by Kenya: see Unidroit, *Diplomatic Conference to Adopt a Mobile Equipment Convention and an Aircraft Protocol: Acts and Proceedings; [Convention on International Interests in Mobile Equipment and Protocol thereto on Matters Specific to Aircraft Equipment]* (UNIDROIT 2006) 878.

[73] cf the occasional practice of referring matters of substance to the Drafting Committee during the Joint Sessions of governmental experts in section 8.2.2.

[74] To ensure objectivity, the chairman intentionally distanced himself from all the informal consultation groups and did not participate in any of them.

informal consultations had been the *main instrument* which had led to the conclusion of the meetings … [in] a very satisfactory manner'.[75]

8.3. Alternatives as an Instrument of Crystallising Negotiations

Throughout the whole period of development of the Convention and its protocols alternative texts of the same provision were produced to facilitate discussion and to emphasise the differences between various views. Alternatives were used by virtually all the working groups, including: (i) the Drafting Group;[76] (ii) the APG;[77] (iii) the SRC;[78] (iv) specialist working groups during the Joint Sessions;[79] (v) the Drafting Committee of the Joint Sessions;[80] and even commentators.[81]

In all instances – but two – the alternatives reached their goal and resulted in the selection of a single option preferred (and revised as necessary) by the relevant working groups and delegates. The two sets of alternative provisions on which no agreement could be reached relate to (i) remedies on insolvency, and (ii) association of mining, agricultural and construction equipment with immovable property. The former can now be found in each of the first three protocols[82] (but not the MAC Protocol), and deserves a separate mention. The latter is specific to the MAC Protocol and was addressed in section 7.3.[83]

All the insolvency-related alternatives originate from the proposal of the AWG to incorporate into the draft Convention an optional 'international insolvency provision', modelled after Section 1110 of the US Bankruptcy Code and aiming to give greater protection to the financier in the event of the insolvency of the debtor.[84] By the start of the First Joint Session, the corresponding provision was

[75] Unidroit, *Diplomatic Conference to Adopt a Mobile Equipment Convention and an Aircraft Protocol: Acts and Proceedings; [Convention on International Interests in Mobile Equipment and Protocol thereto on Matters Specific to Aircraft Equipment]* (UNIDROIT 2006) 907 (emphasis added).

[76] See, eg, alternative drafts of Article 1(2) in Unidroit, *Study LXXII – Doc. 18 (1995)* 5; alternative drafts of Article 7 in Unidroit, *Study LXXII – Doc. 22 (1996)* 4 and in Unidroit, *Study LXXII – Doc. 24 (1996)* iv; alternative drafts of Article 24(2) in Unidroit, *Study LXXII – Drafting Group Fourth Session (1997)* 9; alternative drafts of Articles 6 and 26 in Unidroit, *Study LXXII – Doc. 35 (1997)* ii–iii.

[77] See, eg, alternative drafts of Article XXIII in Unidroit, *Study LXXIID – Doc. 1 (1998)* 14–15; alternative drafts of Article XVI in Unidroit, *Study LXXIID – Doc. 3 (1998)* 11.

[78] See alternative drafts of Article XVII in Appendix III to Unidroit, *Study LXXII – Doc. 41 (1998).*

[79] See three alternative drafts of Article C proposed by the Registration Working Group in Appendix II to Unidroit, *ICAO Ref. LSC/ME/2-WP/17 Unidroit CGE/Int.Int./2-WP/17 (1999)*; Options A and B in paragraph 28 of Unidroit, *Unidroit CGE/Int.Int./3-WP/18 ICAO Ref. LSC/ME/3-WP/18 12/03/00 (2000)* 9.

[80] See, eg, alternative drafts of Article 26 *bis* on the liability of the Registrar in Unidroit, *Unidroit CGE/Int.Int./3-WP/28 Rev. ICAO Ref. LSC/ME/3-WP/28 Rev. 28/03/00 (2000)* 4.

[81] See, eg, alternatives A and B in draft Article 36(4) in Unidroit, *Study LXXII – Doc. 36 (1997)* 53.

[82] See Article XI of the Aircraft Protocol, Article IX of the Rail Protocol, Article XXI of the Space Protocol.

[83] See n 123 in section 7.3.

[84] See Annex 4-B in Unidroit, *Study LXXII – Doc. 16 (1995)* 45.

made part of the draft Aircraft Protocol and contained in a single article, with no alternatives, but subject to the right of each contracting state not to apply the relevant provisions.[85] Discussions at the First Joint Session, however, showed a divergence of opinion: one group of delegates noted that the corresponding insolvency provision encroached significantly on national bankruptcy laws, while others stressed the 'economic importance'[86] of the rule. As a result, the Drafting Committee was instructed to prepare two alternative versions of the same article,[87] which it could not do in time, leaving the second option (Alternative B) empty. Importantly, however, nothing in the language of the alternatives indicates that they were formulated as options from which states could choose: they merely represented two different options for the governmental experts to consider at the next session.

This changed after review of the report of the Insolvency Working Group during the Second Joint Session, which agreed 'to proceed on the basis of offering Contracting States two alternative approaches':[88] a 'hard' option, based on the draft proposed by the AWG allowing automatic transfer of possession to the creditor without court intervention, and a 'soft' version, based on the proposal of the French delegation, which provided for a degree of judicial control and discretion over the exercise of remedies. These two options formed the basis of Alternatives A and B in the first three protocols. Alternative C, which largely follows Alternative A, but allows intervention by the insolvency administrator to suspend the obligation to give the creditor the opportunity to take possession of collateral, unique to the Rail Protocol,[89] appeared after the adoption of the Convention and the Aircraft Protocol, following a proposal by the Rail Working Group,[90] which intended to produce a compromise between the 'hard' and 'soft' options.

Interestingly, the MAC Protocol did not follow the Rail Protocol (on which it was largely based) and – despite the early designs[91] – has become the only protocol to the CTC that does not include multiple alternatives relating to remedies on insolvency. The abolition of Alternatives B and C was a last-minute change adopted during the Pretoria Diplomatic Conference.[92] By November 2019 (ie almost 20 years following the adoption of the Convention) it became clear that the relevant alternatives had served no purpose: there had only been one ratification in the entire history of the treaty that selected any option other than Alternative A. Thus, for the first time the provisions of a protocol relating to remedies on insolvency (in this case, Article X of the MAC Protocol) offer states a clear binary choice between (i) a single set of provisions in the protocol itself, and

[85] See Articles XI and XXX in Unidroit, *Study LXXIID – Doc. 3 (1998).*

[86] See n 73 in section 7.2.2.

[87] See paragraph 123 in Unidroit, *Unidroit CGE/Int.Int./Report ICAO Ref. LSC/ME-Report (1999)* 19.

[88] See paragraph 2.2 in Unidroit, *ICAO Ref. LSC/ME/2-WP/19 Unidroit CGE/Int.Int./2-WP/19 26/8/99 (1999)* 2.

[89] See Article IX of the Rail Protocol.

[90] See Attachment K in Unidroit, *Study LXXIIH – Doc. 7 (2002).*

[91] See draft Article X in Unidroit, *Study 72k – CGE1 – Doc. 2 corr. (2017).*

[92] See Unidroit, *Unidroit 2019 DCME-MAC – Doc. 24 rev. (2019)* 1–2.

(ii) their own insolvency laws (by not making a declaration implementing the protocol's rules).

8.4. Obtaining Industry Support

In 1994, at a very early stage of development of the Convention, UNIDROIT reported an interesting 'phenomenon':

> [A]n ever-lengthening number of international instruments in the business law field which, notwithstanding the most thorough intergovernmental preparation and the very best efforts of international Organisations ... had either failed to enter into force at all or, at best, operated only as between a limited number of States.[93]

This problem highlighted another challenge: to ensure that those who are in a position to exert the necessary pressure on governments (namely, the business circles affected by the new instruments) view the proposed changes as necessary and beneficial to them. In the context of the CTC, the perceived effect of the changes brought about by this treaty was not uniformly understood among the different industries, which resulted in dramatically different levels of support expressed by them.

First attempts to measure the level of interest of various industries go back to Cuming's 1990 Questionnaire circulated among financial institutions, industry associations and concerns (according to UNIDROIT, approximately 1,000 copies were distributed).[94] Among 93 respondents, the clear majority (52) identified themselves as 'lenders' and represented the financial services industry.[95] Over the years, the latter showed considerable support towards the Convention, viewing it as an important instrument for the promotion of asset finance. The banking industry generally looked at the UNIDROIT project through the prism of a risk-averse creditor aiming to achieve a number of objectives, such as: (i) improved access to market information resulting from the establishment of an international register;[96] (ii) cost reduction via elimination of legal risks and keeping in check the costs (both monetary and time-related) associated with the international registration system;[97] (iii) maintaining the stability of the loan market by protecting pre-existing national interests and eliminating confusion from the coexistence of national and international interests;[98] or (iv) strengthening the creditor's position through the promotion of self-help remedies[99] and recovery of legal costs from

[93] Unidroit, *Study LXXIIB – Doc. 1 (1995)* 2.
[94] Unidroit, *Study LXXII – Doc. 3 (1991)* 2.
[95] ibid 3. See also Appendix to the same.
[96] Unidroit, *Study LXXII – Doc. 26 (1996)* 2.
[97] ibid 2–3; Unidroit, *Study LXXII – Doc. 36 Add. 1 (1997)* 1.
[98] Unidroit, *Study LXXII – Doc. 26 (1996)* 3; Unidroit, *Study LXXII – Doc. 36 Add. 1 (1997)* 1–2.
[99] See paragraph 15 in Unidroit, *Study LXXII – Doc. 36 (1997)* 6.

the proceeds of enforcement.[100] The problem of conceptual differences between security interests, on the one hand, and the rights of lessor and conditional seller, on the other,[101] was also picked up within the banking sector,[102] in addition to the active position taken by Leaseurope.[103]

While the above banking concerns were aligned with the text of the Convention, the latter did not incorporate certain creditor-centric recommendations for various policy reasons. The proposal to extend the scope of the CTC to cover a broader range of mobile assets, including lorries and ships,[104] was rejected, in the first instance, to restrict the Convention to assets of very high value[105] and, in the second case, due to the resistance of the shipping circles.[106] The idea of establishment of a minimum threshold value of eligible assets[107] did not materialise to enhance predictability in the application of the CTC.[108] The recommendation to give effect to registration of interests from the moment of transmission of registration information to the registry[109] was rejected for the protection of interests of third parties.[110]

While the value of banking industry support should not be underestimated, the principal stakeholders of a treaty promoting asset financing techniques are, of course, the manufacturers and end users of relevant assets, ie those who produce and put to actual use such collateral. The lack of a shipping protocol is a fine illustration of this fact. This said, the impact of the relevant industry cannot be relegated to treaty promotion and domestic lobbying. In the case of the Aircraft Protocol alone, the involvement of the aviation circles had very practical needs[111] and made possible, among other things: (i) the development of the appropriate definitions of 'aircraft objects';[112] (ii) the selection of appropriate objective criteria (such as carrying capacity, thrust or horsepower) to limit the eligible aircraft objects to assets of high value; (iii) indication of the most appropriate mode of asset identification; and (iv) the incorporation of additional rules specific to the relevant industry (such as the aviation-specific remedy of aircraft de-registration).[113]

[100] Unidroit, *Study LXXII – Doc. 36 Add. 1 (1997)* 2.
[101] See section 2.2.4.
[102] See Unidroit, *Study LXXII – Doc. 26 (1996)* 3; paragraph 15 in Unidroit, *Study LXXII – Doc. 36 (1997)* 6.
[103] See n 42 in section 2.2.4.
[104] Unidroit, *Study LXXII – Doc. 26 (1996)* 3.
[105] See section 3.2.2.
[106] See section 3.4.
[107] Unidroit, *Study LXXII – Doc. 26 (1996)* 3.
[108] See section 3.2.1.
[109] See paragraph 157 in Unidroit, *Study LXXII – Doc. 36 (1997)* 38.
[110] See paragraph 4.153 in Goode, *Convention on International Interests in Mobile Equipment and Protocol thereto on Matters Specific to Aircraft Equipment: Official Commentary* (4th edn, International Institute for the Unification of Private Law (UNIDROIT) 2019) 363–64.
[111] See Unidroit, *Study LXXII – Doc. 40 (1998)* 6–7.
[112] However, a separate reference to 'helicopters' is unfortunate: see section 3.3.3.
[113] See Article IX(1)(a) of the Aircraft Protocol.

In the history of the CTC, no other single industry provided so much support to the project as the aviation sector represented by the AWG. The effect that the aviation industry had on the draft Convention was so significant compared to other sectors that one of the commentators representing the leasing circles ended up expressing its 'reservations regarding the extent to which the future Convention may be considered to be *representative* in view of the intense lobbying carried out by aviation interests'.[114] Furthermore, the role of the AWG was not limited to providing sector-specific expertise and building consensus within the relevant industry group. The resources available to it allowed the AWG to undertake numerous international activities promoting the draft Convention – a practice that caused a great deal of confusion in the run-up to the governmental expert stage.

The promotional activities, which the AWG conducted at the time in cooperation with IATA, included briefings aimed at governmental audiences. Apparently, the invitation letters sent on behalf of the AWG and IATA did not make it sufficiently clear that the two organisations were not acting on behalf of UNIDROIT or ICAO. As a result, a number of governments, upon receipt of such letters of invitation, 'had gained the impression that it was I.A.T.A. and A.W.G. [*sic*] that were driving the project and that the role of Unidroit and I.C.A.O. [*sic*] was limited to doing the paper-work'.[115]

The unfortunate practice (but not the very helpful promotional impact) of such briefings was condemned by the Acting Secretary-General of UNIDROIT, with the AWG and IATA representatives committing to 'avoid recurrences of such confusion and embarrassment in future'.[116] The same matter was raised again during the First Joint Session, which opened with a joint statement by the Secretary-General of UNIDROIT and the director of the ICAO Legal Bureau addressed to all the industry groups 'to respect the procedures of inter-governmental Organisations, in accordance with which relations with member States came within the exclusive purview of the inter-governmental Organisations concerned'.[117] The strongest concluding part of the original statement, which was subsequently removed from the final report as a gesture of goodwill, can still be found in the earlier drafts: 'This was so as to avoid the *unacceptable interferences* with member Governments that had regrettably occurred in the past'.[118]

Following adoption of the CTC and the Aircraft Protocol, the aviation industry (represented by the AWG) continued its efforts in assisting with the promotion and implementation of the two instruments, through various activities, from supporting the Cape Town Convention Academic Project (CTCAP)[119] to, more recently, the development of a Cape Town Convention Compliance Index[120] that

[114] See paragraph 205 in Unidroit, *Study LXXII – Doc. 36 (1997)* 58 (emphasis added).
[115] See paragraph 156 in Unidroit, *Study LXXII – Doc. 41 (1998)* 37.
[116] ibid.
[117] See paragraph 2 in Unidroit, *Unidroit CGE/Int.Int./Report ICAO Ref. LSC/ME-Report (1999)* 3.
[118] See paragraph 2 in Unidroit, *Unidroit CGE/Int.Int./WP/17 ICAO Ref. LSC/ME-WP/28 (1999)* 4 (emphasis added).
[119] 'Cape Town Convention Academic Project' www.ctcap.org.
[120] 'Cape Town Convention Compliance Index' https://ctc-compliance-index.awg.aero/.

monitors and assesses compliance of states parties to the CTC with their respective undertakings under the treaty.

What ended up as a major enterprise for the promotion of aviation financing interests, started from an early initiative by the Boeing Company to take a proactive view and, having consulted with a number of industry participants (the Long-Term Credit Bank of Japan, Ltd, GE Capital Aviation Services Ltd), offer support to the future Convention, but only to the extent that the new instrument would address the needs of the aviation sector through a number of finance-enhancing mechanisms (such as a clear first-to-file priority rule, a modern electronic registry, validity of international interests in bankruptcy, extensive party autonomy, application to both domestic and international transactions, and even to assignments of contract rights). If a comprehensive new instrument meeting these criteria was not possible, the Boeing Company was ready to walk away, recommending the exclusion of aircraft and aircraft engines from the scope of the future Convention altogether.[121] The overall thrust of the feedback presented by the aviation industry did not change after the formal establishment of the AWG (as a joint initiative of the Boeing Company and Airbus Industrie) and its cooperation with IATA: the UNIDROIT instrument was seen as commercially acceptable 'if, and only if, the proposed convention, taken as whole, materially [promoted] the asset-based financing of aviation equipment'.[122]

Overall, the participation of the aviation industry in the development of the CTC had three important characteristics. First, the industry-wide interest group was formed and actively supported the Convention before the formal engagement of the corresponding intergovernmental organisation (ICAO).[123] Second, the composition of the AWG was very diverse and included, apart from major aircraft and engine manufacturers, commercial banks with strong aviation finance practices and leasing companies, providing a more representative view of the industry.[124] Third, the AWG was instrumental in aligning its interests with those of the governments by stressing that the latter themselves often acted as primary risk-takers in aviation finance through the operation of export credit agencies.[125]

The situation was quite different in the shipping sector. As is clear from section 3.4, the fiasco of the idea of a shipping protocol under the Convention was the result of a very strong opposition from three international organisations: IMO, UNCTAD and the CMI. Unlike the aviation industry, the shipping business circles did not come together to form a dedicated interest group similar to the AWG, and occasionally produced individual comments and observations on the draft Convention.[126] Given the very early negative reaction of the shipping international organisations, and their very broad mandates, one can only speculate as to the

[121] See Appendix to the comments by Scott Scherer in Unidroit, *Study LXXII - Doc. 14 Add 1 (1994).*
[122] Unidroit, *Study LXXII - Doc. 32 Add. 2 (1997)* 1.
[123] ICAO was invited to participate in the preparation of the draft Aircraft Protocol in 1997 and hosted one of the APG sessions. See Unidroit, *Study LXXII - Doc. 40 (1998)* 17.
[124] See Annex 1 to Unidroit, *Study LXXII - Doc. 16 (1995)* 33–34.
[125] See ibid 27.
[126] See, eg, Unidroit, *Study LXXII - Doc. 36 Add. 2 (1997)* 1–2.

possibility of a different outcome for the idea of a shipping protocol in case of direct engagement of the shipping industry disregarding the stance taken by IMO, UNCTAD and the CMI. However, this raises the delicate problem of international coordination and the need for collaboration among international organisations, and the pressure to cooperate. It is thus unsurprising that UNIDROIT did not immediately proceed with the idea of a shipping protocol, unwilling to openly disregard the official position of major maritime organisations.[127] It is impossible to say with full certainty which of the two factors was decisive: the stance of these international organisations or the lack of clear industry support. However, for the purposes of this section, let us assume that UNIDROIT was seeking either (i) a consensus within the relevant industry, or, at least, (ii) a position not subject to any major objections from within the industry.

The assumption above appears accurate in the context of the shipping protocol: both legs of the test failed, resulting in the logical decision not to continue with the idea of a dedicated shipping protocol. The same assumption, however, does not work if applied to the history of the Space Protocol, which was adopted despite major objections of parts of the target business sector. In 2008 and 2009, ie at an advance stage of development of the protocol, major satellite operators petitioned the UNIDROIT Secretariat not to proceed with the adoption of the instrument, claiming that it would 'neither benefit the satellite industry nor facilitate space finance'.[128] In the run-up to the Berlin Diplomatic Conference, this proposal was supplemented by a letter[129] allegedly signed by a large group of industry stakeholders requesting no further action to adopt the Space Protocol.[130] The different arguments made in this letter can be reduced to two key statements: (i) the new instrument would not generate economic benefit, and (ii) the existing financing regime was satisfactory and not in need of reform. Despite these and other similar efforts of the industry,[131] the Space Protocol was nevertheless adopted in 2012, generating even more vocal opposition.[132]

This fact calls for reconsideration of the earlier assumption, since, first, there was clearly no consensus within the target business sector and, second, even a clear

[127] More recently, a more subtle approach has been utilised by UNIDROIT, which produced a limited feasibility study analysing the potential benefits of the CTC system for the shipping industry: see Unidroit, *Unidroit 2013 C.D. (92) 5(c)/(d) (2013).*

[128] Unidroit, *Study LXXIIJ – Doc. 17 (2009)* 12.

[129] 'Letter from a Group of Space Industry Representatives to Mr. Martin John Stanford' (9 December 2011) www.geospatialworld.net/wp-content/uploads/Satellite%20Industry%20Letter%20to%20Unidroit%209%20Dec%202011%20%28rev%29.pdf.

[130] The list included 45 entities identified as satellite operators, 12 entities labelled spacecraft manufacturers and launch service providers, 17 entities marked as space insurers and underwriters, 11 entities associated with the financial services sector and 8 'other' satellite and space-related organisations and institutions.

[131] For more evidence of opposition of the satellite industry and additional critique see Mark J Sundahl, *The Cape Town Convention: Its Application to Space Assets and Relation to the Law of Outer Space* (Martinus Nijhoff Publishers 2013) 27.

[132] 'Global Satellite Industry Denounces UNIDROIT Protocol' (9 March 2012) www.casbaa.com/news/industry-news/global-satellite-industry-denounces-unidroit-protocol.

opposition of a particular industry did not affect the decision to adopt the Space Protocol. To accommodate this outcome, it appears that the actual test applied by UNIDROIT in assessing the level of industry support was based on but a single factor: whether or not there existed a *representative* industry view in support of the new instrument (regardless of the existence of objections from parts of the target sector).

The wisdom of this decision remains to be tested in the future, in the light of the number of ratifications of the Space Protocol (which so far amount to zero) and its practical application by end users. In the end, many of the concerns voiced by the satellite industry might end up being overstated: it is immediately noticeable that the comments brought forward by the satellite industry were very vague and not backed by empirical data. Whatever the future has in store, adoption of an international instrument despite the clear opposition of at least part of such instrument's target sector appears unfortunate and should be avoided for two key reasons. First, it is counterproductive to adopt an instrument *right now* in hopes of persuading the opposing industry afterwards, since the latter is likely to engage in activities undermining the relevant instrument *immediately* following its adoption. Evidence of such behaviour can be found in the statement of the Secretary-General of the EMEA Satellite Operators Association (ESOA) adopted following the Berlin Diplomatic Conference:

> We will now work with our colleagues in the satellite industry on other continents to inform nations of the negative impact of the Protocol on this market as they consider ratification.[133]

Second, one should not dismiss the critique of the uncooperative industry on the basis of its vague or unsubstantiated character. In the context of transnational commercial law reform, it is inappropriate to measure the validity of the target sector's *counterarguments* with the same force as during the assessment of the *arguments in favour* of reform formulated by the relevant agency. The reason is simple: the latter is interfering with the ongoing operation of the target sector and thus the onus is on the formulating agency to persuade the relevant stakeholders. This also means that it should be perfectly acceptable for such stakeholders to question the benefits of the reform in abstract terms. One possible (although by no means simple) solution to the problem is an ex ante economic benefit assessment, which can at least alleviate the concerns about extra costs and the lack of tangible gains resulting from the new instrument and, by doing so, transform the substance of the debate from abstract to concrete. This idea is not new,[134] but it remains to be seen whether the perspectives of a possible shipping protocol looming on the horizon[135] will show better use of economic benefit studies.

[133] ibid.

[134] See, eg, the proposal by the United Kingdom to commission a report on the economic impact of the Space Protocol in Unidroit, *Unidroit C.G.E./Space Pr./3/W.P. 12 (2009)* 2.

[135] See n 196 in section 3.4.2.

9

Conclusions

The recent developments in the realm of the Cape Town Convention are very positive: over the years of work on this book both the number of ratifications and the number of registrations in the international registry under the Aircraft Protocol have been growing steadily, while the MAC Protocol has become the first protocol to trigger Article 51. The opposition from the satellite industry to the Space Protocol, while still present, shows elements of a constructive approach. Even the shipping industry displays early signs of interest in the Convention, despite its initial negative reaction. These developments are a tribute to the enormous work performed by UNIDROIT, the various experts and the relevant industries.

This outcome is possible due to the simple fact that the Cape Town Convention has for the most part provided adequate solutions to the challenges associated with its development. There is overwhelming evidence to support this view.

First, the CTC successfully resolved the original *lex situs* problem by establishing a new autonomous concept of 'international interest', while at the same time preserving state sensitivities and avoiding wholesale unification of domestic laws on the basis of functional approach to security interests.

Second, the abolition of the 'internationality' requirement, coupled with the self-contained system of priorities gave the Convention a surprising reach, eliminating much uncertainty in the application of the CTC and avoiding circular priorities.

Third, the Convention has intentionally left the concepts of 'mobility' and 'high value' vague to allow unhindered expansion in the future. This decision has yielded its dividends in the case of the MAC Protocol (but has created other challenges noted below as one of the qualifications).

Fourth, the umbrella structure of the Convention made possible a multiple speeds approach, whereby the relevant industries could proceed at their own pace, but at the same time preserved the integrity and continuity of the whole system created by the CTC.

Fifth, the remedy rules not only provided the necessary protections to the financiers, but were also carefully structured to promote party autonomy and preserve a balance of interests among various stakeholders, including the debtor and other creditors.

Sixth, the international registration system formed a solid basis for the Convention's system of priorities. For some states, the possibility of migration of national interests into the modern international system constituted the key benefit of the CTC regime.

Seventh, the Convention has provided an adequate response to the industry-driven call for greater commercial certainty, while at the same time preserving the sensitivities of states in handling complex issues.

At the same time, in several situations the CTC does not provide a solid response to the relevant challenges.

First, the final text of the Convention did not establish the limits of its scope and did not clarify the concept of 'mobility'. As a result, new protocols (starting with the MAC Protocol) may end up covering stationary objects capable of being transported to another location, contrary to the original design of the CTC. The absence of clearly defined 'gateway' criteria raises the difficult question as to who should perform the role of the 'gatekeeper' of the integrity of the Convention's system in cases of future expansion of its scope (by ensuring that this expansion is not infinite). Both the formulating agency and the relevant industry can be seen as having a particular interest in such expansion due to the mandate of the former and the potential economic gains of the latter. It is conceivable that the difficult task will thus fall on the shoulders of individual governments, but it remains to be seen whether a dispersed group of states could effectively perform the 'gatekeeper' function. At the same time, it might be an opportunity for increased coordination among international organisations active in the field of secured transactions.

Second, in an attempt to achieve a high degree of predictability among private parties, the Convention got rid of some misleading concepts, such as 'good faith' and 'public policy', but retained others (references to reasonableness and materiality).

Third, it has proven impossible to secure the support of a number of key (shipping, satellite) industries. In the first case, this eliminated one of the key asset categories (ships) from the scope of the Convention, despite unconvincing argumentation in favour of such exclusion. In the second case, this gave rise to public opposition to the idea of the Space Protocol. The unifying potential of economic benefit assessment was not fully utilised.

Fourth, the treatment of helicopters and helicopter engines in the Aircraft Protocol is unfortunate, although the problem is partly mitigated by the Official Commentary.

Clearly, these qualifications pale in comparison with the Convention's achievements: the CTC has created a highly effective machinery for regulating international interests in mobile assets. However, the potential of this machinery will only be realised through consistent implementation of the CTC by national courts – a challenge that cannot be overestimated, particularly in the wake of the COVID-19 pandemic of 2020, which has caused unprecedented disruption of air travel across the globe, driving dozens of airlines into financial distress and creating new opportunities for enforcement of the provisions of the Cape Town Convention.

9.1 Lessons for Commercial Treaty-Making

The documentary history of the Cape Town Convention offers several important lessons. Most of them are specific to commercial law treaties, but some may have more general application.

First, there is a need for greater use of economic benefit assessment studies to attract the attention of the target industry, to provide a credible challenge to any stakeholders opposing the new instruments and to give a clear indication of the resulting impact to governments. The methodology of future studies needs to be improved, and studies will benefit from a more comprehensive analysis of the costs associated with the transition to the new instrument.

Second, the target industry plays a key role in the preparation and promotion of commercial law treaties – and the adoption of a commercial law treaty regardless of open opposition from the target industry as a whole, or a substantial part thereof, is undesirable. The onus of disproving any objections – however general or abstract – should be on the formulating agency attempting to change the status quo of the existing legal regime.

Third, the need for greater predictability has made it possible to establish substantive international rules in areas initially considered a 'taboo' (eg insolvency laws), however conceptual problems remain strong in the development of commercial law treaties. The differences of approach between civil and common law jurisdictions and individual state sensitivities dictate the need for compromise solutions at the cost of simplicity and legal certainty.

Fourth, structural and procedural flexibility is a crucial element in building broad international support for new treaties. Dual convention/protocol structures, a multiple-speeds approach and declarations on the most sensitive matters can reduce the scope of state opposition to a new convention. At the same time, the integrity of the regulatory system established by the new instrument must be preserved using various instruments, including a clear identification of scope of the new regime and mandatory declarations.

Fifth, a variety of instruments can be used to enhance the procedural efficiency of the treaty-making process. These include: (i) the engagement of specialist working groups to generate additional knowledge and break deadlocks in negotiations; (ii) efficient use of the expertise provided by the drafting groups, by avoiding the practice of labelling policy matters as drafting issues, but at the same time permitting the drafting team to make new proposals to facilitate discussion; and (iii) use of alternatives to crystallise the main points of objection, make subsequent discussions more focused and – if necessary – to provide greater flexibility to governments during adoption and ratification.

Finally, official or otherwise authorised explanatory materials and commentaries can be used as an instrument for enhancing legal certainty without drafting an international treaty in the style of complex and detailed legislation.

I end this book at the strangest of times. The COVID-19 pandemic has crippled airlines all over the world, and courts that have never heard of the Cape Town Convention suddenly end up applying its provisions as more creditors choose to enforce their rights under the treaty. I am confident the Convention will pass this test of time. But I digress. This book is about the past, not the future. There is so much more to say about the interesting history of the three protocols not currently in force, as well as the CTC itself – alas, I have run out of pages. I am sure different readers will come up with their own conclusions having read the brief account of documentary history in this small book. In my view, the Convention has been a perfect litmus test of what is achievable in a modern commercial law treaty, and a fine illustration of the many pitfalls of harmonising commercial law – pitfalls this book will hopefully help to avoid in the future.

APPENDIX 1

Cape Town Convention Development Timeline: Key Milestones

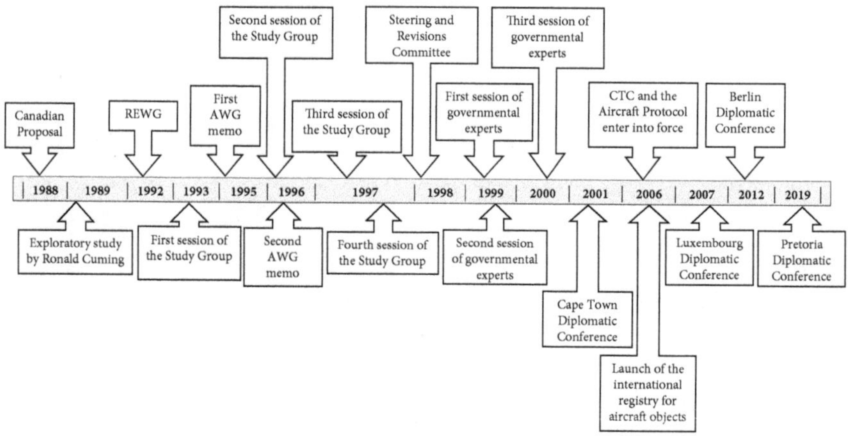

APPENDIX 2

Table of Concordance of Reports and Working Papers

UNIDROIT and Joint UNIDROIT/ICAO, UNIDROIT/OTIF Reports and Working Papers

No	Full title	Short title
1.	Preliminary Draft Uniform Rules on International Financial Leasing, as Adopted by the Unidroit Study Group for the Preparation of Uniform Rules on the Leasing Contract (UNIDROIT 1984 Study LIX - Doc 16, 1984)	Study LIX – Doc. 16 (1984)
2.	Draft Convention on International Financial Leasing as Adopted by a Unidroit Committee of Governmental Experts on 30 April 1987 with Explanatory Report Prepared by the Unidroit Secretariat (UNIDROIT 1987 Study LIX - Doc 48, 1987)	Study LIX – Doc. 48 (1987)
3.	Governing Council 67th Session (Rome, 14 to 17 June 1988) Report on the Session (Prepared by the Secretariat) (UNIDROIT 1988 CD 67 - Doc 18, 1988)	Governing Council C.D. 67 – Doc. 18 (1988)
4.	Governing Council 68th Session (Rome, 10 to 12 April 1989) Report on the Session (Prepared by the Secretariat) (UNIDROIT 1989 CD 68 - Doc 26, 1989)	Governing Council C.D. 68 – Doc. 26 (1989)
5.	International Regulation of Aspects of Security Interests in Mobile Equipment: Study Prepared by Professor Ronald C.C. Cuming (College of Law, University of Saskatchewan) (UNIDROIT 1989 Study LXXII - Doc 1, 1989)	Study LXXII – Doc. 1 (1989)
6.	International Regulation of Aspects of Security Interests in Mobile Equipment: Questionnaire (UNIDROIT 1989 Study LXXII - Doc 2, 1989)	Study LXXII – Doc. 2 (1989)
7.	Analysis of the Replies to the Questionnaire on an International Regulation of Aspects of Security Interests in Mobile Equipment (Prepared by the Unidroit Secretariat) (UNIDROIT 1991 Study LXXII - Doc 3, 1991)	Study LXXII – Doc. 3 (1991)

(continued)

(Continued)

No	Full title	Short title
8.	Basic Issues Identified in Responses to the Questionnaire on an International Regulation of Aspects of Security Interests in Mobile Equipment by Professor Ronald C.C. Cuming (University of Saskatchewan) (UNIDROIT 1992 Study LXXII – Doc 4, 1992)	Study LXXII – Doc. 4 (1992)
9.	Governing Council 70th Session (Rome, 21 to 24 May 1991) Report on the Session (Prepared by the Secretariat) (UNIDROIT 1991 CD (70) 22, 1991)	Governing Council C.D. (70) 22 (1991)
10.	Governing Council 71st Session (Genoa, 22 to 24 June 1992) Report on the Session (Prepared by the Secretariat) (UNIDROIT 1992 CD (71) 18, 1992)	Governing Council C.D. (71) 18 (1992)
11.	Restricted Exploratory Working Group to Examine the Feasibility of Drawing up Uniform Rules on Certain International Aspects of Security Interests in Mobile Equipment: Report (Adopted by the Working Group on 11 March 1992) (UNIDROIT 1992 Study LXXII – Doc 5, 1992)	Study LXXII – Doc. 5 (1992)
12.	Study Group for the Preparation of Uniform Rules on Certain International Aspects of Security Interests in Mobile Equipment: Memorandum for the Attention of the Study Group at its First Session (Prepared by the Unidroit Secretariat) (UNIDROIT 1993 Study LXXII – Doc 6, 1993)	Study LXXII – Doc. 6 (1993)
13.	Study Group for the Preparation of Uniform Rules on Certain International Aspects of Security Interests in Mobile Equipment; Memorandum (for the Attention of the Study Group at its First Session): Addendum (Comments of the German Federal Ministry of Justice) (UNIDROIT 1993 Study LXXII – Doc 6 Add, 1993)	Study LXXII – Doc. 6 Add. (1993)
14.	Study Group for the Preparation of Uniform Rules on Certain International Aspects of Security Interests in Mobile Equipment; Memorandum (for the Attention of the Study Group at its First Session): Addendum (Comments of the European Bank for Reconstruction and Development) (UNIDROIT 1993 Study LXXII – Doc 6 Add 2, 1993)	Study LXXII – Doc. 6 Add. 2 (1993)

(continued)

(Continued)

No	Full title	Short title
15.	Study Group for the Preparation of Uniform Rules on Certain International Aspects of Security Interests in Mobile Equipment; Memorandum (for the Attention of the Study Group at its First Session): Addendum (Comments of the European Federation of Equipment Leasing Company Associations (Leaseurope)) (UNIDROIT 1993 Study LXXII - Doc 6 Add 3, 1993)	Study LXXII – Doc. 6 Add. 3 (1993)
16.	Study Group for the Preparation of Uniform Rules on Certain International Aspects of Security Interests in Mobile Equipment (First Session: Rome, 8–10 March 1993) – Summary Report (Prepared by the Unidroit Secretariat) (UNIDROIT 1993 Study LXXII - Doc 7, 1993)	Study LXXII – Doc. 7 (1993)
17.	Study Group for the Preparation of Uniform Rules on Certain International Aspects of Security Interests in Mobile Equipment: Texts of International Instruments and of a Proposed New International Instrument Regulating the Recognition and Priority of Security Interests in Ships and Inland Navigation Vessels and Appurtenances Thereto (Security Interests Study Group 1st Session Misc 3, 1993)	Security Interests Study Group 1st Session Misc. 3 (1993)
18.	Study Group for the Preparation of Uniform Rules on Certain International Aspects of Security Interests in Mobile Equipment: Some Preliminary Observations on the Process of Developing a Convention on International Security Interests by Professor R.C.C. Cuming (University of Saskatchewan) (Security Interests Study Group 1st Session Misc 5, 1993)	Security Interests Study Group 1st Session Misc. 5 (1993)
19.	Study Group for the Preparation of Uniform Rules on Certain International Aspects of Security Interests in Mobile Equipment; Memorandum on a Proposed Unidroit Convention on Security Interests in Mobile Equipment prepared by Professor R.C.C. Cuming (University of Saskatchewan) (UNIDROIT 1993 Study LXXII - Doc 8, 1993)	Study LXXII – Doc. 8 (1993)
20.	Study Group for the Preparation of Uniform Rules on Certain International Aspects of Security Interests in Mobile Equipment; Comments by Mr Thomas J. Whalen to the Memorandum by Professor R.C.C. Cuming on a Proposed Unidroit Convention on Security Interests in Mobile Equipment (UNIDROIT 1994 Study LXXII - Doc 9, 1994)	Study LXXII – Doc. 9 (1994)

(continued)

(Continued)

No	Full title	Short title
21.	Study Group for the Preparation of Uniform Rules on Certain International Aspects of Security Interests in Mobile Equipment; Comments by Professor C.W. Mooney, Jr. Concerning the Test of Internationality to be Employed in the Proposed Unidroit Convention on Security Interests in Mobile Equipment (UNIDROIT 1994 Study LXXII – Doc 10, 1994)	Study LXXII – Doc. 10 (1994)
22.	Study Group for the Preparation of Uniform Rules on Certain International Aspects of Security Interests in Mobile Equipment; Comments by Mr. J.-H. Roever (European Bank for Reconstruction and Development) to the Memorandum by Professor R.C.C. Cuming on a Proposed Unidroit Convention on Security Interests in Mobile Equipment (UNIDROIT 1994 Study LXXII – Doc 11, 1994)	Study LXXII – Doc. 11 (1994)
23.	Study Group for the Preparation of Uniform Rules on Certain International Aspects of Security Interests in Mobile Equipment: Sub-Committee for the Preparation of a First Draft (First Session: Rome, 14 –16 February 1994) Summary Report (Prepared by the Unidroit Secretariat) (UNIDROIT 1994 Study LXXII – Doc 12, 1994)	Study LXXII – Doc. 12 (1994)
24.	Study Group for the Preparation of Uniform Rules on Certain International Aspects of Security Interests in Mobile Equipment: Sub-Committee for the Preparation of a First Draft (Rome, 14–16 February 1994); Comments by Professor R.D. Vriesendorp (Catholic University of Brabant at Tilburg) to the Memorandum by Professor R.C.C. Cuming Regarding a Proposed Unidroit Convention on Security Interests in Mobile Equipment (Security Interests Study Group Sub-committee 1st Session Misc 2, 1994)	Security Interests Study Group Sub-committee 1st Session Misc. 2 (1994)
25.	Study Group for the Preparation of Uniform Rules on Certain International Aspects of Security Interests in Mobile Equipment: Sub-Committee for the Preparation of a First Draft (Rome, 14–16 February 1994); Comments by The Boeing Company to the Memorandum by Professor R.C.C. Cuming Regarding a Proposed Unidroit Convention on Security Interests in Mobile Equipment (Security Interests Study Group Sub-committee 1st Session Misc 3, 1994)	Security Interests Study Group Sub-committee 1st Session Misc. 3 (1994)

(continued)

(Continued)

No	Full title	Short title
26.	Study Group for the Preparation of Uniform Rules on Certain International Aspects of Security Interests in Mobile Equipment: Sub-Committee for the Preparation of a First Draft (Rome, 14–16 February 1994): Addendum to the Comments by The Boeing Company to the Memorandum of Professor R.C.C. Cuming Regarding a Proposed Convention on Security Interests in Mobile Equipment (Security Interests Study Group Sub-committee 1st Session Misc 3 Add, 1994)	Security Interests Study Group Sub-committee 1st Session Misc. 3 Add. (1994)
27.	Study Group for the Preparation of Uniform Rules on Certain International Aspects of Security Interests in Mobile Equipment: Sub-Committee for the Preparation of a First Draft; Proposals for a First Draft (Drawn up by the Chairman and a Member of the Sub-committee on the Basis of the Provisional Conclusions Reached by the Latter at its First Session) (UNIDROIT 1994 Study LXXII - Doc 13, 1994)	Study LXXII - Doc. 13 (1994)
28.	Study Group for the Preparation of Uniform Rules on Certain International Aspects of Security Interests in Mobile Equipment: Sub-Committee for the Preparation of a First Draft; Proposals for a First Draft (Drawn up by the Chairman and a Member of the Sub-committee on the Basis of the Provisional Conclusions Reached by the Latter at its First Session): Comments (by Members of the Sub-committee and the Study Group and the International Organisations and Professional Associations Represented by Observers Thereon) (UNIDROIT 1994 Study LXXII - Doc 14, 1994)	Study LXXII - Doc. 14 (1994)
29.	Study Group for the Preparation of Uniform Rules on Certain International Aspects of Security Interests in Mobile Equipment: Sub-Committee for the Preparation of a First Draft; Proposals for a First Draft (Drawn up by the Chairman and a Member of the Sub-committee on the Basis of the Provisional Conclusions Reached by the Latter at its First Session): Comments (by Mr Thomas J. Whalen, Professor Rolf Herber and The Boeing Company) (UNIDROIT 1994 Study LXXII - Doc 14 Add 1, 1994)	Study LXXII - Doc. 14 Add 1 (1994)

(continued)

(Continued)

No	Full title	Short title
30.	Study Group for the Preparation of Uniform Rules on Certain International Aspects of Security Interests in Mobile Equipment: Sub-Committee for the Preparation of a First Draft; Proposals for a First Draft (Drawn up by the Chairman and a Member of the Sub-committee on the Basis of the Provisional Conclusions Reached by the Latter at its First Session): Comments by Professor Charles W. Mooney, Jr. and the Legal Committee of the Finance & Leasing Association of the United Kingdom) (UNIDROIT 1994 Study LXXII – Doc 14 Add 2, 1994)	Study LXXII – Doc. 14 Add 2 (1994)
31.	Study Group for the Preparation of Uniform Rules on Certain International Aspects of Security Interests in Mobile Equipment: Sub-Committee for the Preparation of a First Draft; Proposals for a First Draft (Drawn up by the Chairman and a Member of the Sub-committee on the Basis of the Provisional Conclusions Reached by the Latter at its First Session): Comments (by the Banking Federation of the European Union and the Italian Banking Association) (UNIDROIT 1994 Study LXXII – Doc 14 Add 4, 1994)	Study LXXII – Doc. 14 Add 4 (1994)
32.	Meeting of International Organisations Currently Involved in the Preparation of Legislation in the Field of Personal Property Security (Rome, 29 November 1994): Report (Prepared by the Unidroit Secretariat) (UNIDROIT 1995 Study LXXIIB – Doc 1, 1994)	Study LXXIIB – Doc. 1 (1995)
33.	Study Group for the Preparation of Uniform Rules on Certain International Aspects of Security Interests in Mobile Equipment: Sub-Committee for the Preparation of a First Draft (Second Session: Rome, 29 November–1 December 1994) Summary Report (Prepared by the Unidroit Secretariat) (UNIDROIT 1995 Study LXXII – Doc 15, 1995)	Study LXXII – Doc. 15 (1995)
34.	Study Group for the Preparation of Uniform Rules on Certain International Aspects of Security Interests in Mobile Equipment: Sub-Committee for the Preparation of a First Draft; Memorandum Prepared Jointly by Airbus Industrie and The Boeing Company on behalf of an Aviation Working Group (UNIDROIT 1995 Study LXXII – Doc 16, 1995)	Study LXXII – Doc. 16 (1995)

(continued)

(Continued)

No	Full title	Short title
35.	Study Group for the Preparation of Uniform Rules on Certain International Aspects of Security Interests in Mobile Equipment: Sub-Committee for the Preparation of a First Draft; Memorandum Prepared Jointly by Airbus Industrie and The Boeing Company on behalf of an Aviation Working Group: Comments (by Members of the Sub-committee) (UNIDROIT 1995 Study LXXII - Doc 17, 1995)	Study LXXII – Doc. 17 (1995)
36.	Study Group for the Preparation of Uniform Rules on Certain International Aspects of Security Interests in Mobile Equipment: Sub-Committee for the Preparation of a First Draft; Memorandum Prepared Jointly by Airbus Industrie and The Boeing Company on behalf of an Aviation Working Group: Comments (by Members of the Study Group and the International Organisations and Professional Associations Represented by Observers Thereon) (UNIDROIT 1995 Study LXXII - Doc 17 Add 3, 1995)	Study LXXII – Doc. 17 Add. 3 (1995)
37.	Study Group for the Preparation of Uniform Rules on Certain International Aspects of Security Interests in Mobile Equipment: Sub-Committee for the Preparation of a First Draft; Revised Proposals for a First Set of Draft Articles of a Future Unidroit Convention on International Interests in Mobile Equipment (Drawn up by the Drafting Group on the Basis of the Provisional Conclusions Reached by the Sub-committee at its Second Session) (UNIDROIT 1995 Study LXXII - Doc 18, 1995)	Study LXXII – Doc. 18 (1995)
38.	Study Group for the Preparation of Uniform Rules on Certain International Aspects of Security Interests in Mobile Equipment: Sub-Committee for the Preparation of a First Draft; Revised Proposals for a First Set of Draft Articles of a Future Unidroit Convention on International Interests in Mobile Equipment (Drawn up by the Drafting Group on the Basis of the Provisional Conclusions Reached by the Sub-committee at its Second Session): Comments (by a Member of the Drafting Group) (UNIDROIT 1995 Study LXXII - Doc 19, 1995)	Study LXXII – Doc. 19 (1995)

(continued)

(Continued)

No	Full title	Short title
39.	Study Group for the Preparation of Uniform Rules on Certain International Aspects of Security Interests in Mobile Equipment: Sub-Committee for the Preparation of a First Draft; Revised Proposals for a First Set of Draft Articles of a Future Unidroit Convention on International Interests in Mobile Equipment (Drawn up by the Drafting Group on the Basis of the Provisional Conclusions Reached by the Sub-committee at its Second Session): Comments (by Members of the Study Group and the Sub-committee and the International Organisations and Professional Associations Represented by Observers Thereon) (UNIDROIT 1995 Study LXXII - Doc 19 Add, 1995)	Study LXXII – Doc. 19 Add. (1995)
40.	Study Group for the Preparation of Uniform Rules on Certain International Aspects of Security Interests in Mobile Equipment: Sub-Committee for the Preparation of a First Draft; Revised Proposals for a First Set of Draft Articles of a Future Unidroit Convention on International Interests in Mobile Equipment (Drawn up by the Drafting Group on the Basis of the Provisional Conclusions Reached by the Sub-committee at its Second Session): Comments (by Airbus Industrie / The Boeing Company on behalf of an Aviation Working Group) (UNIDROIT 1995 Study LXXII - Doc 19 Add 4, 1995)	Study LXXII – Doc. 19 Add. 4 (1995)
41.	Study Group for the Preparation of Uniform Rules on Certain International Aspects of Security Interests in Mobile Equipment: Sub-Committee for the Preparation of a First Draft (Third Session: Rome, 11–13 October 1995) Summary Report (Prepared by the Unidroit Secretariat) (UNIDROIT 1995 Study LXXII - Doc 21, 1995)	Study LXXII – Doc. 21 (1995)
42.	Study Group for the Preparation of Uniform Rules on Certain International Aspects of Security Interests in Mobile Equipment: Sub-Committee for the Preparation of a First Draft (Third Session: Rome, 11–13 October 1995); Memorandum Prepared Jointly by Airbus Industrie and The Boeing Company on behalf of an Aviation Working Group: Comments (by the Equipment Leasing Association of America) (International Interests Study-Group Sub-committee 3rd Session Misc 1, 1995)	International Interests Study-Group Sub-committee 3rd Session Misc. 1 (1995)

(continued)

(Continued)

No	Full title	Short title
43.	Study Group for the Preparation of Uniform Rules on International Interests in Mobile Equipment: Sub-Committee for the Preparation of a First Draft (Third Session: Rome, 11–13 October 1995) Extract from a Work in Progress by Professor Charles W. Mooney, Jr. on 'Exporting Article 9 of the Uniform Commercial Code in an International Convention: the Local law Conundrum and Possible Solutions Thereto' (International Interests Study Group Sub-committee 3rd Session Misc 3, 1995)	International Interests Study Group Sub-committee 3rd Session Misc. 3 (1995)
44.	Study Group for the Preparation of Uniform Rules on Certain International Aspects of Security Interests in Mobile Equipment: First Set of Draft Articles of a Future Unidroit Convention on International Interests in Mobile Equipment (Established by the Drafting Group of the Sub-committee on 19 December 1995 Pursuant to the Decisions Taken by the Sub-committee of the Study Group at its Third Session) (UNIDROIT 1996 Study LXXII - Doc 22, 1996)	Study LXXII – Doc. 22 (1996)
45.	Study Group for the Preparation of Uniform Rules on Certain International Aspects of Security Interests in Mobile Equipment: Second Memorandum Prepared Jointly by Airbus Industrie and The Boeing Company on behalf of an Aviation Working Group (UNIDROIT 1996 Study LXXII - Doc 23, 1996)	Study LXXII – Doc. 23 (1996)
46.	Study Group for the Preparation of Uniform Rules on Certain International Aspects of Security Interests in Mobile Equipment: First Set of Draft Articles of a Future Unidroit Convention on International Interests in Mobile Equipment (Established by the Drafting Group of the Sub-committee on 19 December 1995 as Revised by the Same on 4 March 1996) (UNIDROIT 1996 Study LXXII - Doc 24, 1996)	Study LXXII Doc. 24 (1996)
47.	Study Group for the Preparation of Uniform Rules on Certain International Aspects of Security Interests in Mobile Equipment: Second Memorandum Prepared Jointly by Airbus Industrie and The Boeing Company on behalf of an Aviation Working Group: Summary of Principal Concepts Prepared by Mr Jeffrey Wool (Expert Consultant to the Study Group on International Aviation Finance Matters) (UNIDROIT 1996 Study LXXII - Doc 25, 1996)	Study LXXII – Doc. 25 (1996)

(continued)

(Continued)

No	Full title	Short title
48.	Study Group for the Preparation of Uniform Rules on International Interests in Mobile Equipment; First Set of Draft Articles of a Future Unidroit Convention on International Interests in Mobile Equipment (Established by the Drafting Group of the Sub-committee on 19 December 1995 as Revised by the Same on 4 March 1996): Comments (by the Cosmic Space Agency of the Russian Federation and the Banking Federation of the European Union) (UNIDROIT 1996 Study LXXII – Doc 26, 1996)	Study LXXII – Doc. 26 (1996)
49.	Study Group for the Preparation of Uniform Rules on International Interests in Mobile Equipment; First Set of Draft Articles of a Future Unidroit Convention on International Interests in Mobile Equipment (Established by the Drafting Group of the Sub-committee on 19 December 1995 as Revised by the Same on 4 March 1996): Comments (by Professor C.W. Mooney, Jr. and Mr T.J. Whalen) (UNIDROIT 1996 Study LXXII – Doc 26 Add 1, 1996)	Study LXXII – Doc. 26 Add. 1 (1996)
50.	Study Group for the Preparation of Uniform Rules on International Interests in Mobile Equipment; First Set of Draft Articles of a Future Unidroit Convention on International Interests in Mobile Equipment (Established by the Drafting Group of the Sub-committee on 19 December 1995 as Revised by the Same on 4 March 1996): Comments (by Ms N. de la Pena, Professor L. Girton and Mr H. Fleisig) (UNIDROIT 1996 Study LXXII – Doc 26 Add 2, 1996)	Study LXXII – Doc. 26 Add. 2 (1996)
51.	Study Group for the Preparation of Uniform Rules on International Interests in Mobile Equipment; First Set of Draft Articles of a Future Unidroit Convention on International Interests in Mobile Equipment (Established by the Drafting Group of the Sub-committee on 19 December 1995 as Revised by the Same on 4 March 1996): Comments (by the European Federation of Equipment Leasing Company Associations, Mr Peter D. Nesgos and Ms Shiva Falsafi) (UNIDROIT 1996 Study LXXII – Doc 26 Add 3, 1996)	Study LXXII – Doc. 26 Add. 3 (1996)
52.	Study Group for the Preparation of Uniform Rules on Certain International Aspects of Security Interests in Mobile Equipment (Second Session: Rome, 12–16 April 1996): Report (Prepared by Unidroit Secretariat) (UNIDROIT 1996 Study LXXII – Doc 27, 1996)	Study LXXII – Doc. 27 (1996)

(continued)

(Continued)

No	Full title	Short title
53.	Study Group for the Preparation of Uniform Rules on Certain International Aspects of Security Interests in Mobile Equipment: Extract from the Report on the 75th Session of the Unidroit Governing Council (Prepared by the Unidroit Secretariat) (UNIDROIT 1996 Study LXXII – Doc 28, 1996)	Study LXXII – Doc. 28 (1996)
54.	Study Group for the Preparation of Uniform Rules on International Interests in Mobile Equipment: Consideration of the Case for the Exclusion of Registered Ships from the Sphere of Application of the Future Convention (Secretariat Memorandum) (UNIDROIT 1996 Study LXXII – Doc 29, 1996)	Study LXXII – Doc. 29 (1996)
55.	Study Group for the Preparation of Uniform Rules on Certain International Aspects of Security Interests in Mobile Equipment: Revised Draft Articles of a Future Unidroit Convention on International Interests in Mobile Equipment (Proposed by the Drafting Group in the Light of the Study Group's Reading at its Second Session of the First set of Draft Articles Established by the Sub-committee in Conjunction with the Recommendations of the Aviation Working Group) with Introductory Remarks (Prepared by the Unidroit Secretariat) (UNIDROIT 1996 Study LXXII – Doc 30, 1996)	Study LXXII – Doc. 30 (1996)
56.	Study Group for the Preparation of Uniform Rules on Certain International Aspects of Security Interests in Mobile Equipment: Second Memorandum Prepared Jointly by Airbus Industrie and The Boeing Company on behalf of an Aviation Working Group: Preliminary Comments by the Russian Federation Aviation Working Group (UNIDROIT 1997 Study LXXII – Doc 31, 1997)	Study LXXII – Doc. 31 (1997)
57.	Study Group for the Preparation of Uniform Rules on International Interests in Mobile Equipment: Revised Draft Articles of a Future Unidroit Convention on International Interests in Mobile Equipment (Proposed by the Drafting Group in the Light of the Study Group's Reading at its Second Session of the First Set of Draft Articles Established by the Sub-committee in Conjunction with the Recommendations of the Aviation Working Group): Comments (by the Aviation Working Group and the International Air Transport Association) (UNIDROIT 1996 Study LXXII – Doc 32, 1996)	Study LXXII – Doc. 32 (1996)

(continued)

(Continued)

No	Full title	Short title
58.	Study Group for the Preparation of Uniform Rules on International Interests in Mobile Equipment: Revised Draft Articles of a Future Unidroit Convention on International Interests in Mobile Equipment (Proposed by the Drafting Group in the Light of the Study Group's Reading at its Second Session of the First Set of Draft Articles Established by the Sub-committee in Conjunction with the Recommendations of the Aviation Working Group): Comments (by Mr S. Masuda) (UNIDROIT 1997 Study LXXII – Doc 32 Add 1, 1997)	Study LXXII – Doc. 32 Add. 1 (1997)
59.	Study Group for the Preparation of Uniform Rules on International Interests in Mobile Equipment: Revised Draft Articles of a Future Unidroit Convention on International Interests in Mobile Equipment (Proposed by the Drafting Group in the Light of the Study Group's Reading at its Second Session of the First Set of Draft Articles Established by the Sub-committee in Conjunction with the Recommendations of the Aviation Working Group): Comments (by the Aviation Working Group and the International Air Transport Association) (UNIDROIT 1997 Study LXXII – Doc 32 Add 2, 1997)	Study LXXII – Doc. 32 Add. 2 (1997)
60.	Study Group for the Preparation of Uniform Rules on International Interests in Mobile Equipment: Revised Draft Articles of a Future Unidroit Convention on International Interests in Mobile Equipment (Proposed by the Drafting Group in the Light of the Study Group's Reading at its Second Session of the First Set of Draft Articles Established by the Sub-committee in Conjunction with the Recommendations of the Aviation Working Group): Comments (by Professor C.W. Mooney, Jr. and Mr T. Whalen) (UNIDROIT 1997 Study LXXII – Doc 32 Add 3, 1997)	Study LXXII – Doc. 32 Add. 3 (1997)
61.	Study Group for the Preparation of Uniform Rules on Certain International Aspects of Security Interests in Mobile Equipment: (Fourth session: Rome, 3–8 November 1997): Preliminary Draft Unidroit Convention on International Interests in Mobile Equipment (as Proposed by the Drafting Group at its Fifth Session, Held in Rome from 4 to 7 November 1997) (International Interests Study Group 4th session Misc 5, 1997)	International Interests Study Group 4th Session Misc. 5 (1997)

(continued)

(Continued)

No	Full title	Short title
62.	Study Group for the Preparation of Uniform Rules on Certain International Aspects of Security Interests in Mobile Equipment: Drafting Group (Fourth session: Würzburg, 24–26 July 1997) Revised Draft Articles of a Future Unidroit Convention on International Interests in Mobile Equipment (Prepared by the Chairman of the Study Group in the Light of the Deliberations of that Group at its Third Session, Held in Rome from 15 to 21 January 1997, and of the Proposals by the Drafting Group at its Third Session, Held in Rome on 17 and 20 January 1997) (UNIDROIT 1997 International Interests/Study Group/Drafting Group/Fourth session/WP 1, 1997)	Study LXXII – Drafting Group Fourth Session (1997)
63.	Study Group for the Preparation of Uniform Rules on Certain International Aspects of Security Interests in Mobile Equipment: Revised Draft Articles of a Future Unidroit Convention on International Interests in Mobile Equipment (as Proposed by the Drafting Group at its Fourth Session, Held in Würzburg from 24 to 26 July 1997) with Introductory Remarks (by the Unidroit Secretariat) (UNIDROIT 1997 Study LXXII – Doc 35, 1997)	Study LXXII – Doc. 35 (1997)
64.	Study Group for the Preparation of Uniform Rules on Certain International Aspects of Security Interests in Mobile Equipment: Revised Draft Articles of a Future Unidroit Convention on International Interests in Mobile Equipment (as Proposed by the Drafting Group at its Fourth Session, Held in Würzburg from 24 to 26 July 1997): Comments (by Members of the Study Group, Advisers Thereto and the International Organisations, Professional Associations and Other Bodies Represented Thereon by Observers as also those Persons and Bodies Having Participated from Outside the Study Group in the Development of the Project) (UNIDROIT 1997 Study LXXII – Doc 36, 1997)	Study LXXII – Doc. 36 (1997)
65.	Study Group for the Preparation of Uniform Rules on Certain International Aspects of Security Interests in Mobile Equipment: Revised Draft Articles of a Future Unidroit Convention on International Interests in Mobile Equipment (as Proposed by the Drafting Group at its Fourth Session, Held in Würzburg from 24 to 26 July 1997): Comments (by the Federal German Association of Banks) (UNIDROIT 1997 Study LXXII – Doc 36 Add 1, 1997)	Study LXXII – Doc. 36 Add. 1 (1997)

(continued)

(Continued)

No	Full title	Short title
66.	Study Group for the Preparation of Uniform Rules on Certain International Aspects of Security Interests in Mobile Equipment: Revised Draft Articles of a Future Unidroit Convention on International Interests in Mobile Equipment (as Proposed by the Drafting Group at its Fourth Session, Held in Würzburg from 24 to 26 July 1997): Comments (by the Intergovernmental Organisation for International Carriage by Rail, the European Company for the Financing of Railroad Rolling Stock, the Danish Shipowners' Association and the Elf Aquitaine Group) (UNIDROIT 1997 Study LXXII – Doc 36 Add 2, 1997)	Study LXXII – Doc. 36 Add. 2 (1997)
67.	Study Group for the Preparation of Uniform Rules on Certain International Aspects of Security Interests in Mobile Equipment: Revised Draft Articles of a Future Unidroit Convention on International Interests in Mobile Equipment (as Proposed by the Drafting Group at its Fourth Session, Held in Würzburg from 24 to 26 July 1997): Comments (by the Aircraft Protocol Group) (UNIDROIT 1997 Study LXXII – Doc 36 Add 3, 1997)	Study LXXII – Doc. 36 Add. 3 (1997)
68.	Study Group for the Preparation of Uniform Rules on Certain International Aspects of Security Interests in Mobile Equipment: Preliminary Draft Unidroit Convention on International Interests in Mobile Equipment (as Established by the Study Group at the Conclusion of its Fourth Session, Held in Rome from 3 to 7 November 1997) (UNIDROIT 1997 Study LXXII – Doc 37, 1997)	Study LXXII – Doc. 37 (1997)
69.	Study Group for the Preparation of Uniform Rules on Certain International Aspects of Security Interests in Mobile Equipment: Working Group to Consider the Legal and Technical Issues Raised by the Establishment of an International Register (First session: Rome, 16–18 April 1996): Summary Report (Prepared by the Unidroit Secretariat) (UNIDROIT 1997 Study LXXIIC – Doc 2, 1997)	Study LXXIIC – Doc. 2 (1997)
70.	Study Group for the Preparation of Uniform Rules on Certain International Aspects of Security Interests in Mobile Equipment: Working Group to Consider the Legal and Technical Issues Raised by the Establishment of an International Register (Second Session: Geneva, 26–28 May 1997): Summary Report (Prepared by the Unidroit Secretariat) (UNIDROIT 1997 Study LXXIIC – Doc 3, 1997)	Study LXXIIC – Doc. 3 (1997)

(continued)

(Continued)

No	Full title	Short title
71.	Steering and Revisions Committee for the Finalisation of the Preliminary Draft Unidroit Convention on International Interests in Mobile Equipment and the Preliminary Protocol Thereto on Matters Specific to Aircraft Equipment: Preliminary Draft Unidroit Convention on International Interests in Mobile Equipment (as Established by the Study Group at the Conclusion of its Fourth Session, held in Rome from 3 to 7 November 1997, and as Revised by the Chairman of the Study Group) (UNIDROIT 1998 Study LXXII – Doc 39, 1998)	Study LXXII – Doc. 39 (1998)
72.	Governing Council (77th Session: Rome, 16–20 February 1998): Extract from the Report on the Session Re Item n 8 on the Agenda: International Interests in Mobile Equipment (UNIDROIT 1998 Etude LXXII – Doc 40, 1998)	Study LXXII – Doc. 40 (1998)
73.	Steering and Revisions Committee (Rome, 27–29 June 1998): Report (Prepared by the Unidroit Secretariat) (UNIDROIT 1998 Study LXXII - Doc 41, 1998)	Study LXXII – Doc. 41 (1998)
74.	Preliminary Draft Unidroit Convention on International Interests in Mobile Equipment (as Established by an Unidroit Study Group and Revised, in Accordance with a Decision Taken by the Unidroit Governing Council at its 77th Session, Held in Rome from 16 to 20 February 1998, by a Steering and Revisions Committee, Meeting in Rome from 27 to 29 June 1998) (UNIDROIT 1998 Study LXXII - Doc 42, 1998)	Study LXXII – Doc. 42 (1998)
75.	Committee of Governmental Experts for the Preparation of a Draft Convention on International Interests in Mobile Equipment and a Draft Protocol on Matters Specific to Aircraft Equipment; Preliminary Draft Unidroit Convention on International Interests in Mobile Equipment and Preliminary Draft Protocol to the Preliminary Draft Unidroit Convention on International Interest in Mobile Equipment on Matters Specific to Aircraft Equipment: Preliminary Observations (Submitted by the Government of the United States of America) (UNIDROIT 1998 Study LXXII - Doc 43 / Study LXXIID - Doc 4, 1998)	Study LXXII – Doc. 43 / Study LXXIID – Doc. 4 (1998)

(continued)

(Continued)

No	Full title	Short title
76.	Committee of Governmental Experts for the Preparation of a Draft Convention on International Interests in Mobile Equipment and a Draft Protocol on Matters Specific to Aircraft Equipment; Preliminary Draft Unidroit Convention on International Interests in Mobile Equipment: Comments (Submitted by the Government of Australia) (UNIDROIT 1998 Study LXXII – Doc 44, 1998)	Study LXXII – Doc. 44 (1998)
77.	Committee of Governmental Experts for the Preparation of a Draft Convention on International Interests in Mobile Equipment and a Draft Protocol on Matters Specific to Aircraft Equipment; Preliminary Draft Unidroit Convention on International Interests in Mobile Equipment and Preliminary Draft Protocol to the Preliminary Draft Unidroit Convention on International Interest in Mobile Equipment on Matters Specific to Aircraft Equipment: Comments (Submitted by the International Air Transport Association and the Aviation Working Group) (UNIDROIT 1998 Study LXXII – Doc 45 / Study LXXIID – Doc 6, 1998)	Study LXXII – Doc. 45 / Study LXXIID – Doc. 6 (1998)
78.	Study Group for the Preparation of Uniform Rules on International Interests in Mobile Equipment; Preliminary Draft Unidroit Convention on International Interests in Mobile Equipment (as Established by the Study Group at the Conclusion of its Fourth Session, Held in Rome from 3 to 7 November 1997: Preliminary Draft Protocol on Matters Specific to Aircraft Equipment (as Established by a Working Group Organised by Mr J. Wool, Expert Consultant to the Study Group on International Aviation Finance Matters, at the Invitation of the President, at the Conclusion of its Second Session, Held in Geneva from 19 to 21 November 1997) (UNIDROIT 1998 Study LXXIID – Doc 1, 1998)	Study LXXIID – Doc. 1 (1998)
79.	Preliminary Draft Protocol to the Preliminary Draft UNIDROIT Convention on International Interests in Mobile Equipment on Matters Specific to Aircraft Equipment (as Established by a Working Group Organised, at the Invitation of the President of the Unidroit Study Group for the Preparation of Uniform Rules on International Interests in Mobile Equipment, and Revised, in Accordance with a Decision Taken by the Unidroit Governing Council at its 77th Session, Held in Rome from 16 to 20 February 1998, by a Steering and Revisions Committee, Meeting in Rome from 27 to 29 June 1998) (UNIDROIT 1998 Study LXXIID – Doc 3, 1998)	Study LXXIID – Doc. 3 (1998)

(continued)

(Continued)

No	Full title	Short title
80.	Committee of Governmental Experts for the Preparation of a Draft Convention on International Interests in Mobile Equipment and a Draft Protocol on Matters Specific to Aircraft Equipment; Preliminary Draft Unidroit Convention on International Interests in Mobile Equipment and Preliminary Draft Protocol to the Preliminary Draft Unidroit Convention on International Interest in Mobile Equipment on Matters Specific to Aircraft Equipment: Comments (Submitted by the Government of Japan) (UNIDROIT 1999 Study LXXII – Doc 49 / Study LXXIID – Doc 9, 1999)	Study LXXII – Doc. 49 / Study LXXIID – Doc. 9 (1999)
81.	UNIDROIT Committee of Governmental Experts for the Preparation of a Draft Convention on International Interests in Mobile Equipment and a Draft Protocol Thereto on Matters Specific to Aircraft Equipment; Sub-Committee of the ICAO Legal Committee on the Study of International Interests in Mobile Equipment (Aircraft Equipment); First Joint Session (Rome, 1–12 February 1999): Report (Unidroit CGE/IntInt/Report ICAO Ref LSC/ME Report, 1999)	Unidroit CGE/ Int.Int./Report ICAO Ref. LSC/ ME-Report (1999)
82.	Drafting Committee Proposal (Submitted by the Delegation of the United States of America) (Unidroit CGE/IntInt ICAO Ref LSC/ME DC-WP/7 5/02/99, 1999)	Unidroit CGE/ Int.Int. ICAO Ref. LSC/ME DC-WP/7 5/02/99 (1999)
83.	Drafting Committee Proposal (Submitted by the Delegation of the United States of America) (Unidroit CGE/IntInt ICAO Ref LSC/ME DC-WP/10 8/02/99, 1999)	Unidroit CGE/Int. Int. ICAO Ref. LSC/ ME DC-WP/10 8/02/99 (1999)
84.	UNIDROIT Committee of Governmental Experts for the Preparation of a Draft Convention on International Interests in Mobile Equipment and a Draft Protocol Thereto on Matters Specific to Aircraft Equipment; Sub-Committee of the ICAO Legal Committee on the Study of International Interests in Mobile Equipment (Aircraft Equipment); Joint Session (Rome, 1–12 February 1999): Information Paper (Submitted Jointly by the Unidroit Secretariat and the ICAO Secretariat) (Unidroit CGE/IntInt/WP/8 ICAO Ref LSC/ME-WP/19 8/02/99, 1999)	Unidroit CGE/ Int.Int./WP/8 ICAO Ref. LSC/ ME-WP/19 (1999)

(continued)

(Continued)

No	Full title	Short title
85.	Consolidated Version of a Preliminary Draft Unidroit Convention on International Interests in Aircraft Equipment Submitted by the German Delegation Integrating the Preliminary Draft Unidroit Convention on International Interests in Mobile Equipment UNIDROIT 1998 Study LXXII – Doc. 42 and the Preliminary Draft Protocol to the Preliminary Draft Unidroit Convention on International Interests in Mobile Equipment on Matters Specific to Aircraft Equipment Unidroit 1998 Study LXXIID – Doc. 3 Established on the Basis of the Preliminary Draft Unidroit Convention on International Interests in Mobile Equipment (as Established by an Unidroit Study Group and Revised, in Accordance with a Decision Taken by the Unidroit Governing Council at its 77th Session, Held in Rome from 16 to 29 February 1998, by a Steering and Revisions Committee, Meeting in Rome from 27 to 29 June 1998) UNIDROIT 1998 Study LXXII – Doc. 42 (Unidroit CGE/IntInt/WP/9 ICAO Ref LSC/ME-WP/20, 1999)	Unidroit CGE/ Int.Int./WP/9 ICAO Ref. LSC/ ME-WP/20 (1999)
86.	UNIDROIT Committee of Governmental Experts for the Preparation of a Draft Convention on International Interests in Mobile Equipment and a Draft Protocol Thereto on Matters Specific to Aircraft Equipment; Sub-Committee of the ICAO Legal Committee on the Study of International Interests in Mobile Equipment (Aircraft Equipment); Draft Report: Plenary Session; 1–12 February 1999 (Unidroit CGE/IntInt/WP/17 ICAO Ref LSC/ME-WP/28 12/02/99, 1999)	Unidroit CGE/ Int.Int./WP/17 ICAO Ref. LSC/ ME-WP/28 (1999)
87.	Sub-Committee of the ICAO Legal Committee on the Study of International Interests in Mobile Equipment (Aircraft Equipment); UNIDROIT Committee of Governmental Experts for the Preparation of a Draft Convention on International Interests in Mobile Equipment and a Draft Protocol Thereto on Matters Specific to Aircraft Equipment; Second Joint Session (Montreal, 24 August–3 September 1999): Report (ICAO Ref LSC/ME/2-Report Unidroit CGE/IntInt/ 2-Report, 1999)	ICAO Ref. LSC/ ME/2-Report Unidroit CGE/ Int.Int./2-Report (1999)

(continued)

(Continued)

No	Full title	Short title
88.	Sub-Committee of the ICAO Legal Committee on the Study of International Interests in Mobile Equipment (Aircraft Equipment); UNIDROIT Committee of Governmental Experts for the Preparation of a Draft Convention on International Interests in Mobile Equipment and a Draft Protocol Thereto on Matters Specific to Aircraft Equipment; Second Joint Session (Montreal, 24 August–3 September 1999): Report (by the Registration Working Group (RWG)) (ICAO Ref LSC/ME/2-WP/17 Unidroit CGE/IntInt/2-WP/17, 1999)	ICAO Ref. LSC/ME/2-WP/17 Unidroit CGE/Int.Int./2-WP/17 (1999)
89.	Sub-Committee of the ICAO Legal Committee on the Study of International Interests in Mobile Equipment (Aircraft Equipment); UNIDROIT Committee of Governmental Experts for the Preparation of a Draft Convention on International Interests in Mobile Equipment and a Draft Protocol Thereto on Matters Specific to Aircraft Equipment; Second Joint Session (Montreal, 24 August–3 September 1999): Insolvency Working Group Report (ICAO Ref LSC/ME/2-WP/19 Unidroit CGE/IntInt/2 WP/19 26/8/99, 1999)	ICAO Ref. LSC/ME/2-WP/19 Unidroit CGE/Int.Int./2-WP/19 26/8/99 (1999)
90.	UNIDROIT Committee of Governmental Experts for the Preparation of a Draft Convention on International Interests in Mobile Equipment and a Draft Protocol Thereto on Matters Specific to Aircraft Equipment; Sub-Committee of the ICAO Legal Committee on the Study of International Interests in Mobile Equipment (Aircraft Equipment); Third Joint Session (Rome, 20–31 March 2000): Report (Unidroit CGE/IntInt/3-Report ICAO Ref LSC/ME/3-Report, 2000)	Unidroit CGE/Int.Int./3-Report ICAO Ref. LSC/ME/3-Report (2000)
91.	UNIDROIT Committee of Governmental Experts for the Preparation of a Draft Convention on International Interests in Mobile Equipment and a Draft Protocol Thereto on Matters Specific to Aircraft Equipment; Sub-Committee of the ICAO Legal Committee on the Study of International Interests in Mobile Equipment (Aircraft Equipment); Third Joint Session (Rome, 20–31 March 2000): Ad hoc Drafting Group (Rome 25–27 November 1999), Report (Unidroit CGE/IntInt/3-WP/2 ICAO Ref LSC/ME/3-WP/2, 2000)	Unidroit CGE/Int.Int./3-WP/2 ICAO Ref. LSC/ME/3-WP/2 (2000)

(continued)

(Continued)

No	Full title	Short title
92.	UNIDROIT Committee of Governmental Experts for the Preparation of a Draft Convention on International Interests in Mobile Equipment and a Draft Protocol Thereto on Matters Specific to Aircraft Equipment; Sub-Committee of the ICAO Legal Committee on the Study of International Interests in Mobile Equipment (Aircraft Equipment); Third Joint Session (Rome, 20–31 March 2000): Preliminary Comments (Submitted by the Government of France) (Unidroit CGE/IntInt/3-WP/4 ICAO Ref LSC/ME/3-WP/4, 2000)	Unidroit CGE/ Int.Int./3-WP/4 ICAO Ref. LSC/ ME/3-WP/4 (2000)
93.	UNIDROIT Committee of Governmental Experts for the Preparation of a Draft Convention on International Interests in Mobile Equipment and a Draft Protocol Thereto on Matters Specific to Aircraft Equipment; Sub-Committee of the ICAO Legal Committee on the Study of International Interests in Mobile Equipment (Aircraft Equipment); Third Joint Session (Rome, 20–31 March 2000): Comments (Submitted by the Secretariat of UNCITRAL) (Unidroit CGE/IntInt/3-WP/10 ICAO Ref LSC/ME/3-WP/10 2000)	Unidroit CGE/ Int.Int./3-WP/10 ICAO Ref. LSC/ ME/3-WP/10 (2000)
94.	UNIDROIT Committee of Governmental Experts for the Preparation of a Draft Convention on International Interests in Mobile Equipment and a Draft Protocol Thereto on Matters Specific to Aircraft Equipment; Sub-Committee of the ICAO Legal Committee on the Study of International Interests in Mobile Equipment (Aircraft Equipment); Third Joint Session (Rome, 20–31 March 2000): Remedies and Interim Relief (Submitted by the ICAO Secretariat) (Unidroit CGE/IntInt/3-WP/12 ICAO Ref LSC/ME/3-WP/12, 2000)	Unidroit CGE/ Int.Int./3-WP/12 ICAO Ref. LSC/ ME/3-WP/12 (2000)
95.	UNIDROIT Committee of Governmental Experts for the Preparation of a Draft Convention on International Interests in Mobile Equipment and a Draft Protocol Thereto on Matters Specific to Aircraft Equipment; Sub-Committee of the ICAO Legal Committee on the Study of International Interests in Mobile Equipment (Aircraft Equipment); Third Joint Session (Rome, 20–31 March 2000): Proposal Regarding the Substantive Sphere of Application of the Preliminary Draft Convention (Submitted by the UNIDROIT Secretariat) (Unidroit CGE/IntInt/3-WP/14 ICAO Ref LSC/ME/3-WP/14 2000)	Unidroit CGE/ Int.Int./3-WP/14 ICAO Ref. LSC/ ME/3-WP/14 (2000)

(continued)

(Continued)

No	Full title	Short title
96.	UNIDROIT Committee of Governmental Experts for the Preparation of a Draft Convention on International Interests in Mobile Equipment and a Draft Protocol Thereto on Matters specific to Aircraft Equipment; Sub-Committee of the ICAO Legal Committee on the Study of International Interests in Mobile Equipment (Aircraft Equipment); Third Joint Session (Rome, 20–31 March 2000): Proposal (Submitted by the French Delegation) (Unidroit CGE/IntInt/3-WP/17 ICAO Ref LSC/ME/3-WP/17 12/03/00, 2000)	Unidroit CGE/ Int.Int./3-WP/17 ICAO Ref. LSC/ ME/3-WP/17 12/03/00 (2000)
97.	UNIDROIT Committee of Governmental Experts for the Preparation of a Draft Convention on International Interests in Mobile Equipment and a Draft Protocol Thereto on Matters Specific to Aircraft Equipment; Sub-Committee of the ICAO Legal Committee on the Study of International Interests in Mobile Equipment (Aircraft Equipment); Third Joint Session (Rome, 20–31 March 2000): Public International Law Working Group (Rome, 20 and 21 March 2000): Report (Unidroit CGE/IntInt/3-WP/18 ICAO Ref LSC/ME/3-WP/18 22/03/00, 2000)	Unidroit CGE/ Int.Int./3-WP/18 ICAO Ref. LSC/ ME/3-WP/18 12/03/00 (2000)
98.	UNIDROIT Committee of Governmental Experts for the Preparation of a Draft Convention on International Interests in Mobile Equipment and a Draft Protocol Thereto on Matters Specific to Aircraft Equipment; Sub-Committee of the ICAO Legal Committee on the Study of International Interests in Mobile Equipment (Aircraft Equipment); Third Joint Session (Rome, 20–31 March 2000): Special Working Group on Article 14 of the Preliminary Draft Convention and Selected Aspects of Article X of the Preliminary Draft Aircraft Protocol: Report (Unidroit CGE/IntInt/3-WP/24 ICAO Ref LSC/ME/3-WP/24 2000)	Unidroit CGE/ Int.Int./3-WP/24 ICAO Ref. LSC/ ME/3-WP/24 (2000)
99.	UNIDROIT Committee of Governmental Experts for the Preparation of a Draft Convention on International Interests in Mobile Equipment and a Draft Protocol Thereto on Matters specific to Aircraft Equipment; Sub-Committee of the ICAO Legal Committee on the Study of International Interests in Mobile Equipment (Aircraft Equipment); Third Joint Session (Rome, 20–31 March 2000): Proposal (Submitted by the Delegation of the United States of America): Comments on Article 14 of the Preliminary Draft Convention and Article X of the Preliminary Draft Aircraft Protocol (Unidroit CGE/IntInt/3-WP/25 ICAO Ref LSC/ME/3-WP/25 23/03/00, 2000)	Unidroit CGE/ Int.Int./3-WP/25 ICAO Ref. LSC/ ME/3-WP/25 (2000)

(continued)

(Continued)

No	Full title	Short title
100.	UNIDROIT Committee of Governmental Experts for the Preparation of a Draft Convention on International Interests in Mobile Equipment and a Draft Protocol Thereto on Matters Specific to Aircraft Equipment; Sub-Committee of the ICAO Legal Committee on the Study of International Interests in Mobile Equipment (Aircraft Equipment); Third Joint Session (Rome, 20–31 March 2000): Special Working Group on Article 3 of the Preliminary Draft Convention; Second Report (Unidroit CGE/IntInt/3-WP/27 Corr ICAO Ref LSC/ME/3-WP/27 27/03/00, 2000)	Unidroit CGE/ Int.Int./3-WP/27 Corr. ICAO Ref. LSC/ME/3-WP/27 27/03/00 (2000)
101.	UNIDROIT Committee of Governmental Experts for the Preparation of a Draft Convention on International Interests in Mobile Equipment and a Draft Protocol Thereto on Matters Specific to Aircraft Equipment; Sub-Committee of the ICAO Legal Committee on the Study of International Interests in Mobile Equipment (Aircraft Equipment); Third Joint Session (Rome, 20–31 March 2000): Drafting Committee/Restricted Group Monday 27 March 2000 Public International Law Provisions (Unidroit CGE/IntInt/3-WP/28 Rev ICAO Ref LSC/ME/3-WP/28 Rev 28/03/00, 2000)	Unidroit CGE/Int. Int./3-WP/28 Rev. ICAO Ref. LSC/ ME/3-WP/28 Rev. 28/03/00 (2000)
102.	UNIDROIT Committee of Governmental Experts for the Preparation of a Draft Convention on International Interests in Mobile Equipment and a Draft Protocol Thereto on Matters Specific to Aircraft Equipment; Sub-Committee of the ICAO Legal Committee on the Study of International Interests in Mobile Equipment (Aircraft Equipment); Third Joint Session (Rome, 20–31 March 2000): Proposal for Revised Text of Chapter IX of the Preliminary Draft Convention (Unidroit CGE/ IntInt/3-WP/31 ICAO Ref LSC/ME/3-WP/31 29/03/00, 2000)	Unidroit CGE/ Int.Int./3-WP/31 ICAO Ref. LSC/ ME/3-WP/31 Rev. 29/03/00 (2000)
103.	UNIDROIT Committee of Governmental Experts for the Preparation of a Draft Convention on International Interests in Mobile Equipment and a Draft Protocol Thereto on Matters Specific to Aircraft Equipment; Sub-Committee of the ICAO Legal Committee on the Study of International Interests in Mobile Equipment (Aircraft Equipment); Third Joint Session (Rome, 20–31 March 2000): Drafting Committee: Report (Unidroit CGE/IntInt/3-WP/40 ICAO Ref LSC/ME/3-WP/40 30/03/00, 2000)	Unidroit CGE/ Int.Int./3-WP/40 ICAO Ref. LSC/ ME/3-WP/40 30/03/00 (2000)

(continued)

(Continued)

No	Full title	Short title
104.	Committee of Governmental Experts for the Preparation of a Draft Protocol to the Convention on International Interests in Mobile Equipment on Matters Specific to Railway Rolling Stock; Second Joint Session (Rome, 17–19 June 2002) Report (Prepared by the Secretariats of Unidroit and OTIF) (Unidroit 2003 Study LXXIIH – Doc 7, 2002)	Study LXXIIH – Doc. 7 (2002)
105.	Committee of Governmental Experts for the Preparation of a Draft Protocol to the Convention on International Interests in Mobile Equipment on Matters Specific to Railway Rolling Stock; Preliminary Draft Protocol on Matters Specific to Railway Rolling Stock (as Reviewed by the Drafting Committee at its Second Session, Held in Rome, 23 to 25 October 2002) (Unidroit 2003 Study LXXIIH – Doc 8, 2003)	Study LXXIIH – Doc. 8 (2003)
106.	Committee of Governmental Experts for the Preparation of a Draft Protocol to the Convention on International Interests in Mobile Equipment on Matters Specific to Railway Rolling Stock; Third Joint Session (Berne, 5–13 May 2003) Report (Prepared by the Secretariats of OTIF and Unidroit) (Unidroit 2003 Study LXXIIH – Doc 13, 2003)	Study LXXIIH – Doc. 13 (2003)
107.	Governing Council 86th Session (Rome, 16–18 April 2007) Item No. 8 on the Agenda: International Interests in Mobile Equipment: Preparation of an Additional Protocol to the Cape Town Convention on Matters Specific to Agricultural, Construction and Mining Equipment (Prepared by the Unidroit Secretariat) (Unidroit 2007 CD (86) 8 (d), 2007)	Governing Council C.D. (86) 8 (d) (2007)
108.	Steering Committee to Build Consensus around the Provisional Conclusions Reached by the Government/ Industry Meeting Regarding the Preliminary Draft Space Assets Protocol held in New York on 19 and 20 June 2007 Second Meeting; Paris, 14/15 May 2009: Summary Report (Prepared by the Unidroit Secretariat) (Unidroit 2009 Study LXXIIJ – Doc 17, 2009)	Study LXXIIJ – Doc. 17 (2009)
109.	Unidroit Committee of Governmental Experts for the Preparation of a Draft Protocol to the Convention on International Interests in Mobile Equipment on Matters Specific to Space Assets; Third Session: Rome, 7/11 December 2009 (Unidroit 2009 CGE/Space Pr/3/WP 12, 2009)	Unidroit C.G.E./ Space Pr./3/W.P. 12 (2009)

(continued)

(Continued)

No	Full title	Short title
110.	Governing Council 92nd Session; Rome, 8–10 May 2013: Item No. 5 on the Agenda: International Interests in Mobile Equipment – (b) Possible Preparation of Other Protocols to the Cape Town Convention (i) Agricultural, Mining and Construction Equipment (Memorandum Prepared by the Secretariat) (Unidroit 2013 CD (92) 5(b), 2013)	Unidroit 2013 C.D. (92) 5(b) (2013)
111.	Governing Council 92nd Session; Rome, 8–10 May 2013: Item No. 5 on the Agenda: International Interests in Mobile Equipment – (b) Possible Preparation of other Protocols to the Cape Town Convention (ii) Ships and Maritime Transport Equipment (iii) Off-shore Wind Power Generation and Similar Equipment (Memorandum Prepared by the Secretariat) (Unidroit 2013 CD (92) 5(c)/(d), 2013)	Unidroit 2013 C.D. (92) 5(c)/(d) (2013)
112.	MAC Protocol Study Group; 3rd Meeting; Rome, 19–21 October 2015: Report (Prepared by the Unidroit Secretariat) (Unidroit 2015 Study 72K – SG3 – Doc 5, 2015)	Study 72k – SG3 – Doc. 5 (2015)
113.	Preparatory Commission for the Establishment of the International Registry for Space Assets Pursuant to the Space Protocol: Fourth Session (Rome, 10–11 December 2015); Summary Report of the Fourth Session (Unidroit 2015 Prep Comm Space/4/Doc 7 rev, 2015)	Unidroit 2015 Prep. Comm. Space/4/ Doc. 7 rev. (2015)
114.	MAC Protocol Committee of Governmental Experts; First Session; Rome, 20–24 March 2017: Report (Prepared by the Unidroit Secretariat) (Unidroit 2017 Study 72K – CGE1 – Report, 2017)	Study 72k – CGE1 – Report (2017)
115.	MAC Protocol Committee of Governmental Experts; First Session; Rome, 20–24 March 2017: Preliminary Draft Protocol to the Convention on International Interests in Mobile Equipment on Matters Specific to Agricultural, Construction and Mining Equipment (Unidroit 2017 Study 72K – CGE1 – Doc 2 corr, 2017)	Study 72k – CGE1 – Doc. 2 corr. (2017)
116.	MAC Protocol Committee of Governmental Experts; First Session; Rome, 20–24 March 2017: Legal Analysis (Prepared by the Unidroit Secretariat) (Unidroit 2016 Study 72K – CGE1 – Doc 4, 2017)	Study 72k – CGE1 – Doc. 4 (2017)
117.	MAC Protocol Committee of Governmental Experts; First Session; Rome, 20–24 March 2017: Spreadsheet Detailing Harmonized System Codes Proposed by the Study Group for Inclusion in the Annexes to the Preliminary Draft MAC Protocol (Prepared by the Unidroit Secretariat) (Unidroit 2017 Study 72K – CGE1 – Doc 5 corr, 2017)	Study 72k – CGE1 – Doc. 5 corr (2017)

(continued)

(Continued)

No	Full title	Short title
118.	MAC Protocol Committee of Governmental Experts; First Session; Rome, 20–24 March 2017: Committee of Governmental Experts for the Preparation of a Draft Fourth Protocol to the Convention on International Interests in Mobile Equipment on Matters Specific to Agricultural, Construction and Mining Equipment: Comments (Submitted by the Government of the United Kingdom) (Unidroit 2017 Study 72K – CGE1 – Doc. 9)	Study 72k – CGE1 – Doc. 9 (2017)
119.	Potential Economic Benefits of Proposed MAC Protocol: Background Paper (Submitted by the US Department of Commerce on Request of the Unidroit Secretariat) (Unidroit 2017 Study 72K – CGE1 – Doc 10, 2017)	Study 72K – CGE 1 – Doc. 10 (2017)
120.	Diplomatic Conference for the Adoption of the Draft Protocol to the Convention on International Interests in Mobile Equipment on Matters Specific to Mining, Agricultural and Construction Equipment (the 'MAC Protocol'): Summary Report for 14 November 2019 (Unidroit 2019 DCME-MAC – Doc. 24 rev., 2019)	Unidroit 2019 DCME-MAC – Doc. 24 rev. (2019)
121.	Preparatory Commission for the Establishment of the International Registry for MAC Equipment Pursuant to the MAC Protocol: First Session (Rome, 21–22 May 2020); Summary Report of the First Session (Unidroit 2020 MACPC/1/Doc. 9, June 2020)	Unidroit 2020 MACPC/1/Doc. 9 rev. (2020)

Other reports and working papers

No	Full title	Short title
1.	Report of the Secretary-General: Study on Security Interests (A/CN.9/131) (United Nations Commission on International Trade Law Yearbook Volume VIII: 1977, 1978)	Report of the Secretary-General: Study on Security Interests (A/CN.9/131) (1978)
2.	United Nations, UNCITRAL Legislative Guide on Secured Transactions	UNCITRAL Legislative Guide on Secured Transactions (2010)
3.	CMI, Yearbook 2015 (New York I: Documents for the Conference (Published by CMI Headquarter; Dijckkaai 8, 2000 Antwerpen, Belgium), 2016)	CMI Yearbook 2015

BIBLIOGRAPHY

'Cape Town Convention Academic Project' www.ctcap.org

'Cape Town Convention Compliance Index' https://ctc-compliance-index.awg.aero/

'Letter from a Group of Space Industry Representatives to Mr Martin John Stanford' (9 December 2011) www.geospatialworld.net/wp-content/uploads/Satellite%20Industry%20Letter%20to%20Unidroit%209%20Dec%202011%20%28rev%29.pdf

'Global Satellite Industry Denounces UNIDROIT Protocol' (9 March 2012) www.casbaa.com/news/industry-news/global-satellite-industry-denounces-unidroit-protocol

Akseli O, *International Secured Transactions Law: Facilitation of Credit and International Conventions and Instruments* (Routledge 2011)

Böger O, 'The Cape Town Convention and Proprietary Security over Ships' (2014) 19 *Uniform Law Review* 24

——, 'The Case for a New Protocol to the Cape Town Convention Covering Security over Ships' (2016) 5 *Cape Town Convention Journal* 73

CMI, *Yearbook 2015* (New York I: Documents for the Conference (published by CMI Headquarter; Dijckkaai 8, 2000 Antwerp, Belgium), 2016)

Cowan R, 'Comparison of the Aircraft and MAC International Registries' (2018) 7 *Cape Town Convention Journal* 21

Deschamps M, 'The Perfection and Priority Rules of the Cape Town Convention and the Aircraft Protocol: A Comparative Law Analysis' (2013) 2 *Cape Town Convention Journal* 51

Goode R, 'From Acorn to Oak Tree: the Development of the Cape Town Convention and Protocols' (2012) 17 *Uniform Law Review* 599

——, 'The Priority Rules Under the Cape Town Convention and Protocols' (2012) 1 *Cape Town Convention Journal* 95

——, *Convention on International Interests in Mobile Equipment and Protocol thereto on Matters Specific to Space Assets: Official Commentary* (International Institute for the Unification of Private Law (UNIDROIT) 2013)

——, *Convention on International Interests in Mobile Equipment and Luxembourg Protocol thereto on Matters Specific to Railway Rolling Stock: Official Commentary* (2nd edn, International Institute for the Unification of Private Law (UNIDROIT) 2014)

——, *Convention on International Interests in Mobile Equipment and Protocol thereto on Matters Specific to Aircraft Equipment: Official Commentary* (4th edn, International Institute for the Unification of Private Law (UNIDROIT) 2019)

Hanley D, 'The Relationship between the Geneva and Cape Town Conventions' (2015) 4 *Cape Town Convention Journal* 103

Kozuka S and Taniguchi F, 'An Economic Assessment of the Space Assets Protocol to the Cape Town Convention' (2011) 16 *Uniform Law Review* 927

Kronke H, 'International Uniform Commercial Law Conventions: Advantages, Disadvantages, Criteria for Choice' (2000) 5 *Uniform Law Review* 13

Linetsky V, *Economic Benefits of the Cape Town Treaty* (2009)

——, *Accession to the Cape Town Convention by the UK: An Economic Impact Assessment Study* (2010)

McPhillips R and others, 'Comparative Analysis of Aircraft, Rail and Space International Registries and Their Regulatory Provisions' (2016) 5 *Cape Town Convention Journal* 29

Mooney CW, 'Cape Town Convention's Improbable-but-Possible Progeny Part One: An International Secured Transactions Registry of General Application, The Essay' (2014) 55 *Va J Int'l L* 163

OECD, *Sector Understanding on Export Credits for Civil Aircraft* (2007)
Rosen H, 'Public Service and the Cape Town Convention' (2013) 2 *Cape Town Convention Journal* 131
Saunders A, Srinivasan A and Walter I, 'Innovation in International Law and Global Finance: Estimating the Financial Impact of the Cape Town Convention' (2006) http://ssrn.com/abstract=894027
Saunders A and others, 'The Economic Implications of International Secured Transactions Law Reform: A Case Study' (1999) 20 *U Pa J Int'lL* 309
Saunders A and Walter I, *Proposed Unidroit Convention on International Interests in Mobile Equipment as Applicable to Aircraft Equipment through the Aircraft Equipment Protocol: Economic Impact Assessment* (A Study Prepared Under the Auspices of INSEAD and the New York University Salomon Center, 1998)
Spagnolo L, *CISG Exclusion and Legal Efficiency* (Kluwer Law International 2014)
Sundahl MJ, 'The Cape Town Approach: A New Method of Making International Law' (2006) 44 *Colum J Transnat'l L* 339
——, *The Cape Town Convention: Its Application to Space Assets and Relation to the Law of Outer Space* (Martinus Nijhoff Publishers 2013)
The Legal Advisory Panel of the Aviation Working Group, *Practitioners' Guide to the Cape Town Convention and The Aircraft Protocol* (2015)
Unidroit, 'Declarations Lodged by The People's Republic of China (PRC) under the Cape Town Convention at the Time of the Deposit of its Instrument of Ratification' www.unidroit.org/status-2001capetown?id=463
——, 'Declarations Lodged by the Republic of Panama under the Cape Town Convention at the Time of the Deposit of its Instrument of Ratification' www.unidroit.org/status-2001capetown?id=484
——, 'Declarations Lodged by the Republic of Turkey under the Cape Town Convention at the Time of the Deposit of its Instrument of Ratification' www.unidroit.org/status-2001capetown?id=492
——, 'Declarations Lodged by the United Mexican States under the Cape Town Convention at the Time of the Deposit of its Instrument of Accession' www.unidroit.org/status-2001capetown?id=476
——, 'Declarations Lodged by Ukraine under the Cape Town Convention at the Time of the Deposit of its Instrument of Accession' www.unidroit.org/status-2001capetown?id=493
——, *Preliminary Draft Uniform Rules on International Financial Leasing, as Adopted by the Unidroit Study Group for the Preparation of Uniform Rules on the Leasing Contract* (UNIDROIT 1984 Study LIX – Doc 16, 1984)
——, *Draft Convention on International Financial Leasing as Adopted by a Unidroit Committee of Governmental Experts on 30 April 1987 with Explanatory Report Prepared by the Unidroit Secretariat* (UNIDROIT 1987 Study LIX – Doc 48, 1987)
——, *Governing Council 67th Session (Rome, 14 to 17 June 1988) Report on the Session (Prepared by the Secretariat)* (UNIDROIT 1988 CD 67 – Doc 18, 1988)
——, *Governing Council 68th Session (Rome, 10 to 12 April 1989) Report on the Session (Prepared by the Secretariat)* (UNIDROIT 1989 CD 68 – Doc 26, 1989)
——, *International Regulation of Aspects of Security Interests in Mobile Equipment: Questionnaire* (UNIDROIT 1989 Study LXXII – Doc 2, 1989)
——, *International Regulation of Aspects of Security Interests in Mobile Equipment: Study Prepared by Professor Ronald C.C. Cuming (College of Law, University of Saskatchewan)* (UNIDROIT 1989 Study LXXII – Doc 1, 1989)
——, *Analysis of the Replies to the Questionnaire on an International Regulation of Aspects of Security Interests in Mobile Equipment (Prepared by the Unidroit Secretariat)* (UNIDROIT 1991 Study LXXII – Doc 3, 1991)
——, *Governing Council 70th Session (Rome, 21 to 24 May 1991) Report on the Session (Prepared by the Secretariat)* (UNIDROIT 1991 CD (70) 22, 1991)
——, *Basic Issues Identified in Responses to the Questionnaire on an International Regulation of Aspects of Security Interests in Mobile Equipment by Professor Ronald C.C. Cuming (University of Saskatchewan)* (UNIDROIT 1992 Study LXXII – Doc 4, 1992)
——, *Governing Council 71st Session (Genoa, 22 to 24 June 1992) Report on the Session (Prepared by the Secretariat)* (UNIDROIT 1992 CD (71) 18, 1992)

——, *Restricted Exploratory Working Group to Examine the Feasibility of Drawing up Uniform Rules on Certain International Aspects of Security Interests in Mobile Equipment: Report (Adopted by the Working Group on 11 March 1992)* (UNIDROIT 1992 Study LXXII – Doc 5, 1992)

——, *Study Group for the Preparation of Uniform Rules on Certain International Aspects of Security Interests in Mobile Equipment (First Session: Rome, 8–10 March 1993) – Summary Report (Prepared by the Unidroit Secretariat)* (UNIDROIT 1993 Study LXXII – Doc 7, 1993)

——, *Study Group for the Preparation of Uniform Rules on Certain International Aspects of Security Interests in Mobile Equipment: Memorandum for the Attention of the Study Group at its First Session (Prepared by the Unidroit Secretariat)* (UNIDROIT 1993 Study LXXII – Doc 6, 1993)

——, *Study Group for the Preparation of Uniform Rules on Certain International Aspects of Security Interests in Mobile Equipment: Some Preliminary Observations on the Process of Developing a Convention on International Security Interests by Professor R.C.C. Cuming (University of Saskatchewan)* (Security Interests Study Group 1st Session Misc 5, 1993)

——, *Study Group for the Preparation of Uniform Rules on Certain International Aspects of Security Interests in Mobile Equipment: Texts of International Instruments and of a Proposed New International Instrument Regulating the Recognition and Priority of Security Interests in Ships and Inland Navigation Vessels and Appurtenances Thereto* (Security Interests Study Group 1st Session Misc 3, 1993)

——, *Study Group for the Preparation of Uniform Rules on Certain International Aspects of Security Interests in Mobile Equipment; Memorandum (for the Attention of the Study Group at its First Session): Addendum (Comments of the European Bank for Reconstruction and Development)* (UNIDROIT 1993 Study LXXII – Doc 6 Add 2, 1993)

——, *Study Group for the Preparation of Uniform Rules on Certain International Aspects of Security Interests in Mobile Equipment; Memorandum (for the Attention of the Study Group at its First Session): Addendum (Comments of the European Federation of Equipment Leasing Company Associations (Leaseurope))* (UNIDROIT 1993 Study LXXII – Doc 6 Add 3, 1993)

——, *Study Group for the Preparation of Uniform Rules on Certain International Aspects of Security Interests in Mobile Equipment; Memorandum (for the Attention of the Study Group at its First Session): Addendum (Comments of the German Federal Ministry of Justice)* (UNIDROIT 1993 Study LXXII – Doc 6 Add, 1993)

——, *Study Group for the Preparation of Uniform Rules on Certain International Aspects of Security Interests in Mobile Equipment; Memorandum on a Proposed Unidroit Convention on Security Interests in Mobile Equipment prepared by Professor R.C.C. Cuming (University of Saskatchewan)* (UNIDROIT 1993 Study LXXII – Doc 8, 1993)

——, *Meeting of International Organisations Currently Involved in the Preparation of Legislation in the Field of Personal Property Security (Rome, 29 November 1994): Report (Prepared by the Unidroit Secretariat)* (UNIDROIT 1995 Study LXXIIB – Doc 1, 1994)

——, *Study Group for the Preparation of Uniform Rules on Certain International Aspects of Security Interests in Mobile Equipment: Sub-Committee for the Preparation of a First Draft (First Session: Rome, 14–16 February 1994) Summary Report (Prepared by the Unidroit Secretariat)* (UNIDROIT 1994 Study LXXII – Doc 12, 1994)

——, *Study Group for the Preparation of Uniform Rules on Certain International Aspects of Security Interests in Mobile Equipment: Sub-Committee for the Preparation of a First Draft (Rome, 14–16 February 1994): Addendum to the Comments by The Boeing Company to the Memorandum of Professor R.C.C. Cuming Regarding a Proposed Convention on Security Interests in Mobile Equipment* (Security Interests Study Group Sub-committee 1st Session Misc 3 Add, 1994)

——, *Study Group for the Preparation of Uniform Rules on Certain International Aspects of Security Interests in Mobile Equipment: Sub-Committee for the Preparation of a First Draft (Rome, 14–16 February 1994); Comments by Professor R.D. Vriesendorp (Catholic University of Brabant at Tilburg) to the Memorandum by Professor R.C.C. Cuming Regarding a Proposed Unidroit Convention on Security Interests in Mobile Equipment* (Security Interests Study Group Sub-committee 1st Session Misc 2, 1994)

——, *Study Group for the Preparation of Uniform Rules on Certain International Aspects of Security Interests in Mobile Equipment: Sub-Committee for the Preparation of a First Draft (Rome, 14–16 February 1994); Comments by The Boeing Company to the Memorandum by Professor R.C.C. Cuming Regarding a Proposed Unidroit Convention on Security Interests in Mobile Equipment* (Security Interests Study Group Sub-committee 1st Session Misc 3, 1994)

——, *Study Group for the Preparation of Uniform Rules on Certain International Aspects of Security Interests in Mobile Equipment: Sub-Committee for the Preparation of a First Draft; Proposals for a First Draft (Drawn up by the Chairman and a Member of the Sub-committee on the Basis of the Provisional Conclusions Reached by the Latter at its First Session)* (UNIDROIT 1994 Study LXXII – Doc 13, 1994)

——, *Study Group for the Preparation of Uniform Rules on Certain International Aspects of Security Interests in Mobile Equipment: Sub-Committee for the Preparation of a First Draft; Proposals for a First Draft (Drawn up by the Chairman and a Member of the Sub-committee on the Basis of the Provisional Conclusions Reached by the Latter at its First Session): Comments (by Members of the Sub-committee and the Study Group and the International Organisations and Professional Associations Represented by Observers Thereon)* (UNIDROIT 1994 Study LXXII – Doc 14, 1994)

——, *Study Group for the Preparation of Uniform Rules on Certain International Aspects of Security Interests in Mobile Equipment: Sub-Committee for the Preparation of a First Draft; Proposals for a First Draft (Drawn up by the Chairman and a Member of the Sub-committee on the Basis of the Provisional Conclusions Reached by the Latter at its First Session): Comments (by Mr Thomas J. Whalen, Professor Rolf Herber and The Boeing Company)* (UNIDROIT 1994 Study LXXII – Doc 14 Add 1, 1994)

——, *Study Group for the Preparation of Uniform Rules on Certain International Aspects of Security Interests in Mobile Equipment: Sub-Committee for the Preparation of a First Draft; Proposals for a First Draft (Drawn up by the Chairman and a Member of the Sub-committee on the Basis of the Provisional Conclusions Reached by the Latter at its First Session): Comments (by the Banking Federation of the European Union and the Italian Banking Association)* (UNIDROIT 1994 Study LXXII – Doc 14 Add 4, 1994)

——, *Study Group for the Preparation of Uniform Rules on Certain International Aspects of Security Interests in Mobile Equipment: Sub-Committee for the Preparation of a First Draft; Proposals for a First Draft (Drawn up by the Chairman and a Member of the Sub-committee on the Basis of the Provisional Conclusions Reached by the Latter at its First Session): Comments by Professor Charles W. Mooney, Jr. and the Legal Committee of the Finance & Leasing Association of the United Kingdom)* (UNIDROIT 1994 Study LXXII – Doc 14 Add 2, 1994)

——, *Study Group for the Preparation of Uniform Rules on Certain International Aspects of Security Interests in Mobile Equipment; Comments by Mr Thomas J. Whalen to the Memorandum by Professor R.C.C. Cuming on a Proposed Unidroit Convention on Security Interests in Mobile Equipment* (UNIDROIT 1994 Study LXXII – Doc 9, 1994)

——, *Study Group for the Preparation of Uniform Rules on Certain International Aspects of Security Interests in Mobile Equipment; Comments by Mr. J.-H. Roever (European Bank for Reconstruction and Development) to the Memorandum by Professor R.C.C. Cuming on a Proposed Unidroit Convention on Security Interests in Mobile Equipment* (UNIDROIT 1994 Study LXXII – Doc 11, 1994)

——, *Study Group for the Preparation of Uniform Rules on Certain International Aspects of Security Interests in Mobile Equipment; Comments by Professor C.W. Mooney, Jr. Concerning the Test of Internationality to be Employed in the Proposed Unidroit Convention on Security Interests in Mobile Equipment* (UNIDROIT 1994 Study LXXII – Doc 10, 1994)

——, *Study Group for the Preparation of Uniform Rules on Certain International Aspects of Security Interests in Mobile Equipment: Sub-Committee for the Preparation of a First Draft (Second Session: Rome, 29 November–1 December 1994) Summary Report (Prepared by the Unidroit Secretariat)* (UNIDROIT 1995 Study LXXII – Doc 15, 1995)

——, *Study Group for the Preparation of Uniform Rules on Certain International Aspects of Security Interests in Mobile Equipment: Sub-Committee for the Preparation of a First Draft (Third Session: Rome, 11–13 October 1995) Summary Report (Prepared by the Unidroit Secretariat)* (UNIDROIT 1995 Study LXXII – Doc 21, 1995)

——, *Study Group for the Preparation of Uniform Rules on Certain International Aspects of Security Interests in Mobile Equipment: Sub-Committee for the Preparation of a First Draft (Third Session: Rome, 11–13 October 1995); Memorandum Prepared Jointly by Airbus Industrie and The Boeing Company on behalf of an Aviation Working Group: Comments (by the Equipment Leasing Association of America)* (International Interests Study-Group Sub-committee 3rd Session Misc 1, 1995)

——, *Study Group for the Preparation of Uniform Rules on Certain International Aspects of Security Interests in Mobile Equipment: Sub-Committee for the Preparation of a First Draft; Memorandum Prepared Jointly by Airbus Industrie and The Boeing Company on behalf of an Aviation Working Group* (UNIDROIT 1995 Study LXXII – Doc 16, 1995)

——, *Study Group for the Preparation of Uniform Rules on Certain International Aspects of Security Interests in Mobile Equipment: Sub-Committee for the Preparation of a First Draft; Memorandum Prepared Jointly by Airbus Industrie and The Boeing Company on behalf of an Aviation Working Group: Comments (by Members of the Study Group and the International Organisations and Professional Associations Represented by Observers Thereon)* (UNIDROIT 1995 Study LXXII – Doc 17 Add 3, 1995)

——, *Study Group for the Preparation of Uniform Rules on Certain International Aspects of Security Interests in Mobile Equipment: Sub-Committee for the Preparation of a First Draft; Memorandum Prepared Jointly by Airbus Industrie and The Boeing Company on behalf of an Aviation Working Group: Comments (by Members of the Sub-committee)* (UNIDROIT 1995 Study LXXII – Doc 17, 1995)

——, *Study Group for the Preparation of Uniform Rules on Certain International Aspects of Security Interests in Mobile Equipment: Sub-Committee for the Preparation of a First Draft; Revised Proposals for a First Set of Draft Articles of a Future Unidroit Convention on International Interests in Mobile Equipment (Drawn up by the Drafting Group on the Basis of the Provisional Conclusions Reached by the Sub-committee at its Second Session)* (UNIDROIT 1995 Study LXXII – Doc 18, 1995)

——, *Study Group for the Preparation of Uniform Rules on Certain International Aspects of Security Interests in Mobile Equipment: Sub-Committee for the Preparation of a First Draft; Revised Proposals for a First Set of Draft Articles of a Future Unidroit Convention on International Interests in Mobile Equipment (Drawn up by the Drafting Group on the Basis of the Provisional Conclusions Reached by the Sub-committee at its Second Session): Comments (by a Member of the Drafting Group)* (UNIDROIT 1995 Study LXXII – Doc 19, 1995)

——, *Study Group for the Preparation of Uniform Rules on Certain International Aspects of Security Interests in Mobile Equipment: Sub-Committee for the Preparation of a First Draft; Revised Proposals for a First Set of Draft Articles of a Future Unidroit Convention on International Interests in Mobile Equipment (Drawn up by the Drafting Group on the Basis of the Provisional Conclusions Reached by the Sub-committee at its Second Session): Comments (by Airbus Industrie / The Boeing Company on behalf of an Aviation Working Group)* (UNIDROIT 1995 Study LXXII – Doc 19 Add 4, 1995)

——, *Study Group for the Preparation of Uniform Rules on Certain International Aspects of Security Interests in Mobile Equipment: Sub-Committee for the Preparation of a First Draft; Revised Proposals for a First Set of Draft Articles of a Future Unidroit Convention on International Interests in Mobile Equipment (Drawn up by the Drafting Group on the Basis of the Provisional Conclusions Reached by the Sub-committee at its Second Session): Comments (by Members of the Study Group and the Sub-committee and the International Organisations and Professional Associations Represented by Observers Thereon)* (UNIDROIT 1995 Study LXXII – Doc 19 Add, 1995)

——, *Study Group for the Preparation of Uniform Rules on International Interests in Mobile Equipment: Sub-Committee for the Preparation of a First Draft (Third Session: Rome, 11–13 October 1995) Extract from a Work in Progress by Professor Charles W. Mooney, Jr. on "Exporting Article 9 of the Uniform Commercial Code in an International Convention: the Local law Conundrum and Possible Solutions Thereto"* (International Interests Study Group Sub-committee 3rd Session Misc 3, 1995)

——, *Study Group for the Preparation of Uniform Rules on Certain International Aspects of Security Interests in Mobile Equipment (Second Session: Rome, 12–16 April 1996): Report (Prepared by Unidroit Secretariat)* (UNIDROIT 1996 Study LXXII – Doc 27, 1996)

——, *Study Group for the Preparation of Uniform Rules on Certain International Aspects of Security Interests in Mobile Equipment: Extract from the Report on the 75th Session of the Unidroit Governing Council (Prepared by the Unidroit Secretariat)* (UNIDROIT 1996 Study LXXII – Doc 28, 1996)

——, *Study Group for the Preparation of Uniform Rules on Certain International Aspects of Security Interests in Mobile Equipment: First Set of Draft Articles of a Future Unidroit Convention on International Interests in Mobile Equipment (Established by the Drafting Group of the Sub-committee on 19 December 1995 as Revised by the Same on 4 March 1996)* (UNIDROIT 1996 Study LXXII – Doc 24, 1996)

——, *Study Group for the Preparation of Uniform Rules on Certain International Aspects of Security Interests in Mobile Equipment: First Set of Draft Articles of a Future Unidroit Convention on International Interests in Mobile Equipment (Established by the Drafting Group of the Sub-committee on 19 December 1995 Pursuant to the Decisions Taken by the Sub-committee of the Study Group at its Third Session)* (UNIDROIT 1996 Study LXXII – Doc 22, 1996)

——, *Study Group for the Preparation of Uniform Rules on Certain International Aspects of Security Interests in Mobile Equipment: Revised Draft Articles of a Future Unidroit Convention on International Interests in Mobile Equipment (Proposed by the Drafting Group in the Light of the Study Group's Reading at its Second Session of the First set of Draft Articles Established by the Sub-committee in Conjunction with the Recommendations of the Aviation Working Group) with Introductory Remarks (Prepared by the Unidroit Secretariat)* (UNIDROIT 1996 Study LXXII – Doc 30, 1996)

——, *Study Group for the Preparation of Uniform Rules on Certain International Aspects of Security Interests in Mobile Equipment: Second Memorandum Prepared Jointly by Airbus Industrie and The Boeing Company on behalf of an Aviation Working Group* (UNIDROIT 1996 Study LXXII – Doc 23, 1996)

——, *Study Group for the Preparation of Uniform Rules on Certain International Aspects of Security Interests in Mobile Equipment: Second Memorandum Prepared Jointly by Airbus Industrie and The Boeing Company on behalf of an Aviation Working Group: Summary of Principal Concepts Prepared by Mr Jeffrey Wool (Expert Consultant to the Study Group on International Aviation Finance Matters)* (UNIDROIT 1996 Study LXXII – Doc 25, 1996)

——, *Study Group for the Preparation of Uniform Rules on International Interests in Mobile Equipment: Consideration of the Case for the Exclusion of Registered Ships from the Sphere of Application of the Future Convention (Secretariat Memorandum)* (UNIDROIT 1996 Study LXXII – Doc 29, 1996)

——, *Study Group for the Preparation of Uniform Rules on International Interests in Mobile Equipment: Revised Draft Articles of a Future Unidroit Convention on International Interests in Mobile Equipment (Proposed by the Drafting Group in the Light of the Study Group's Reading at its Second Session of the First Set of Draft Articles Established by the Sub-committee in Conjunction with the Recommendations of the Aviation Working Group): Comments (by the Aviation Working Group and the International Air Transport Association)* (UNIDROIT 1996 Study LXXII – Doc 32, 1996)

——, *Study Group for the Preparation of Uniform Rules on International Interests in Mobile Equipment; First Set of Draft Articles of a Future Unidroit Convention on International Interests in Mobile Equipment (Established by the Drafting Group of the Sub-committee on 19 December 1995 as Revised by the Same on 4 March 1996): Comments (by Ms N. de la Pena, Professor L. Girton and Mr H. Fleisig)* (UNIDROIT 1996 Study LXXII – Doc 26 Add 2, 1996)

——, *Study Group for the Preparation of Uniform Rules on International Interests in Mobile Equipment; First Set of Draft Articles of a Future Unidroit Convention on International Interests in Mobile Equipment (Established by the Drafting Group of the Sub-committee on 19 December 1995 as Revised by the Same on 4 March 1996): Comments (by Professor C.W. Mooney, Jr. and Mr T.J. Whalen)* (UNIDROIT 1996 Study LXXII – Doc 26 Add 1, 1996)

——, *Study Group for the Preparation of Uniform Rules on International Interests in Mobile Equipment; First Set of Draft Articles of a Future Unidroit Convention on International Interests in Mobile Equipment (Established by the Drafting Group of the Sub-committee on 19 December 1995 as Revised by the Same on 4 March 1996): Comments (by the Cosmic Space Agency of the Russian Federation and the Banking Federation of the European Union)* (UNIDROIT 1996 Study LXXII – Doc 26, 1996)

——, *Study Group for the Preparation of Uniform Rules on International Interests in Mobile Equipment; First Set of Draft Articles of a Future Unidroit Convention on International Interests in Mobile Equipment (Established by the Drafting Group of the Sub-committee on 19 December 1995 as Revised by the Same on 4 March 1996): Comments (by the European Federation of Equipment Leasing Company Associations, Mr Peter D. Nesgos and Ms Shiva Falsafi)* (UNIDROIT 1996 Study LXXII – Doc 26 Add 3, 1996)

——, *Study Group for the Preparation of Uniform Rules on Certain International Aspects of Security Interests in Mobile Equipment: (Fourth session: Rome, 3–8 November 1997): Preliminary Draft Unidroit Convention on International Interests in Mobile Equipment (as Proposed by the Drafting Group at its Fifth Session, Held in Rome from 4 to 7 November 1997)* (International Interests Study Group 4th session Misc 5, 1997)

——, *Study Group for the Preparation of Uniform Rules on Certain International Aspects of Security Interests in Mobile Equipment: Drafting Group (Fourth session: Würzburg, 24–26 July 1997) Revised Draft Articles of a Future Unidroit Convention on International Interests in Mobile Equipment (Prepared by the Chairman of the Study Group in the Light of the Deliberations of that Group at its Third Session, Held in Rome from 15 to 21 January 1997, and of the Proposals by the Drafting Group at its Third Session, Held in Rome on 17 and 20 January 1997)* (UNIDROIT 1997 International Interests/Study Group/Drafting Group/Fourth session/ WP 1, 1997)

——, *Study Group for the Preparation of Uniform Rules on Certain International Aspects of Security Interests in Mobile Equipment: Preliminary Draft Unidroit Convention on International Interests in Mobile Equipment (as Established by the Study Group at the Conclusion of its Fourth Session, Held in Rome from 3 to 7 November 1997)* (UNIDROIT 1997 Study LXXII – Doc 37, 1997)

——, *Study Group for the Preparation of Uniform Rules on Certain International Aspects of Security Interests in Mobile Equipment: Revised Draft Articles of a Future Unidroit Convention on International Interests in Mobile Equipment (as Proposed by the Drafting Group at its Fourth Session, Held in Würzburg from 24 to 26 July 1997) with Introductory Remarks (by the Unidroit Secretariat)* (UNIDROIT 1997 Study LXXII – Doc 35, 1997)

——, *Study Group for the Preparation of Uniform Rules on Certain International Aspects of Security Interests in Mobile Equipment: Revised Draft Articles of a Future Unidroit Convention on International Interests in Mobile Equipment (as Proposed by the Drafting Group at its Fourth Session, Held in Würzburg from 24 to 26 July 1997): Comments (by Members of the Study Group, Advisers Thereto and the International Organisations, Professional Associations and Other Bodies Represented Thereon by Observers as also those Persons and Bodies Having Participated from Outside the Study Group in the Development of the Project)* (UNIDROIT 1997 Study LXXII – Doc 36, 1997)

——, *Study Group for the Preparation of Uniform Rules on Certain International Aspects of Security Interests in Mobile Equipment: Revised Draft Articles of a Future Unidroit Convention on International Interests in Mobile Equipment (as Proposed by the Drafting Group at its Fourth Session, Held in Würzburg from 24 to 26 July 1997): Comments (by the Aircraft Protocol Group)* (UNIDROIT 1997 Study LXXII – Doc 36 Add 3, 1997)

——, *Study Group for the Preparation of Uniform Rules on Certain International Aspects of Security Interests in Mobile Equipment: Revised Draft Articles of a Future Unidroit Convention on International Interests in Mobile Equipment (as Proposed by the Drafting Group at its Fourth Session, Held in Würzburg from 24 to 26 July 1997): Comments (by the Federal German Association of Banks)* (UNIDROIT 1997 Study LXXII – Doc 36 Add 1, 1997)

——, *Study Group for the Preparation of Uniform Rules on Certain International Aspects of Security Interests in Mobile Equipment: Revised Draft Articles of a Future Unidroit Convention on International Interests in Mobile Equipment (as Proposed by the Drafting Group at its Fourth Session, Held in Würzburg from 24 to 26 July 1997): Comments (by the Intergovernmental Organisation for International Carriage by Rail, the European Company for the Financing of Railroad Rolling Stock, the Danish Shipowners' Association and the Elf Aquitaine Group)* (UNIDROIT 1997 Study LXXII – Doc 36 Add 2, 1997)

——, *Study Group for the Preparation of Uniform Rules on Certain International Aspects of Security Interests in Mobile Equipment: Second Memorandum Prepared Jointly by Airbus Industrie and The Boeing Company on behalf of an Aviation Working Group: Preliminary Comments by the Russian Federation Aviation Working Group* (UNIDROIT 1997 Study LXXII - Doc 31, 1997)

——, *Study Group for the Preparation of Uniform Rules on Certain International Aspects of Security Interests in Mobile Equipment: Working Group to Consider the Legal and Technical Issues Raised by the Establishment of an International Register (First session: Rome, 16–18 April 1996): Summary Report (Prepared by the Unidroit Secretariat)* (UNIDROIT 1997 Study LXXIIC - Doc 2, 1997)

——, *Study Group for the Preparation of Uniform Rules on Certain International Aspects of Security Interests in Mobile Equipment: Working Group to Consider the Legal and Technical Issues Raised by the Establishment of an International Register (Second Session: Geneva, 26–28 May 1997): Summary Report (Prepared by the Unidroit Secretariat)* (UNIDROIT 1997 Study LXXIIC - Doc 3, 1997)

——, *Study Group for the Preparation of Uniform Rules on International Interests in Mobile Equipment: Revised Draft Articles of a Future Unidroit Convention on International Interests in Mobile Equipment (Proposed by the Drafting Group in the Light of the Study Group's Reading at its Second Session of the First Set of Draft Articles Established by the Sub-committee in Conjunction with the Recommendations of the Aviation Working Group): Comments (by Mr S. Masuda)* (UNIDROIT 1997 Study LXXII - Doc 32 Add 1, 1997)

——, *Study Group for the Preparation of Uniform Rules on International Interests in Mobile Equipment: Revised Draft Articles of a Future Unidroit Convention on International Interests in Mobile Equipment (Proposed by the Drafting Group in the Light of the Study Group's Reading at its Second Session of the First Set of Draft Articles Established by the Sub-committee in Conjunction with the Recommendations of the Aviation Working Group): Comments (by Professor C.W. Mooney, Jr. and Mr T. Whalen)* (UNIDROIT 1997 Study LXXII - Doc 32 Add 3, 1997)

——, *Study Group for the Preparation of Uniform Rules on International Interests in Mobile Equipment: Revised Draft Articles of a Future Unidroit Convention on International Interests in Mobile Equipment (Proposed by the Drafting Group in the Light of the Study Group's Reading at its Second Session of the First Set of Draft Articles Established by the Sub-committee in Conjunction with the Recommendations of the Aviation Working Group): Comments (by the Aviation Working Group and the International Air Transport Association)* (UNIDROIT 1997 Study LXXII - Doc 32 Add 2, 1997)

——, *Committee of Governmental Experts for the Preparation of a Draft Convention on International Interests in Mobile Equipment and a Draft Protocol on Matters Specific to Aircraft Equipment; Preliminary Draft Unidroit Convention on International Interests in Mobile Equipment and Preliminary Draft Protocol to the Preliminary Draft Unidroit Convention on International Interest in Mobile Equipment on Matters Specific to Aircraft Equipment: Comments (Submitted by the International Air Transpot Association and the Aviation Working Group)* (UNIDROIT 1998 Study LXXII - Doc 45 / Study LXXIID - Doc 6, 1998)

——, *Committee of Governmental Experts for the Preparation of a Draft Convention on International Interests in Mobile Equipment and a Draft Protocol on Matters Specific to Aircraft Equipment; Preliminary Draft Unidroit Convention on International Interests in Mobile Equipment and Preliminary Draft Protocol to the Preliminary Draft Unidroit Convention on International Interest in Mobile Equipment on Matters Specific to Aircraft Equipment: Preliminary Observations (Submitted by the Government of the United States of America)* (UNIDROIT 1998 Study LXXII - Doc 43 / Study LXXIID - Doc 4, 1998)

——, *Committee of Governmental Experts for the Preparation of a Draft Convention on International Interests in Mobile Equipment and a Draft Protocol on Matters Specific to Aircraft Equipment; Preliminary Draft Unidroit Convention on International Interests in Mobile Equipment: Comments (Submitted by the Government of Australia)* (UNIDROIT 1998 Study LXXII - Doc 44, 1998)

——, *Governing Council (77th Session: Rome, 16–20 February 1998): Extract from the Report on the Session Re Item n 8 on the Agenda: International Interests in Mobile Equipment* (UNIDROIT 1998 Etude LXXII - Doc 40, 1998)

——, *Preliminary Draft Protocol to the Preliminary Draft UNIDROIT Convention on International Interests in Mobile Equipment on Matters Specific to Aircraft Equipment (as Established by a Working Group Organised, at the Invitation of the President of the Unidroit Study Group for the Preparation of Uniform Rules on International Interests in Mobile Equipment, and Revised, in Accordance with a Decision Taken by the Unidroit Governing Council at its 77th Session, Held in Rome from 16 to 20 February 1998, by a Steering and Revisions Committee, Meeting in Rome from 27 to 29 June 1998)* (UNIDROIT 1998 Study LXXIID – Doc 3, 1998)

——, *Preliminary Draft Unidroit Convention on International Interests in Mobile Equipment (as Established by an Unidroit Study Group and Revised, in Accordance with a Decision Taken by the Unidroit Governing Council at its 77th Session, Held in Rome from 16 to 20 February 1998, by a Steering and Revisions Committee, Meeting in Rome from 27 to 29 June 1998)* (UNIDROIT 1998 Study LXXII – Doc 42, 1998)

——, *Steering and Revisions Committee (Rome, 27–29 June 1998): Report (Prepared by the Unidroit Secretariat)* (UNIDROIT 1998 Study LXXII – Doc 41, 1998)

——, *Steering and Revisions Committee for the Finalisation of the Preliminary Draft Unidroit Convention on International Interests in Mobile Equipment and the Preliminary Protocol Thereto on Matters Specific to Aircraft Equipment: Preliminary Draft Unidroit Convention on International Interests in Mobile Equipment (as Established by the Study Group at the Conclusion of its Fourth Session, held in Rome from 3 to 7 November 1997, and as Revised by the Chairman of the Study Group)* (UNIDROIT 1998 Study LXXII – Doc 39, 1998)

——, *Study Group for the Preparation of Uniform Rules on International Interests in Mobile Equipment; Preliminary Draft Unidroit Convention on International Interests in Mobile Equipment (as Established by the Study Group at the Conclusion of its Fourth Session, Held in Rome from 3 to 7 November 1997): Preliminary Draft Protocol on Matters Specific to Aircraft Equipment (as Established by a Working Group Organised by Mr J. Wool, Expert Consultant to the Study Group on International Aviation Finance Matters, at the Invitation of the President, at the Conclusion of its Second Session, Held in Geneva from 19 to 21 November 1997)* (UNIDROIT 1998 Study LXXIID – Doc 1, 1998)

——, *Committee of Governmental Experts for the Preparation of a Draft Convention on International Interests in Mobile Equipment and a Draft Protocol on Matters Specific to Aircraft Equipment; Preliminary Draft Unidroit Convention on International Interests in Mobile Equipment and Preliminary Draft Protocol to the Preliminary Draft Unidroit Convention on International Interest in Mobile Equipment on Matters Specific to Aircraft Equipment: Comments (Submitted by the Government of Japan)* (UNIDROIT 1999 Study LXXII – Doc 49 / Study LXXIID – Doc 9, 1999)

——, *Consolidated Version of a Preliminary Draft Unidroit Convention on International Interests in Aircraft Equipment Submitted by the German Delegation Integrating the Preliminary Draft Unidroit Convention on International Interests in Mobile Equipment UNIDROIT 1998 Study LXXII – Doc. 42 and the Preliminary Draft Protocol to the Preliminary Draft Unidroit Convention on International Interests in Mobile Equipment on Matters Specific to Aircraft Equipment Unidroit 1998 Study LXXIID – Doc. 3 Established on the Basis of the Preliminary Draft Unidroit Convention on International Interests in Mobile Equipment (as Established by an Unidroit Study Group and Revised, in Accordance with a Decision Taken by the Unidroit Governing Council at its 77th Session, Held in Rome from 16 to 29 February 1998, by a Steering and Revisions Committee, Meeting in Rome from 27 to 29 June 1998) UNIDROIT 1998 Study LXXII – Doc. 42* (Unidroit CGE/IntInt/WP/9 ICAO Ref LSC/ME-WP/20, 1999)

——, *Drafting Committee Proposal (Submitted by the Delegation of the United States of America)* (Unidroit CGE/IntInt ICAO Ref LSC/ME DC-WP/10 8/02/99, 1999)

——, *Drafting Committee Proposal (Submitted by the Delegation of the United States of America)* (Unidroit CGE/IntInt ICAO Ref LSC/ME DC-WP/7 5/02/99, 1999)

——, *Sub-Committee of the ICAO Legal Committee on the Study of International Interests in Mobile Equipment (Aircraft Equipment); UNIDROIT Committee of Governmental Experts for the Preparation of a Draft Convention on International Interests in Mobile Equipment and a Draft Protocol Thereto on Matters Specific to Aircraft Equipment; Second Joint Session (Montreal, 24 August–3 September 1999): Insolvency Working Group Report* (ICAO Ref LSC/ME/2-WP/19 Unidroit CGE/IntInt/2-WP/19 26/8/99, 1999)

——, *Sub-Committee of the ICAO Legal Committee on the Study of International Interests in Mobile Equipment (Aircraft Equipment); UNIDROIT Committee of Governmental Experts for the Preparation of a Draft Convention on International Interests in Mobile Equipment and a Draft Protocol Thereto on Matters Specific to Aircraft Equipment; Second Joint Session (Montreal, 24 August–3 September 1999): Report* (ICAO Ref LSC/ME/2-Report Unidroit CGE/IntInt/2-Report, 1999)

——, *Sub-Committee of the ICAO Legal Committee on the Study of International Interests in Mobile Equipment (Aircraft Equipment); UNIDROIT Committee of Governmental Experts for the Preparation of a Draft Convention on International Interests in Mobile Equipment and a Draft Protocol Thereto on Matters Specific to Aircraft Equipment; Second Joint Session (Montreal, 24 August–3 September 1999): Report (by the Registration Working Group (RWG))* (ICAO Ref LSC/ME/2-WP/17 Unidroit CGE/IntInt/2-WP/17, 1999)

——, *UNIDROIT Committee of Governmental Experts for the Preparation of a Draft Convention on International Interests in Mobile Equipment and a Draft Protocol Thereto on Matters Specific to Aircraft Equipment; Sub-Committee of the ICAO Legal Committee on the Study of International Interests in Mobile Equipment (Aircraft Equipment); Draft Report: Plenary Session; 1–12 February 1999* (Unidroit CGE/IntInt/WP/17 ICAO Ref LSC/ME-WP/28 12/02/99, 1999)

——, *UNIDROIT Committee of Governmental Experts for the Preparation of a Draft Convention on International Interests in Mobile Equipment and a Draft Protocol Thereto on Matters Specific to Aircraft Equipment; Sub-Committee of the ICAO Legal Committee on the Study of International Interests in Mobile Equipment (Aircraft Equipment); First Joint Session (Rome, 1–12 February 1999): Report* (Unidroit CGE/IntInt/Report ICAO Ref LSC/ME-Report, 1999)

——, *UNIDROIT Committee of Governmental Experts for the Preparation of a Draft Convention on International Interests in Mobile Equipment and a Draft Protocol Thereto on Matters Specific to Aircraft Equipment; Sub-Committee of the ICAO Legal Committee on the Study of International Interests in Mobile Equipment (Aircraft Equipment); Joint Session (Rome, 1–12 February 1999): Information Paper (Submitted Jointly by the Unidroit Secretariat and the ICAO Secretariat)* (Unidroit CGE/IntInt/WP/8 ICAO Ref LSC/ME-WP/19 8/02/99, 1999)

——, *UNIDROIT Committee of Governmental Experts for the Preparation of a Draft Convention on International Interests in Mobile Equipment and a Draft Protocol Thereto on Matters Specific to Aircraft Equipment; Sub-Committee of the ICAO Legal Committee on the Study of International Interests in Mobile Equipment (Aircraft Equipment); Third Joint Session (Rome, 20–31 March 2000): Ad hoc Drafting Group (Rome 25–27 November 1999), Report* (Unidroit CGE/IntInt/3-WP/2 ICAO Ref LSC/ME/3-WP/2, 2000)

——, *UNIDROIT Committee of Governmental Experts for the Preparation of a Draft Convention on International Interests in Mobile Equipment and a Draft Protocol Thereto on Matters Specific to Aircraft Equipment; Sub-Committee of the ICAO Legal Committee on the Study of International Interests in Mobile Equipment (Aircraft Equipment); Third Joint Session (Rome, 20–31 March 2000): Comments (Submitted by the Secretariat of UNCITRAL)* (Unidroit CGE/IntInt/3-WP/10 ICAO Ref LSC/ME/3-WP/10 2000)

——, *UNIDROIT Committee of Governmental Experts for the Preparation of a Draft Convention on International Interests in Mobile Equipment and a Draft Protocol Thereto on Matters Specific to Aircraft Equipment; Sub-Committee of the ICAO Legal Committee on the Study of International Interests in Mobile Equipment (Aircraft Equipment); Third Joint Session (Rome, 20–31 March 2000): Drafting Committee/Restricted Group Monday 27 March 2000 Public International Law Provisions* (Unidroit CGE/IntInt/3-WP/28 Rev ICAO Ref LSC/ME/3-WP/28 Rev 28/03/00, 2000)

——, *UNIDROIT Committee of Governmental Experts for the Preparation of a Draft Convention on International Interests in Mobile Equipment and a Draft Protocol Thereto on Matters Specific to Aircraft Equipment; Sub-Committee of the ICAO Legal Committee on the Study of International Interests in Mobile Equipment (Aircraft Equipment); Third Joint Session (Rome, 20–31 March 2000): Drafting Committee: Report* (Unidroit CGE/IntInt/3-WP/40 ICAO Ref LSC/ME/3-WP/40 30/03/00, 2000)

——, *UNIDROIT Committee of Governmental Experts for the Preparation of a Draft Convention on International Interests in Mobile Equipment and a Draft Protocol Thereto on Matters Specific to Aircraft Equipment; Sub-Committee of the ICAO Legal Committee on the Study of International Interests in Mobile Equipment (Aircraft Equipment); Third Joint Session (Rome, 20–31 March 2000): Preliminary Comments (Submitted by the Government of France)* (Unidroit CGE/IntInt/3-WP/4 ICAO Ref LSC/ME/3-WP/4, 2000)

——, *UNIDROIT Committee of Governmental Experts for the Preparation of a Draft Convention on International Interests in Mobile Equipment and a Draft Protocol Thereto on Matters specific to Aircraft Equipment; Sub-Committee of the ICAO Legal Committee on the Study of International Interests in Mobile Equipment (Aircraft Equipment); Third Joint Session (Rome, 20–31 March 2000): Proposal (Submitted by the Delegation of the United States of America): Comments on Article 14 of the Preliminary Draft Convention and Article X of the Preliminary Draft Aircraft Protocol* (Unidroit CGE/IntInt/3-WP/25 ICAO Ref LSC/ME/3-WP/25 23/03/00, 2000)

——, *UNIDROIT Committee of Governmental Experts for the Preparation of a Draft Convention on International Interests in Mobile Equipment and a Draft Protocol Thereto on Matters specific to Aircraft Equipment; Sub-Committee of the ICAO Legal Committee on the Study of International Interests in Mobile Equipment (Aircraft Equipment); Third Joint Session (Rome, 20–31 March 2000): Proposal (Submitted by the French Delegation)* (Unidroit CGE/IntInt/3-WP/17 ICAO Ref LSC/ME/3-WP/17 12/03/00, 2000)

——, *UNIDROIT Committee of Governmental Experts for the Preparation of a Draft Convention on International Interests in Mobile Equipment and a Draft Protocol Thereto on Matters Specific to Aircraft Equipment; Sub-Committee of the ICAO Legal Committee on the Study of International Interests in Mobile Equipment (Aircraft Equipment); Third Joint Session (Rome, 20–31 March 2000): Proposal for Revised Text of Chapter IX of the Preliminary Draft Convention* (Unidroit CGE/IntInt/3-WP/31 ICAO Ref LSC/ME/3-WP/31 29/03/00, 2000)

——, *UNIDROIT Committee of Governmental Experts for the Preparation of a Draft Convention on International Interests in Mobile Equipment and a Draft Protocol Thereto on Matters Specific to Aircraft Equipment; Sub-Committee of the ICAO Legal Committee on the Study of International Interests in Mobile Equipment (Aircraft Equipment); Third Joint Session (Rome, 20–31 March 2000): Proposal Regarding the Substantive Sphere of Application of the Preliminary Draft Convention (Submitted by the UNIDROIT Secretariat)* (Unidroit CGE/IntInt/3-WP/14 ICAO Ref LSC/ME/3-WP/14 2000)

——, *UNIDROIT Committee of Governmental Experts for the Preparation of a Draft Convention on International Interests in Mobile Equipment and a Draft Protocol Thereto on Matters Specific to Aircraft Equipment; Sub-Committee of the ICAO Legal Committee on the Study of International Interests in Mobile Equipment (Aircraft Equipment); Third Joint Session (Rome, 20–31 March 2000): Public International Law Working Group (Rome, 20 and 21 March 2000): Report* (Unidroit CGE/IntInt/3-WP/18 ICAO Ref LSC/ME/3-WP/18 22/03/00, 2000)

——, *UNIDROIT Committee of Governmental Experts for the Preparation of a Draft Convention on International Interests in Mobile Equipment and a Draft Protocol Thereto on Matters Specific to Aircraft Equipment; Sub-Committee of the ICAO Legal Committee on the Study of International Interests in Mobile Equipment (Aircraft Equipment); Third Joint Session (Rome, 20–31 March 2000): Remedies and Interim Relief (Submitted by the ICAO Secretariat)* (Unidroit CGE/IntInt/3-WP/12 ICAO Ref LSC/ME/3-WP/12, 2000)

——, *UNIDROIT Committee of Governmental Experts for the Preparation of a Draft Convention on International Interests in Mobile Equipment and a Draft Protocol Thereto on Matters Specific to Aircraft Equipment; Sub-Committee of the ICAO Legal Committee on the Study of International Interests in Mobile Equipment (Aircraft Equipment); Third Joint Session (Rome, 20–31 March 2000): Report* (Unidroit CGE/IntInt/3-Report ICAO Ref LSC/ME/3-Report, 2000)

——, *UNIDROIT Committee of Governmental Experts for the Preparation of a Draft Convention on International Interests in Mobile Equipment and a Draft Protocol Thereto on Matters Specific to Aircraft Equipment; Sub-Committee of the ICAO Legal Committee on the Study of International Interests in Mobile Equipment (Aircraft Equipment); Third Joint Session (Rome, 20–31 March 2000): Special Working Group on Article 3 of the Preliminary Draft Convention; Second Report* (Unidroit CGE/IntInt/3-WP/27 Corr ICAO Ref LSC/ME/3-WP/27 27/03/00, 2000)

——, *UNIDROIT Committee of Governmental Experts for the Preparation of a Draft Convention on International Interests in Mobile Equipment and a Draft Protocol Thereto on Matters Specific to Aircraft Equipment; Sub-Committee of the ICAO Legal Committee on the Study of International Interests in Mobile Equipment (Aircraft Equipment); Third Joint Session (Rome, 20–31 March 2000): Special Working Group on Article 14 of the Preliminary Draft Convention and Selected Aspects of Article X of the Preliminary Draft Aircraft Protocol: Report* (Unidroit CGE/IntInt/3-WP/24 ICAO Ref LSC/ME/3-WP/24 2000)

——, *Committee of Governmental Experts for the Preparation of a Draft Protocol to the Convention on International Interests in Mobile Equipment on Matters Specific to Railway Rolling Stock; Second Joint Session (Rome, 17–19 June 2002) Report (Prepared by the Secretariats of Unidroit and OTIF)* (Unidroit 2003 Study LXXIIH – Doc 7, 2002)

——, *Committee of Governmental Experts for the Preparation of a Draft Protocol to the Convention on International Interests in Mobile Equipment on Matters Specific to Railway Rolling Stock; Preliminary Draft Protocol on Matters Specific to Railway Rolling Stock (as Reviewed by the Drafting Committee at its Second Session, Held in Rome, 23 to 25 October 2002)* (Unidroit 2003 Study LXXIIH – Doc 8, 2003)

——, *Committee of Governmental Experts for the Preparation of a Draft Protocol to the Convention on International Interests in Mobile Equipment on Matters Specific to Railway Rolling Stock; Third Joint Session (Berne, 5–13 May 2003) Report* (Prepared by the Secretariats of OTIF and Unidroit) (Unidroit 2003 Study LXXIIH – Doc 13, 2003)

——, *Diplomatic Conference to Adopt a Mobile Equipment Convention and an Aircraft Protocol: Acts and Proceedings; [Convention on International Interests in Mobile Equipment and Protocol thereto on Matters Specific to Aircraft Equipment]* (UNIDROIT 2006)

——, *Governing Council 86th Session (Rome, 16–18 April 2007) Item No. 8 on the Agenda: International Interests in Mobile Equipment: Preparation of an Additional Protocol to the Cape Town Convention on Matters Specific to Agricultural, Construction and Mining Equipment (Prepared by the Unidroit Secretariat)* (Unidroit 2007 CD (86) 8 (d), 2007)

——, *Steering Committee to Build Consensus around the Provisional Conclusions Reached by the Government/Industry Meeting Regarding the Preliminary Draft Space Assets Protocol held in New York on 19 and 20 June 2007 Second Meeting; Paris, 14/15 May 2009: Summary Report* (Prepared by the Unidroit Secretariat) (Unidroit 2009 Study LXXIIJ – Doc 17, 2009)

——, *Unidroit Committee of Governmental Experts for the Preparation of a Draft Protocol to the Convention on International Interests in Mobile Equipment on Matters Specific to Space Assets; Third Session: Rome, 7/11 December 2009* (Unidroit 2009 CGE/Space Pr/3/WP 12, 2009)

——, *Governing Council 92nd Session; Rome, 8–10 May 2013: Item No. 5 on the Agenda: International Interests in Mobile Equipment – (b) Possible Preparation of Other Protocols to the Cape Town Convention (i) Agricultural, Mining and Construction Equipment (Memorandum Prepared by the Secretariat)* (Unidroit 2013 CD (92) 5(b), 2013)

——, *Governing Council 92nd Session; Rome, 8–10 May 2013: Item No. 5 on the Agenda: International Interests in Mobile Equipment – (b) Possible Preparation of other Protocols to the Cape Town Convention (ii) Ships and Maritime Transport Equipment (iii) Off-shore Wind Power Generation and Similar Equipment (Memorandum Prepared by the Secretariat)* (Unidroit 2013 CD (92) 5(c)/(d), 2013)

——, *MAC Protocol Study Group; 3rd Meeting; Rome, 19–21 October 2015: Report (Prepared by the Unidroit Secretariat)* (Unidroit 2015 Study 72K – SG3 – Doc 5, 2015)

——, *Preparatory Commission for the Establishment of the International Registry for Space Assets Pursuant to the Space Protocol: Fourth Session (Rome, 10–11 December 2015); Summary Report of the Fourth Session* (Unidroit 2015 Prep Comm Space/4/Doc 7 rev, 2015)

——, *MAC Protocol Committee of Governmental Experts; First session; Rome, 20–24 March 2017: Committee of Governmental Experts for the Preparation of a Draft Fourth Protocol to the Convention on International Interests in Mobile Equipment on Matters Specific to Agricultural, Construction and Mining Equipment: Comments (Submitted by the Government of the United Kingdom)* (Unidroit 2017 Study 72K – CGE1 – Doc 9, 2017)

——, *MAC Protocol Committee of Governmental Experts; First Session; Rome, 20–24 March 2017: Legal Analysis (Prepared by the Unidroit Secretariat)* (Unidroit 2016 Study 72K – CGE1 – Doc 4, 2017)

——, *MAC Protocol Committee of Governmental Experts; First Session; Rome, 20–24 March 2017: Preliminary Draft Protocol to the Convention on International Interests in Mobile Equipment on Matters Specific to Agricultural, Construction and Mining Equipment* (Unidroit 2017 Study 72K – CGE1 – Doc 2 corr, 2017)

——, *MAC Protocol Committee of Governmental Experts; First Session; Rome, 20–24 March 2017: Report (Prepared by the Unidroit Secretariat)* (Unidroit 2017 Study 72K – CGE1 – Report, 2017)

——, *MAC Protocol Committee of Governmental Experts; First Session; Rome, 20–24 March 2017: Spreadsheet Detailing Harmonized System Codes Proposed by the Study Group for Inclusion in the Annexes to the Preliminary Draft MAC Protocol (Prepared by the Unidroit Secretariat)* (Unidroit 2017 Study 72K – CGE1 – Doc 5 corr, 2017)

——, *Potential Economic Benefits of Proposed MAC Protocol: Background Paper (Submitted by the US Department of Commerce on Request of the Unidroit Secretariat)* (Unidroit 2017 Study 72K – CGE1 – Doc 10, 2017)

——, *Diplomatic Conference for the Adoption of the Draft Protocol to the Convention on International Interests in Mobile Equipment on Matters Specific to Mining, Agricultural and Construction Equipment (the 'MAC Protocol'): Summary Report for 14 November 2019* (Unidroit 2019 DCME-MAC – Doc. 24 rev., 2019)

——, *Preparatory Commission for the Establishment of the International Registry for MAC Equipment Pursuant to the MAC Protocol: First Session (Rome, 21–22 May 2020); Summary Report of the First Session* (Unidroit 2020 MACPC/1/Doc. 9, June 2020)

United Nations, *Report of the Secretary-General: Study on Security Interests (A/CN.9/131)* (United Nations Commission on International Trade Law Yearbook Volume VIII: 1977, 1978)

——, *UNCITRAL Legislative Guide on Secured Transactions* (2010)

Wool J, 'The Case for a Commercial Orientation of the Proposed UNIDROIT Convention as Applied to Aircraft Equipment' (1999) 4 *Uniform Law Review* 289

——, 'Economic Analysis and Harmonised Modernisation of Private Law' (2003) 8 *Uniform Law Review* 389

——, 'Treaty Design, Implementation, and Compliance Benchmarking Economic Benefit – a Framework as Applied to the Cape Town Convention' (2012) 17 *Uniform Law Review* 633

INDEX

www.ingramcontent.com/pod-product-compliance
Lightning Source LLC
Chambersburg PA
CBHW071258180926
51613CB00001B/62
* 9 7 8 1 5 0 9 9 3 9 7 7 0 *